THE LAST RESCUE

THE LAST RESCUE

How Faith and Love Saved a Navy SEAL Sniper

HOWARD WASDIN

WITH JOEL KILPATRICK

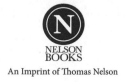

NELSON
BOOKS

An Imprint of Thomas Nelson

Published in Nashville, Tennessee, by Nelson Books, an imprint of Thomas Nelson. Nelson Books and Thomas Nelson are registered trademarks of HarperCollins Christian Publishing, Inc.

Thomas Nelson titles may be purchased in bulk for educational, business, fund-raising, or sales promotional use. For information, please e-mail SpecialMarkets@ThomasNelson.com.

Unless otherwise noted, Scripture quotations are taken from the Holy Bible, New International Version®, NIV®. Copyright © 1973, 1978, 1984, 2011 by Biblica, Inc.™ Used by permission of Zondervan. All rights reserved worldwide. www.zondervan.com

Scripture quotations marked NLT are from *Holy Bible*, New Living Translation. © 1996. Used by permission of Tyndale House Publishers, Inc., Wheaton, Illinois 60189. All rights reserved.

Scriptures marked NKJV are from THE NEW KING JAMES VERSION. © 1982 by Thomas Nelson, Inc. Used by permission. All rights reserved.

**Library of Congress Cataloging-in-Publication Data
is on file with the Library of Congress.**

ISBN: 978-1-5955-5594-6

Printed in the United States of America

14 15 16 17 18 19 RRD 6 5 4 3 2 1

Greater love has no one than this, than to
lay down one's life for his friends.
—JOHN 15:13 NKJV

CONTENTS

PROLOGUE

HOWARD

"Dad, she's gone. Raquel is gone."

"What do you mean, she's gone?" I asked from my helpless vantage point in a hotel room in Utah, a thousand miles away.

"She didn't come home last night," he said. "I kept waiting and waiting. Her car was gone. Finally, I looked in your room and her closet is empty. She took all her stuff."

There was an unusual urgency in Blake's voice. *Gone?* I thought. *She can't just be gone. People don't just up and leave their families.*

"Are you sure she took all her stuff? Maybe she's just out with friends, or at the dry cleaners," I said.

"Dad, there's nothing left."

Those words captured the truth better than he knew.

Howard Wasdin, supposed tactical genius, elite warrior, survivor of the *Black Hawk Down* Battle of Mogadishu, had just seen this op go down in flames. It was 1998. Slowly, the events of the past few months clicked into focus, and I realized that all the signs had been there. As in the past, I had simply chosen to ignore the truth until it whacked me in the face.

All I'd ever wanted, beneath the macho exterior and the constant striving for achievement, was to belong to a loving family. Instead, I had spent my life watching families around me fall apart. Now it was happening again right before my eyes. And there was nothing I could do.

God, please, not again, I prayed. *Why does it always end this way?*

My biggest concern was not for myself, but for Blake. We were living in Tennessee with Raquel, my second wife, a woman I had married mostly because I enjoyed her family. We had met on the police force in a community near Miami and moved away to start a new life. The trouble was, I wasn't the rock star in rural Tennessee that I had been in Miami. The men and women on our old police force had been fascinated by my SEAL experiences and my tactical background. They treated me like a minor celebrity. I lapped up their hero worship like a thirsty dog laps up water, not realizing how shallow that kind of adulation can be. Our mutually beneficial relationship kept my ego inflated and gave them stories to tell their friends.

But hero worship had distorted Raquel's view of me, and my view of her. In Tennessee, nobody was knocking on my door to shake my hand and thank me for my service to the country. Nobody knew who I was at the grocery store. Instead of a figure of awe, I was just a normal guy. My own view had been equally warped because I thought I could do anything—even start a romantic relationship based on virtually nothing and build it into something that would stand the test of time.

Those notions were now gone, just like Raquel was gone. The promise of love I had felt for her was as empty as the clothes hangers swinging in her abandoned closet. Howard Wasdin, war hero, proud veteran of the US Navy SEALs, had been left by his second wife. That does a lot for a guy's self-image.

The worst part was that Blake, who was fourteen, had started to bond with Raquel. God made boys to need their mothers, and when your real mother isn't around, you'll lean on whoever is nearby. For a while Raquel had been that person, especially when I was away. I enjoyed getting home and watching them talk after school and over dinner. They had created their own relationship, a way of interacting, daily routines together. They seemed to be forging the kind of bonds I had always hoped for in a family. The kind of bonds I hadn't been able to create myself.

Now I was far from home and our household was collapsing. My employer, a specialized body-armor company, had sent me to a bigwig golf tournament in Salt Lake City. I was their tactical body-armor expert and was traveling all the time to promote and demonstrate the bulletproof vests we form-fitted to each of our customers. That included the Kevlar that had saved my life. I loved the job. It put biscuits on the table and was the most interesting thing I'd done since my career with SEAL Team Six had ended abruptly in the Battle of Mogadishu five years earlier. Having several inches of bone instantly removed from your leg by an enemy gunman sort of changes your career options.

The leg had healed okay, but the rest of my life was, shall we say, a work in progress.

"Where are you now?" I asked Blake, going into reaction-and-recovery mode. I may have failed at building a family, but I knew how to protect.

"At the neighbors' house," he said. I breathed easier. The neighbor family, which included a son Blake's age, had welcomed Blake into their home on many occasions for dinner or just to relax. He was in good hands there.

"Okay, stick with them and I'll figure this out when I come home," I said. "I'm sorry about all this, Blake. Are you going to be okay?"

"I'm fine," he said, as if to indicate I should worry about her, not him. Typical male: *Nothing wrong here. She's the one who freaked out—worry about that.*

"You hold tight," I said. "Call me if she comes back."

"Okay," he said. We both knew she wouldn't.

I sat there in the empty hotel room feeling like I'd been kicked in the stomach. A tender trust had blown up in Blake's face. While Raquel was there, he had responded to her attention and care. Now she had scarred his heart, betrayed his confidence, and pushed him one step closer to the kind of person I had become: hard, wary, cynical.

Since that day in Mogadishu, I had fallen into rhythms of wandering, drifting from one job, one city, one relationship to another. It was like someone had snapped the rudder off my boat. Whether I went fast or slow, it didn't seem to matter. I never got anywhere. I didn't want Blake becoming familiar with those rhythms. My life's mission now was to protect his heart while it was still young and had hope. I didn't want him to turn out like me, craving love but never connecting. I didn't want him to experience the abandonment that haunted me.

At that moment, I decided never to have a real relationship again. Even if I dated, it would never be serious. My new family would be Blake and me, plus my daughter Rachel, who I only saw occasionally as she lived with her mother. I would defend them from anything that might hurt them. I would guard them with my life. I would build a wall around their emotions so nobody could get to them. I would never grow close to a woman again—because that might breach the wall. I would refuse anyone access to their hearts.

You can imagine how healthy that was for my dating life.

The truth was, I still had a whole lot of love and nowhere to spend it. I'd always been blessed with natural affection and enthusiasm for other people. Pets and children love me. Even at the heights of my arrogance, I felt real compassion for people, though I believed in my own implicit superiority, a delusion that was slowly blowing up in my face. The more I allowed myself to love, the more love filled my life. In Mogadishu I even discovered that the bond I had with warriors of other branches of the military could be stronger than what I had with my own SEAL team members because we fought side by side. When a SEAL guy bonds with a Delta Force guy, it's got to be real.

But back home, there was usually no one to receive my love except for the kids. When you don't have enough places to give your love, it tends to harden like food in the back of the pantry. So that night I quit the love game and resigned myself to being an aging warrior whose best days were behind him. Life was going to suck, but I would keep going for the sake of my kids. More than anything, I would protect them, and myself, from the kind of pain all of us had experienced before. On that op, I would not fail.

I didn't know God had a plan to drop an angel into my life—short, redheaded, and with a take-no-crap attitude—and use her to rewrite my future. With her gentle and butt-kicking guidance, I would go from drifting failure to the kind of success that seemed completely absurd when I was sitting in a ditch in Somalia waiting to die. She would cause my heart to bloom in ways it hadn't since I was a kid. She would help me find my rudder and sail toward the life and family I'd always wanted.

But that was still a thousand prayers away. First, God had some wars for me to fight.

DEBBIE

"You're kidding—he's gone?" my friend asked.

"He's gone," I said. "Left last night. Wasn't going to say anything to me or Eryn."

"So it's over?" she asked, studying me cautiously.

"Yes," I said. "I hate to say it, but it's over."

"Really over?"

"Really, really over," I assured her.

She sipped her coffee and shook her head.

"Wow. I'm not sure what to even say. How are you feeling?"

"Depends. What time is it?"

We laughed.

I had discovered in recent weeks that people don't know what to say to someone going through a separation or divorce. Do they mourn or rejoice with you? It's always sad to hear about people going their separate ways. I felt like mourning the end of one life and rejoicing at the start of a new one. On the bright side, I was free of the failed relationship that had lasted twelve years. All the recriminations, belittling comments, senseless arguments, division, and lack of intimacy—all that was gone now. I could clear my head and breathe again. The world was a much bigger place than I had remembered, and I was ready to explore and smile and laugh again.

On the other hand, I felt like a total failure. If I was the sensible, levelheaded person I fancied myself to be, why had I chosen the disastrously wrong guy? How could someone like me be so blind? I thought I did other things pretty well: raising my daughter, building my career, cultivating friendships. How had I made such a huge blunder on the biggest relational choice of all? And who was to say I wouldn't make it again? Could I still be so easily fooled? My confidence was shattered. I never planned for divorce, never expected it, and basically threw my life under the bus to avoid it. Now reality had caught up with me and crushed me like roadkill.

"I'm just trying to take it one step at a time," I told my friend. "It's like learning to live again. You forget what it's like to make all your own decisions. You forget what it's like not to be married."

"Good or bad?" she asked.

"Mm. Both," I said. She nodded as if trying to understand, but I knew she couldn't. She had a happy marriage and a good husband. I wouldn't have understood either, unless it had happened to me.

"So, when do you think you'll start dating?" she asked almost casually. I couldn't suppress a laugh.

"Never."

She cocked her head to one side as if to say, "Seriously?"

"It's way too early, and why take the chance of picking the wrong guy again?" I said. "I've already proven I can't tell a good one from a bad one. I served years in marriage prison for that decision. Besides, who would want to date me?"

She frowned at my assessment.

"Are you kidding me, Debbie? You are the cutest, sweetest thing. Men will be beating down your door."

"Thanks, but I really just don't see it. I'm not up for it."

"But what if God has someone out there for you," she pleaded almost dreamily, "the right guy, the one you've been waiting for? You can't shut the door on everyone just 'cause you had one bad experience."

I couldn't burst her bubble quickly enough. There would be no more fairy tales for me.

"Mr. Right is a figment of the female imagination," I said confidently. "He exists in deodorant commercials and chick flicks and that's about it. Anyway, I wouldn't expect to find the right guy in Jesup, Georgia."

My words dampened her mood, and I felt a little bad for that. As a naturally optimistic person, I had found myself lately in the odd position of telling people not to have any hope. Everyone wants to believe in second chances, to root for the underdog, to help you off the mat so you can fight on. But the mat was feeling mighty comfortable to me, especially compared to the possibility of going through another wrecked relationship.

One thing I was certain about: I was not the marrying type. Other friends could stay home and snuggle with their husbands and eat popcorn in bed, but that wasn't my path. It was safer to stand on the seashore and let others navigate the rough stuff. I had done my tour of duty and I was finished. My life would be about my daughter, my friends, and my career. That would have to be enough.

"Well," my friend sighed, "I'd better be getting back. Rob's expecting me."

Her words pained me, though she didn't know it. The hardest thing about my new singleness was the loneliness, though I had been lonely in my marriage for a long time. My happily married friends didn't know how lucky they were even to sleep in the same beds as their husbands, a luxury I had been denied for years, even while married.

Yeah, I'd found a strange one.

"Okay," I said, feigning contentment so as not to put the weight of my loneliness on her. "I sure enjoyed seeing you."

"Me too. We'll have to get together again," she promised, then mustered her optimism. "I still say there's someone out there for you."

I laughed in spite of myself.

"I deal with numbers all day, and I'm pretty sure the chances of that are slim to none," I said, "but thanks for thinking the best."

That night at home, my eight-year-old daughter, Eryn, and I watched lighthearted sitcoms after dinner, but my mind wandered and began assembling the pieces of the perfect man—a loving husband, a faithful partner, an uplifting companion, a good-looking hunk. When the image was complete, I realized it was too perfect, too outrageously unreal to resemble anyone living on this planet. I sighed and let the dream go.

You won't find that one on the dating scene. This is your life now. It could be a lot worse. Thank you, God, for the blessings I have.

Eryn was already in her little bed. I turned off the TV and made my way to my bedroom in the dark.

What I couldn't see was that God had a big, challenging adventure around the corner—and that through many trials he would answer every prayer I'd ever prayed for love and family.

ONE

A GOOD-LOOKING CORPSE

Mogadishu was hot, tense, and as volatile as the waters off the bay where sharks circled and occasionally dined on careless US soldiers. From a command center at an airfield near the ocean, members of SEAL Team Six and other elite forces were engaged in a prolonged, simmering confrontation with the local warlord who had run the city with violence and bribes until we got there and messed up his plans.

We were winning the war handily until one day in October 1993, in one of the most infamous battles in modern times, we ran head-long into a calamity that caused our government to turn tail and run, leaving behind a mess that would haunt us for decades.

Before that day, I was living in a safe house in the city with several other US operatives, monitoring the situation among the Somali people. The house belonged to a doctor, but he and his family had fled the country at the onset of violence. Thankfully, he left a cook who somehow turned the city's slim food pickings into gourmet meals each night. We needed those, because the days were punishing.

We were on our feet from sunup to sundown, dealing with

everyone from clan chiefs to low-level informants sympathetic to the US cause or just hungry for pay-offs. Some of these folks came to the house in secrecy to make deals, and other times we went to them because it was too dangerous for them to travel to us. Some helped us for the money. Others held to a more noble cause: their country, their families, a stable society, justice for all. I admired those types because they put their lives on the line for an ideal. It motivated us to do whatever we could to help them wriggle out from under the hand of their mini-despot.

As a SEAL I enjoyed kicking down doors, but at that point we were focused more on gathering intelligence, taking the local temperature, monitoring how well the bad guys' recruiting efforts were going, and talking with possible informants. One big accomplishment of those weeks was discovering how the bad guys had been sending signals for mortar attacks on our airfields. We put the kibosh on that pretty quickly, and they were forced to scramble and change tactics. Up to that point, our efforts had been mostly cat-and-mouse, our hands tied by a feckless United Nations force and its lying, avaricious Italian contingent. The opinion on the American side was unanimous: we wanted to send in the big guns, win the war, and go home. That order hadn't come yet.

Word had gotten out that the Americans were paying for information, so people emerged from the woodwork to make an easy buck. One of my many jobs was to determine if the information we were getting was accurate or a bunch of Bravo Sierra. That often required an impromptu interrogation, knee-to-knee with volunteer informants, in which I promised them, "If what you tell me isn't exactly as you say, I'm going to come back and find you, and there will be consequences. I'm about to put American lives at risk based on what you say." I'd look them square in the eye and often they would admit, "I'm not a hundred percent sure." I'd get up and say, "I'll come back when you are a hundred percent sure. Have a nice day."

It's amazing how having a cup of tea and a simple, if strongly worded, conversation with local people brings out the truth. Once you know where people live, they don't tend to lie to you. I felt our efforts were going pretty well. We'd come back to the safe house exhausted every evening and ready for one of those meals from the doctor's cook.

But with the windows open in our safe house, we began to notice that the smell of something rotting engulfed the area every night. It was like someone had opened a crypt. We also heard death moans. They sound different from standard moans of pain. With death moans you can hear life leaving the body. It was spine chilling.

We finally got curious and disgusted enough to hunt around for the odor's source. We discovered that the family next door had a son whose leg had been blown off by a land mine while he was walking to school through a playground. Rival factions planted mines in playgrounds, hoping to wipe out the next generation of warriors before they could reach adulthood. This boy had lost his leg but not his life—yet. Every night the family put the boy on the porch so they could get some sleep without gagging on the stench from his necrotic tissue.

The kid was clearly going to die. If not for us.

One night as the smell wafted in, we quietly crept to the back door of the family's house. It was nicer than the typical Somali huts, which were assembled from available boards and pieces of metal, things Americans would toss in the trash without a thought. We didn't know who was inside, friend or foe, so we did a hard entry, kicking open the door and taking control of the house. There were three people: a mom, a dad, and some sort of aunt. At least that's what I took them to be. We had no idea who they were or where their sympathies lay. They could have been affiliated with the wrong clan, or with Al Qaeda. It didn't matter to me. Once the house was secure, our mission was humanitarian, not military.

Treating the enemy well is what separates us from them. Even then I knew that love is stronger than any other force. There are only so many bullets to go around, but if love and respect took up residence on all sides, all war would end. Love was why I was doing a rogue op, at the risk of getting my peepee whacked by my higher-ups.

The smell was almost overpowering, and now we saw the source: a boy whose right leg was wrapped in blood-soaked rags. His eyes registered both fear and a plea for help. We grabbed the parents, flexi-cuffed them, and put them on their knees with their foreheads against the wall. To get up they would need to make a double motion, first pulling their foreheads away from the wall, which would alert us to their actions. They never resisted, but were clearly perplexed and afraid.

The boy was on his way out. We found out later that he was being treated by a witch doctor, which was not improving his situation. We could have scrubbed his leg with a yard broom and urinated on it and it would have done more good. There was no time for relaxing and giving him a good bedside manner, so we went about the work efficiently and speedily. I unwrapped the leg and scrubbed away the necrotic tissue. My partner put antibacterial salve on the tissue and began an IV drip. Instead of sitting around waiting for it to drip in, we pushed the liquid in quickly, which did no harm but must have felt strange to the boy.

Before they knew what had happened, we were gone. The moans lessened just a bit that night.

The next night we returned to administer another rogue treatment, and the family was again startled, but less so. We treated him again, the boy watching us with wide eyes the whole time, and left under cover of night. *Whatever you do for the least of these,* I thought, remembering scriptures I'd learned in childhood. I hadn't lived perfectly according to Jesus' words, not by a long shot; but I understood compassion. If I felt the heart of God in anything, it was in helping the helpless.

We skipped a night to avoid setting a pattern. The third time we burst in, the parents were already on their knees and had hot water ready to prepare tea for us to drink. We had brought an interpreter this time and they told us, "We know you're here to help." In their own way they brought out the fine china, so to speak, treating us as honored guests. That tea cost them dearly and they gave it like the widow's mite. That night we took a little more time, instructed them how to change bandages, gave them some salve and medications, and didn't flexi-cuff them. The smell of rotting tissue had all but gone away. I also discovered that the boy's gums were bleeding; he had scurvy. I made a note of it in case we came back.

About that time the US strategy shifted to winning hearts and minds. We had mostly taken out the rival clan and brought safety to the streets; now we could begin helping the community in other ways. Our clandestine mission became semiofficial, and we began going to the boy's house in the light of day, varying the times so the bad guys couldn't plan for us. I brought him a bag of oranges to treat his scurvy, which is caused by a deficiency of vitamin C. I also gave him my MREs (meals ready to eat), making sure to remove pork patties because it was a Muslim country.

We stayed longer and gave him a little more TLC. I blanched his fingers and toes to see if blood was circulating, took my time peeling back layers of bandages, scrubbed more gently. The family did everything to welcome us, bowing their heads, putting their hands together, and backing up as if greeting royalty. They started doing a particular sequence of movements—touch the heart, touch the head, and open a hand toward you—that conveyed a powerful visual form of respect.

I was the one who picked the boy up and moved him around the house because he was comfortable with me. I learned he was fourteen years old. He probably weighed half of what the poorest fourteen-year-old in the poorest American neighborhood weighed. We established a debride station where we scrubbed the wound, and I would often take him outside for some sunshine. As long as I was close to him, he seemed happy and relaxed.

The smell had abated to the point that the family could keep him inside at night. Through the interpreter, the family let us know they were happy. Interestingly, they didn't talk about us as individuals but as "America." "We're happy that America is here." "We are so grateful that America is helping our son." "We want to say thank you to America." They would repeatedly bow, putting their hands to their hearts and heads in a now-familiar motion. What touched me most was the love and affection I felt in that household. This boy had a dad who loved him, which put him ahead of me.

I had never known my biological dad, and the thought always nagged me: How would my life and upbringing have been different, maybe better and less violent, if my real dad had raised me? I thought perhaps I would never know the answer and never see the man who was my father, but the question still surfaced every time we burst into that house. The example of this humble little family in a tragically torn-up country moved my heart because they had something so many people, including me, did not grow up with: an abundance of love.

Moved by these thoughts, I treated the boy and his family special. Once I brought him a bunch of Hershey's Kisses I'd received in a care package from home. He absolutely loved them. He may have been the only kid in Somalia to eat Hershey's Kisses that week, or year.

One day after changing his bandages I spent time doing range of motion movements with his legs. He wasn't walking, so to keep his body in good working condition I flexed his knees, hips, and ankle, taking his thin limbs in my hands and gently rotating them. He observed what was happening carefully as if he wanted to repeat it later when he was alone. The only sound was of our breathing and the table creaking slightly under his emaciated frame. I felt connected to this kid as if he were my own. What he thought of me, I didn't know.

Somalis are not outwardly emotional people, at least in my experience. I never saw them hug each other. Perhaps the war had driven them inside themselves. But when I was getting ready to leave that day, the boy grabbed my hand as I got up from his bed. I thought he might want to tell me something through the interpreter before I left, but he just looked at me, his eyes piercing mine with unspoken meaning. It was like staring into deep pools of gratitude. When I'd first met him, those eyes were glazed and shallow. Now he was a little boy again, the life inside of him pouring out toward me. I squeezed his hand, said something reassuring, and walked out, my heart riding high in my chest.

I went to sleep that night feeling more fulfilled than at any time since arriving for the mission. I didn't know it was the last time I would ever see the boy, or that soon I would be in far worse shape than he.

The next day we got a frag order to vacate the safe house. A frag order implies imminent danger and requires you to vacate without delay, taking only what is essential. We ripped charts off the wall depicting in detail where our agents were, and friendly and unfriendly houses. If we were attacked in the bug out I would find a way to eat the charts. We grabbed the voice-encryption machines and had a thermite grenade ready to incinerate them if we got overtaken. Within minutes we were in Humvees hauling back to the compound at the airfield. We arrived safely and walked into the hangar with several weeks' worth of beard on our faces. Everyone there was clean-cut and military issue. We stood out like vagrants at the royal ball, grinning.

The Battle of Mogadishu seemed at first like it would be a routine op. We massively outgunned the enemy with our 19 aircraft, 12 vehicles, and 160 men. We had crazy amounts of technology, training, manpower, and plain-old bullets. It was the best of the US military against a ragtag, drugged-up, Third World militia. I would have taken those odds any day.

Our objective was to capture two militia leaders from an enemy building and leave. Sounds simple, and I thought it would be. Not that they wanted to come with us, but overwhelming them didn't seem like a problem.

I was driving a "cutvee," a Humvee without a top, windows, or doors, and no special armor except a Kevlar blanket underneath to protect us from bombs. In the vehicle were three other SEAL Team Six guys and three Rangers. We missed the official briefing because we'd been in town setting up CIA repeaters and this op had popped up quickly, but our commander approached the cutvee and briefed us there. "Shouldn't take long. Good luck. See you when you get back," he concluded, slapping me on the shoulder.

We joined the convoy heading to the Olympic Hotel, and soon I found myself taking up a firing position in an alley where I would protect the Delta guys as they went in. I saw two enemy snipers, one behind a ground-level wall and the other five stories up on a veranda. I couldn't get a clear shot on them so a Delta sniper and I moved positions. I was suspicious already: the enemy seemed too well prepared. They were already firing on the target building where Delta assaulted. This smelled like a setup. But for the moment, my job was to protect our guys by taking out these snipers.

I didn't know that a mile west of us, the militia had gathered at a market to distribute smuggled weapons and ammo. A mile east, foreign fighters had arrived. We had driven into an ambush. The day wouldn't get any quieter.

The enemy ground sniper stuck his rifle over the wall and aimed his scope at the Rangers in my convoy. He had a good shooting position, with only his head exposed. I squeezed the trigger and relieved him of duty. His gun fell to the ground.

On the fifth-story veranda, two enemy fighters were firing AK-47s into the back of the target house where Delta assaulters were. The Delta operator and I moved forward twice to get into position, and then I lay prone while he protected the perimeter around me. I laid an ambush of my own, putting the red dot of my sight on the spot where the bad guy had last appeared. I waited for him to pop into view. When he did, my bullet hit his upper torso, sending him toppling through the doorway. He didn't reappear. A second gunman made the same mistake, stepping into my dot. I gave him the same treatment. If we hadn't nailed those snipers, they would have caused havoc among our Delta guys, shooting them like fish in a barrel.

A command came over the radio: return to the convoy. As I

jogged through the alley to the cutvee, a ricochet hit me on the back of the left knee, knocking me to the dirt. The pain was worse than I thought it would be, and for a moment I couldn't move. It was the first time I had ever been shot. I got up and made it to the cutvee, where a medic stuffed my leg full of gauze. Within minutes I was on my feet shooting again. No harm done. If anything, my sense of invincibility climbed a little bit higher.

The blue skies were now filled with smoke from burning tires, a signal from the enemy to other fighters to join them and a way to obscure our vision. Enemy fighters with AK-47s were everywhere. As soon as I capped one, another would pop up like a game of Whack-a-Mole. RPGs ripped through the air with a shriek, leaving an acrid odor. One of the RPGs took out one of our 5-ton trucks. We blew the rest of the truck up with a thermite grenade so it wouldn't fall into enemy hands.

Then we heard over the radio that an RPG had taken down a Black Hawk. Our mission changed instantly from a high-value target snatch to a rescue op. Our guys were alive and on the ground. We loaded up our convoy and headed toward the crash site.

The enemy was much better armed and better prepared than we had expected. Trucks with high-powered guns bolted to the backs traced the paths of the urban labyrinth and popped out at us from alleyways and side streets. Every one of our trucks was getting hit, and we were spending as much time hauling each other to safety as shooting. Some of the wounded kept working to resupply us with ammo.

We were soon enveloped in confusion. Slow, deadly confusion. Our convoy moved in fits and starts toward the crash site. The drivers were trying to take orders from the guys in the helicopters, but we kept going in circles. All the while, the enemy fired on us from positions on all sides—ground level, windows, and rooftops, from behind and in front. Our cutvee began to look like latticework. I shot back as often as I breathed, taking down militia fighters as they approached on every side, but there always seemed to be more. They dug trenches and burned stuff in the middle of the road to stop us, and while we tried to circumnavigate the fires, they ambushed us repeatedly. Women walked shoulder to shoulder as they approached us with gunmen hiding behind their colorful, outstretched robes. The women would suddenly pull in their robes and the gunmen would shoot. After a while, we treated those women like the enemy combatants they were.

More information came over the radio: a second helicopter was downed by an RPG. Now there were two crash sites. We tried to drive there to protect the guys who had survived the crash, but our vehicles were taking hard hits. Guys who weren't dead were carrying shrapnel or bleeding from their wounds. Dead gunners were replaced with live ones. Half our leaders were wounded. We began to run out of ammunition.

We had been told in SEAL training: "If you live through one ambush, go home, get in your rocking chair, and thank God for the rest of your life." Now we were going in circles, seeing the same buildings over and over, providing a fat, slow target for foreign fighters and local militia. Worst of all, some of our guys were at crash sites waiting for us to rescue them. If we didn't get there, the militia would literally hack them to pieces.

The enemy paid a heavy price but seemed to regenerate on the spot. Our helicopters, the Hughes MD 500s that we called "little birds," were swooping in and buzzing the fighters to keep them away from our downed guys. That meant the birds had run out of ammo.

United States bravery and self-sacrifice were on full display, but this thing was not going our way.

I drove the cutvee through the mad streets of Mogadishu. My primary weapon, a CAR-15, was out of ammo so I pulled a SIG SAUER 9mm from the holster. As our convoy inched through the streets, a gunman stepped into a doorway and pointed his AK-47 at me. I aimed my gun right back at him and double-tapped the trigger. I had made that shot a thousand times in training, but today I rushed it. The bullets struck above his head and gave him a moment to dial me in. I saw him pull the trigger in slow motion.

His round hit me in the right leg below the knee. I felt the impact but no pain. I took an extra half second to aim and sent two bullets into his face. He collapsed, dead. *Should have done that the first time.*

It was either eerie coincidence or divine irony that his bullet hit me just inches above where the Somali boy's injury was. Same leg. Same essential problem. A bomb had shattered that boy's childhood and family; the bullet shattered my leg bone and the very foundation of who I was. In the time it took the bullet to exit that muzzle, tear through the metal cutvee body, and strike my flesh and bone, I went from tactical god to mere mortal in my own mind.

Amazingly, for a period of hours, it was more likely that the boy would survive than I would.

My right leg was dangling backward, held on by tatters of flesh. I drove us out of there with my left foot until we came to a place where we weren't receiving so much incoming fire. My SEAL team members pulled me into the passenger seat and propped my injured leg on the hood with my left leg beside it as a brace. At any moment, the shards of bone might cut through an artery. I could bleed to death within minutes.

"I'm going to get you home," one of the Team guys told me.

I had been strangely naïve about my own mortality: eager to die for my country and the Teams, but delusional about my own invincibility. To quote a certain movie heroine, I had come to believe I was impervious to bullets. Past experience bolstered that opinion. How many people perform 752 parachute jumps, including dangerous ones at night and from high altitudes, without even spraining a toe? Or go on countless ops without a scratch?

I'd seen guys injured in all sorts of scenarios: falling off the end of fast ropes when inserting on a target from a helicopter, dislocating a shoulder (and ending a career) climbing a caving ladder into a helicopter, getting shot to my left and right, and banging themselves up skydiving. I came to believe that my tactical superiority had spared me time and again, which is why when the bullet from the AK-47 hit my right leg, my reaction was almost disbelief. The lack of pain made it easier to reject reality. When injuries are that bad, your body shuts down the pain transmissions. But I couldn't help seeing my right leg lying unnaturally sideways on the cutvee hood.

As we proceeded with three flat tires, a second bullet brought the reality home, striking my left foot near the ankle. I had never felt such pain, and I screamed inside my head, *God! What are you trying to tell me?!* If he wanted my attention, he had it now.

Shortly after that, our cutvee died. We were stranded on the side of the road with six or seven enemy fighters coming toward us. I pointed my pistol at them as they approached, but my injuries affected my aim, and I was down to my last magazine. I wasn't much use anymore.

This is it, I thought. *This is what it feels like to die in battle. I only wish I had told Blake and Rachel I loved them more often.*

Blake was eight and Rachel was three. I wished hard that I could hug them just one more time. They would never know the thoughts going through my mind now, or how I had tried to survive just so I could see them again. If my heart beat for anything, it was for my children.

Just then a US Quick Reaction Force vehicle drove by, and for a moment I thought we would be rescued. But it kept going down the road. My hopes dimmed. Then the vehicle reversed direction and came back for us. The enemy gunmen fled. There were no bullets left in my pistol when they loaded us up and took us back to the hangar.

I was one of forty or fifty wounded guys getting treatment at the triage site. My mutilated right leg bled freely. One Ranger opened the back of his Humvee and blood poured onto the ground like water. Eighteen Americans died that day, and eighty-four were wounded.

While I lay there wondering if I would survive, a CIA operative, Mike, found me and offered words of comfort. Then he asked, "Anything I can do for you?"

I thought for a moment. "That kid at Lido," I said. Lido was the name of the neighborhood where the safe house was. "Make sure he's taken care of. Give him a wheelchair."

"Will do," Mike said. He patted my shoulder and left.

The next few days were a blur of surgeries and hospital rooms. The status of my leg was uncertain, and I would taste death before it was through.

When people read the history books, the Battle of Mogadishu will be considered a failed op. One thing that would not appear in the history books is what I consider my most successful mission in Somalia: the unapproved treatment of a dying boy who lived next to our safe house. Saving his life was as important to me as supporting and defending our guys in the fight. I still don't feel worthy of either privilege.

After Mogadishu, many of my friends and fellow warriors, like Delta Force's Dan Busch, a great Christian man whose faith changed my life, went into the ground immortalized as heroes, and rightly so. Me—I went to live with my in-laws in rural Georgia to start my recovery and tend to my suppurating wounds.

*

We had a saying in the Teams: "Live fast, die young, and leave a good-looking corpse." It was a half joke, but also my actual career plan. I had always believed that I would die a SEAL. I could not imagine living to old age. It never crossed my mind. I simply envisioned doing one op after another until one day, due to no tactical error on my part, an op went bad and I died in glory, perhaps saving the lives of my team members or innocent people. That wasn't just my best-case scenario, it was my only scenario. I had no plan B. The idea of living past the age of forty was laughable to me.

Now it was late 1993 and I was thirty-two years old. God or circumstances had thrust me into an unknown future, and I was poorly prepared for it.

My right leg should have been amputated, but I had begged the surgeon to try to salvage it. I'd made such a scene on the operating table that they'd let me stay awake during the surgery while he proceeded to stack the bone pieces together like ill-fitting Legos, hoping they would fuse together to form something like a tibia again. My right leg was not so much a leg anymore as an assemblage of parts thrown together with hope, spit, and a little medical know-how. I say that with no disrespect to the surgeons, who did an awesome job. Even they would have said it was a Hail Mary. Amputation, they always seemed to remind me, was a looming possibility. There was no way of knowing if the leg would start acting like a leg, if the parts would agree, if the bone and tissue would grow, if the blood would flow, and most importantly, if infection would be avoided.

That last part—avoiding infection—was all on me, and it almost made me the last casualty of the Battle of Mogadishu.

Healing was slow, and not just for the leg. As much as I hated to admit it, the diagnosis on all fronts of life was uncertain. I found myself living in the guest bedroom of my in-laws' brick house on a dirt road in the Southern countryside, surrounded by pine forests and marshland. Only a few relatives lived nearby. It was a thirty-minute trip just to get a loaf of bread.

The new environment proved unforgiving. Stairs led to the porch and could not be managed by my wheelchair. The doorways inside were narrow, as they are in older homes, so some rooms, including the bathrooms, were off-limits to me. I spent the better part of a month peeing into a bottle and yearning for the day I could sit on a toilet like a normal human being. As we said in the Teams, nothing is more overrated than sex or more underrated than a good crap.

My right leg was gripped by an external fixator, a metal scaffolding with pins holding the bone in place while it fused together. (Google it and be ready for what you might see.) It feels like your leg is in a vice all the time. To reconstruct my right leg they had filleted my calf muscle, filled the hole with bone pieces, then taken a skin graft from my upper right thigh and laid it over that. A bag of bolts. The skin grafts hurt as bad as anything because the pain was all on the surface where the nerves are. My left ankle was injured too. At the time, that hurt worse than anything. The wound wasn't so bad that it caused the body to block the pain, so every signal flowed to the brain in a constant cascade of agony. I wasn't angry until I got shot through the left foot.

My wife, Katherine, had learned she was pregnant shortly after I went to Somalia, and I was overjoyed. But now Katherine and I couldn't sleep in the same bed because if anything bumped my leg, it sent a blaring trumpet solo of pain up and down my body. At a restaurant one night when I dared to go out with the family, someone passed by and accidentally banged my leg as it stuck out from my wheelchair. The pain was so bad I almost passed out.

The typical American lifestyle suddenly seemed unpleasant, ignorant, and ungrateful. People didn't appreciate things as basic as running water and available medical care. By the grace of God we were born Americans; none of us deserves to live like kings and queens, but we do. How often are we thankful for it? We don't have land mines in our playgrounds. Our parents don't put us on the porch at night to die. Somehow we feel entitled to life's best, just by virtue of our existence. That attitude, which I had shared for many years, was repellent to me now. Where was our gratitude toward God? Toward each other? Had I really been that selfish too?

I found it difficult to connect with people because of what I had experienced. There's tremendous mental whiplash when one day you're taking enemy fire with a full battalion—including helicopters, Humvees, and the assorted weaponry that put such fearsome teeth in the US arsenal—and a week later you find yourself in a quiet rural home with a wife you once knew and people who don't quite know what to do with you. Conversations derailed after just a few sentences. After all, what did we have in common? "I had a great time at the mall last week. They have a couple of new stores open." "Oh really?

Let's see—last week I was lobbing bullets into guys' chests from a concealed position one thousand yards away." Silence.

I did not have recurring dreams or flashbacks, but I was faced with a whole new set of tactical challenges: getting out of bed unharmed, brushing my teeth, washing my face, and tending to my wounds to avoid the dreaded staph infection, which was now more dangerous than the injury itself. When you have a life-threatening injury, everything about your routine becomes critically important. I found ways to leverage myself around by holding the door and the sink, or a doorjamb, or a bedpost. The titanium wheelchair my Team members bought me was hugely helpful.

Pin care became the most important part of my day. Usually the doctors train the family to assist with pin care, but nobody in my family had the stomach for it. Not only that, but there were well-defined roles in the Mormon community to which we belonged: women took care of the kids and the house. Men worked and took care of business. Caring for my wounds fell squarely into the category of things I should be able to manage all by myself. My role wasn't to put manageable stuff like that on other people.

In a way I admired this strict adherence to rules and roles. I had married Katherine largely because of the strong, family-oriented community she belonged to. By contrast, my own upbringing had been chaotic, noncommunicative, and painful for body and soul. I had chosen to go through recovery in Georgia so I could be with family and build on whatever foundation Katherine and I had left. If I had stayed in Virginia Beach, the Team guys and doctors would have helped me through physical and psychological recovery. These guys had fought by my side and would have laid down their lives for me.

In Georgia, I had a wife who was used to living without me,

because that was the kind of life I had created for us. My own failed leadership as a husband came back to haunt me now. Katherine would not dote on me, and why would she? I had never wanted her to before. But now I had serious needs that were new to both of us. Those needs exposed our lack of relational foundation. Instead of drawing us closer, my weaknesses now drove us apart. It gave me the first glimpse into our relationship's future.

My brother-in-law, Ricky, wanted to help, bless his heart, but gagged and almost fainted at the sight of my wounds. I truly appreciated him for trying.

Every morning my first job was to reckon with my bastardized leg, the bane of my days and an ugly, unavoidable reminder that my life as a rock star had just fallen apart. In tactical fashion, I had surveyed the house and concluded it was a breeding ground for the germs that could infect my leg and threaten my life. Most of the house was carpeted, which was terrible. The kitchen had linoleum, but kitchens are as bad as bathrooms when it comes to pathogens. Only the living room had a hardwood floor, which was cleaner than anything else and easy to get around on in my wheelchair. That's where I did my wound care.

I greeted each day by inspecting my bandages. Overnight seepage always discolored the gauze with translucent body fluids. The skin grafts in particular seemed to drain heavily, leaving a brown stain that reminded me of menstrual pads. I mocked myself for being on a perpetual period. Carefully I peeled away the layers of bandages, exposing the ugly graft with its metal staples. I cleaned the grafted area with Betadine and Neosporin. Then it was time for pin care. The four-inch metal pins were now the most dangerous pieces of real estate on my body because they led directly to the bone and provided enterprising bacteria a highway to all the marrow and tissue it could eat. My job was to defend the opening where the pins entered my flesh. I did this also with Betadine and Neosporin, and by carefully shaving away the hair around the pins. Hair follicles, little microscopic terrorist camps, were breeding grounds for bacteria.

I tended the pins with ultimate care, slowly wiping around them with disinfectant in ever-widening circles from the inside out. I shaved deliberately and with millimeter precision. It reminded me of the way I cared for my equipment and weapons, cleaning and testing even the smallest piece before heading out on an op. Only now the critical pieces were my own body.

God, why did this happen? I would ask silently. *What's the point? Why do I have to go through this?*

When I finished with pin care, I tended to my left foot. The bullet had removed a little valley of flesh, which was now packed with skin plugs and gauze. I would bring my leg up behind me in a hurdler's stretch, lying flat on the floor. With the left foot next to me at hip level, I could carefully remove the old gauze and plugs, pack in the new, and cover it with a type of moleskin to protect the skin from getting infected. It hurt a lot less than the graft and pins.

Then it was time for breakfast if I could stomach it.

I knew with my limited medical background how necessary and important wound care was, but it didn't make the task any less dreadful. As I went through my slow, intimate routine, I would often think of the boy in Mogadishu. In my mind's eye I could see his wounds, first illuminated by flashlight on the dark porch that night. They really were in virtually the same place as mine—right leg below the knee. I could even feel the silence that would gather as I swabbed and cleaned out his dead tissue. I could hear his sharp inhalations as he gritted his teeth and swallowed a scream.

I thought of his family living together in that house. They always seemed content and happy together, even in their country's precarious situation. They were willing to touch and comfort him, to move him from one room to another, to tell him they loved him. I yearned for that kind of touch, that kind of family spirit. I could have taken one day's worth of that love and stretched it over weeks and I would have been happy. Now I faced the most difficult part of recovery on my own with a family who seemed strangely distant. It felt like the atmosphere from my childhood home had come to rest over us. The love, for some reason, was gone.

Many days during my recovery I would rather have left a good-looking corpse than deal with a deteriorating leg and a deteriorating life. It wasn't to avoid the pain, but because dying in battle defending my brothers and our mission seemed far more honorable. *If only that sniper had aimed a little higher,* I sometimes thought. *What use was a career-ending leg wound?*

I also wondered why God would send an angel—or, rather, a couple of softhearted warriors—to that boy in Mogadishu while leaving me to care for my wounds alone. Couldn't he send someone to sit by my side, give a kind word, and perhaps make sure I was reaching the parts of my leg that were hard to shave because they were out of my sight? Any sign of concern would have meant the world.

One day I got a call from Mike, the CIA guy.

"We took care of your boy," he said. "We got him a wheelchair, just like you asked. He's doing fine."

With that, the Battle of Mogadishu came to an end for me.

But a question began to gnaw at me more painfully each day: Was that boy worth more to God than I was?

TWO

THE MIRACLE

Every day in late 1993 I drove myself to the hospital for an agoniz-
ing date with the whirlpool. I would make my way gingerly down
the porch steps and into the car, where I used my injured left foot to
operate the gas pedal and the brake, just as I had in Mogadishu after
getting shot.

The physical therapists at the hospital were a gift from God. They
not only treated my leg with great care but made me feel like I was
worth something at a time when no one else would even glance at my
injuries without wincing. "Hey, champ," they would say as I wheeled
myself in. "Welcome back. Let's get to work."

But the whirlpool treatment, called debriding, was hell. Weeks
before, I had been on the other side of this interaction; now I felt in
my own body the pain the boy in Mogadishu had felt when I scrubbed
his wounds. I made the same kinds of sharp inhalations, gritting my
teeth and holding the pain inside as the stabbing hot water swirled
and the doctors removed the necrotic tissue. I realized what it meant
to silently beg someone to be just a little gentler.

They started each whirlpool treatment by taking off the bandages as I did at home and removing any obvious dead tissue with a pair of tweezers. Then I put the leg into the ovular whirlpool where the water heated up rapidly. A water jet behind my knee churned the water and cleaned the wound on the left foot. After a while a ring of dead tissue would form around the whirlpool's water line, just like a ring in the bathtub, except this was made up of my own dead flesh. The water would go from clear to milky gray. I looked at the ring every time and wondered, *Who has to clean that off when I leave?* I was thankful to whoever it was.

It also occurred to me, though I was less familiar with the Bible at that point, that the cleansing of my tissues pointed to a spiritual truth about my life as well. It wasn't just my physical body that was injured; I had deep soul wounds as well. Maybe something larger was going on—maybe God had initiated a cleansing of body and soul that I hadn't asked for and didn't want at the time. Perhaps brokenness was the path toward wholeness in some way I didn't understand.

After all, hadn't I caused that Somali boy pain in the service of healing? Didn't the Bible say that "by his wounds we are healed" (Isa. 53:5)? The Great Physician knows personally that healing is a painful process. If the greatest act ever to take place on earth—the sacrifice of a perfect man in an excruciating death on a cross—was the only way to redeem humanity, why would it be any different for me personally? What if suffering of this sort was indeed the only way toward the redemption I ached for? After all, the Psalms say, strangely, "Let the bones you have crushed rejoice" (Ps. 51:8), indicating that after great pain come times of rejoicing, redemption, renewal.

I tried not to dwell on those thoughts too much because I didn't want that to be true, and if it were true, it was too painful to bear. I was simply trying to get through each day; thoughts about the bigger picture only overwhelmed me.

After thirty minutes my leg would come out as red as the hot dogs my stepfather, Leon, and I used to eat when we were fending for ourselves for dinner. Then came the fun part—the doctors took a brush and augured out the wound until the capillaries bled. It was as fun as it sounds. Debriding treatment was a whole different experience from the other side.

In spite of the pain, I looked forward to going to the hospital. I was the only combat-related injury they had seen since Desert Storm, and often the physical therapists would invite friends to come by while I was there just to see someone who'd been through actual battle. It wasn't uncommon for me to be sitting in the whirlpool with people across the room looking at me like, "There's a guy who's really been in the stuff." I enjoyed it not as an ego stroke but as a welcome feeling of appreciation.

The longer my recovery went on, the more I began to lose the war of the mind. Gone was my routine of daily running, workouts, training exercises, and various adventures with the Teams. Now my life was confined to a thousand square feet of indoor space in rural Georgia. My days were about pain, pin care, disillusionment, and unsatisfying sleep.

Katherine always seemed to be passing by. She kept a clean house, did the dishes and the laundry, but she kept her distance from me. We weren't at odds so much as we were incommunicado. It was like we had both bought into the SEAL and SEAL wife ethic: Tough it out. Do your part. Get through it. That was working less and less for me. I had a broken wing and needed someone to show they cared that I survived. Katherine was not volunteering, and given the way I had essentially abandoned her in our marriage, I didn't blame her one bit.

Still, I missed what we once had. We had both stopped being vibrant and happy as when we were young. I don't recall her face brightening one time when I rolled into the room.

Now and then she would stop by the couch or bed and share a few words, but mostly it was, "How's everything going? Okay, take care of yourself." Our words had the form of kindness, but neither of us put much heart behind them. I had no real idea how to re-create the connections I wanted. Nobody had taught me how to treat a wife or lead a family. I had never seen it done well. I had been mostly absent from Katherine's life for years, putting the Teams first. Now I had come home to find my relational bank account empty. To make it worse, I was determined to live up to the myth of Howard Wasdin, war hero and tactical genius. That meant not admitting I needed help. I basically sat around quietly waiting for someone to volunteer. If I'd have known better, I would have voiced my need for help before things got worse.

Ricky, my brother-in-law, was a priceless gift. He would come over after work and drive me around in his truck so I could see nature again. I'd always been more comfortable outdoors than inside. The ocean and sky were my home and workplace. Ricky would drive us through the woods and stop where the forest was cleared for the gas lines. The farmers planted food in the clearings and deer came out in the early morning or right before sunset to feed on the crops. We would sit there in the truck and look down both sides, watching the deer slowly emerge in the buttery light, dip their heads to the ground, and eat. It was beautiful. I felt God's peace in those moments, his gentleness and his sovereignty over all creation, including my own situation. There also was no doubt in my mind that Ricky loved me. He didn't have to take me around to see beauty, but he did.

Back home I couldn't shower because the fixator couldn't have water on it, so I sponged off, which was always unsatisfying. I also did plyometrics to stay in shape. Push-ups weren't allowed, but I did hundreds of sit-ups a day. I had an isolation bar to work my chest. I also put my legs on the coffee table and used my arms to raise and lower my body, working the triceps like a gymnast on a pommel horse.

Katherine's mom was a good cook, a kind person, and a soap opera addict. Every day at a certain time she would commandeer the television to watch her shows. Instead of wheeling myself out of the room, I started watching with her. Before long, I found myself as hooked as she was. I actually spent time wondering what would happen next on *The Young and the Restless*. Anyone who says those shows aren't addictive is lying.

Years later I was having lunch with friends and a TV was playing in the corner of the restaurant. Out of the blue I said, "I can't believe Victor is still on *The Young and the Restless*. He must be ninety-seven years old." My friend looked at me like, "How on earth do you know anything about that show?" I just grinned and kept eating.

Soap operas and visits to the hospital for debriding weren't enough to carry me. As optimism slipped away, I slept at odd hours and wondered why God had spared me when better guys were dead. It sounds like a cliché, but I didn't feel I deserved to be alive or happy. I felt I deserved to die and that being miserable now was divine retribution. Some mistake had been made in heaven. God had spared my life, and I would pay for everything I had done—the killing, the neglect of my family, my many sins.

One of the worst moments came when I first ventured out of the house to the grocery store and a heavy-set woman rounded the corner of the aisle and encountered my fixated leg. She grimaced and told me I shouldn't take that thing in public.

Such a small comment; such a large impact. She probably didn't think about it, except maybe to mention it to someone at home, but I found it devastating. It was like she spoke for the entire community. I didn't go out in public again for weeks. I had fashioned a cage of emotions and locked myself into it.

*

A few weeks after coming home, memorial services were held for Dan Busch and others who had died in Mogadishu. I was determined to go, and the military sent an aircraft to pick me up. But the morning of the service I woke up feeling like hammered crap. I thought my emotions must have gotten the best of me, but there were also unmistakable physical symptoms. One moment my body felt as if it were on fire, the next it was freezing. What I didn't know was that my doctor was frantically trying to reach me because my latest blood results had come back. I had a staph infection and was on my way to dying. Staph doesn't waste any time.

The diligent, thorough pin care I had done hadn't worked. Bacteria had traveled down the screws into my bone. I had been wishing for the grave, and in the army hospital after the memorial service I almost got my wish. The doctor was angry when we arrived. "Where have you been? We've been trying to contact your house, but you weren't there," he said, then put two shots into my butt, started an IV line, and began treatment. Suddenly I felt myself lift out of my body and float up near the ceiling. It was fascinating because I had never believed in such experiences. I had been close to dying in a ditch in Somalia and hadn't experienced any such thing. Now I was seeing myself from a vantage point near the ceiling, looking down on my body in the bed. I was definitely not a good-looking corpse. Still, it was so peaceful drifting away. *I'm dying*, I thought. *That's what this is.*

A cousin of mine had experienced something similar before being brought back with paddles. I'd always scoffed. I was a Christian, but in everyday life I only believed in things I could handle: tactics, explosives, guns, det-cord. I was like people from Missouri: Show me. Don't get all mystical. But while floating outside of my body I felt no fever, no pain. Nobody else was there and I saw no light. It was just me looking down at myself in that hospital room.

Then, just like that, I was back in my body. The pain was back, the sick-all-over feeling, the pressure in my right leg from the fixator. I went in and out of consciousness for the next day or two as the doctors pulled me back from the brink. Maybe I experienced it for a reason, to make me more tolerant. Now when I read about little kids going to heaven, I think, *Well, maybe they did.*

I survived staph, but it set back my journey of healing. At my forty-day appointment, which doctors consider a milestone to see how healing is progressing, the doctor came in and snapped the X-ray into the light board so we could both see it. He wasn't happy, and I saw why. My leg looked like a bad jigsaw puzzle. It had hardly progressed. The only difference I saw between this X-ray and the one taken right after my surgery was that they had removed the copper and metal bits from the tissue. The bone looked the same. The fixator, the pin care, the stacked bone pieces—none of it was working.

"I can tell you with some certainty, Howard, that you'll never run again, and at this point the bone is not knitting together as we hoped, probably due to staph," he said. "If the X-ray is not better three weeks from now . . . we'll have to do something else."

He didn't say what that "something else" was, and I was too afraid to ask. I knew he meant amputation, but I didn't want to make it real. Emotionally, this was the worst blow I had felt since my childhood.

"Thanks, Doc," I managed to say and wheeled myself back to the car to drive myself home.

Every negative feeling I'd entertained over the previous month came roaring back like an out-of-control freight train. Not only had I not died in glory, but my friends were now gone, I was physically disabled, I couldn't even sleep with my wife or take a shower, my marriage was in shambles, and I was paying in spades for years of building a career and neglecting my family. The next morning I lowered myself from the wheelchair onto the hardwood floor and started removing the bandages. I got through some of the cleaning and then it occurred to me, *Why am I doing this? Who is it for? Me? Her? Say I lose my leg or even my life. What does it matter now? Can I even change the outcome? I did my best and still got staph. Why try?*

I paused with the razor in my hand. I felt like putting it away and letting the future bring what it would. The house was quiet. Nobody would know I had neglected the leg. If I died, they would be blessed with the life insurance.

In my heart I knew I was making a life-or-death decision.

Some sense of duty or a last flicker of an impulse to live passed through my soul. Joylessly, I looked down at the leg and with robotic movements began shaving around the pins, applying new bandages, repacking the left foot wound, and going on with my day.

I was looking for an angel, but she was still a long way off.

*

Word got out that my leg wasn't healing. It may have been through the Mormon church we belonged to or my childhood church, First Baptist Church of Screven, but soon I heard that an urgent prayer request had gone out countywide. People everywhere were praying that my condition would improve, that the bones would start to grow together, that I could avoid amputation. I even began to see signs in shop windows that said, "Welcome home, Howard, our hometown hero" and "Pray for Howard Wasdin." Prayer alerts went out in the newspaper and on the radio. I was grateful for all of it. It was like God himself had rallied the community around me.

I was still going to the whirlpool a couple of times a week, and there I ran into a guy whose example challenged my own dim view of life. He was eighty-five years old, a retired veteran, and had just undergone a hip replacement. His hip socket had worn out, and when he tried to walk it had been bone on bone, very painful. He was sitting in a larger whirlpool to increase circulation around the hip after the surgery. We struck up a conversation.

"I didn't want to have surgery, but I wasn't ready to be in a wheel-chair," he said, sounding jolly.

I was amazed that a guy that old would have such an invasive surgery. Just being put to sleep at any age is a risk. But his upbeat attitude seemed to have carried him through. "I feel so good, I should have done this twenty years ago," he said. "I get around great now. Best thing I ever did."

There in front of me was the future—not mine, exactly, but an example I could follow. He was fifty years older than I was and his zeal for life was undiminished. I felt like a slug by comparison, wallowing in my own pity back home. His example stayed in my mind and worked its way into my attitude. He didn't know it, but that conversation changed my life.

With the community praying and my hope getting just a little brighter, I went in for more X-rays a few weeks later. It was the moment of truth. The doctor came in looking flustered, the old X-rays in one hand, the new ones in the other. He punched both sets into the light box, side by side.

Night and day.

"I've never seen anything like it," he said. "Do you see this? The bone has formed here in just three weeks. Look at the old one—nothing. Now look where it is today—fused solid, back together. It's like your leg decided to start working again."

The difference was obvious even to me. The bone from a few weeks before looked like a jumble of pieces. Now it was one solid piece. It was beautiful.

"Here," the doctor continued, pointing to other areas of newly formed bone. "Here as well. Do you see? It's extraordinary." He shook his head. "It just doesn't happen that fast. Do you realize how lucky you are?"

"Yes, I do," I said. In my mind I was shouting, *Thank you, God!* I knew I had experienced a miracle as real as anything in the Bible. It was a result of the community's united prayer.

I went home jubilant and told everyone what had happened. Word spread that my leg had miraculously healed, and the prayers turned to rejoicing. I knew that God was at work even in the darkest time of my life. It was a major boost.

I would soon see just how strong my leg was. One day some weeks later, the doctor came in looking at another X-ray and said something strange: "The pins aren't doing their job anymore. Your bone is all soggy where they connect to it. We may as well take them out."

When the pins first go in, they have what is called "intimate contact" with the bone. After a while the bone grows softer around the pins, rendering them useless. My pins were now floating in the bone, not holding anything tight. It was a normal part of the healing.

Without giving me any anesthetic, the doctor took a tool that looks like a vise grip and began to unscrew the pins. The pain was more psychological than physical. I watched with strange fascination as the long screws emerged from my flesh.

But after removing the fixator, the doctor did something that scared me to death.

"Let's see how stable this thing is," he said, then grabbed my leg above and below the fracture site and put shearing force on the bone to see how it responded. I nearly came out of my skin with fear that the leg would snap in half like a twig. When you've immobilized your limb and treated it so delicately for so long, you can't believe there is any strength left in it. It was like watching someone manhandle a baby.

As he pushed and yanked, I felt no pain at all. The leg withstood his pressure. I was amazed at my body's resilience. The bone really had grown back.

They put the leg in a cast, and I went home to experience another miracle: my first shower in months. My niece brought home a plastic bag I could slip over the cast, which made it mostly waterproof. Until you've gone months without bathing standing up, you can't appreciate it. Hot water hit the back of my head, my face, my back. All I could think was, *This is the best thing I have ever experienced. This is heaven.*

Somehow I had made it through.

Blake swears I took off my own cast while grilling pork chops on the back porch. Months after the fixator came off, I had such a bad itch that I kept asking him to fetch screwdrivers, coat hangers, anything to reach inside the cast for some relief. Finally I said, "Bring me some cutters." He handed them to me and I cut the whole thing off. It was about time anyway.

I do remember sitting alone and looking at both legs side by side. My left leg looked young, muscular, pink. My right leg looked hairless, atrophied, and colorless. It was half the size of my good leg. I could see where the pin holes had been, the ugly patch of skin where the grafts had taken hold, and the baseball-size wound where the bullet had entered. The whole thing looked ridiculous, and I was disgusted. *This is as good as I could heal—me, the superhuman Howard Wasdin?* I thought. *This is pathetic. Doesn't this leg know who I am? How dare my leg not cooperate with my future plans.*

I had held to the secret hope that I could get back with the Teams and resume my previous lifestyle. When the doctors told me I wouldn't be able to run or carry a one-hundred-pound rucksack, or a two-hundred-pound person, I inwardly disregarded it. Now, looking at the spaghetti noodle attached to my hip, that dream began to slip away. I had survived, but it was possible my career had not. I began to reckon with the fact that my future might not be with SEAL Team Six. I had no idea what else to do.

The miracle of my leg's restoration, and the encouragement I got from the community, stoked my natural optimism. God had sent some angels—the guys at the hospital, Ricky, the old guy in the hot tub— to bring me through the hardest time of my life. I began to see hope for the future, whatever form that took. I also began to believe that if my leg had healed miraculously, so could my marriage.

I looked forward to having the new baby. Katherine remained distant, but I quietly hoped the baby's arrival would be an inflection point for us, putting us on an upward trajectory. Maybe it would mend our broken love and restore some of the trust. I anticipated the birth the way a kid looks forward to a day at Disneyland.

I didn't know it would bring a true surprise.

THREE

THE NEW BABY

It was looking to be one of the best days of my life.

It was the spring of 1994 and I was still in a full-length cast, feeling pathetic hobbling around on crutches, unable to load my own moving van. But that didn't matter because I was about to be a father again. My wife was in a hospital in Liberty County, Georgia. I had just gotten news that she had gone into labor. I was hustling around our family's storage unit in Virginia Beach, and a bunch of SEAL Team Six buddies were loading my family's worldly possessions into a twenty-four-foot van so Katherine, Blake, Rachel, and I could live near family in Georgia more or less permanently. I couldn't carry anything that sunny day so I leaned on my crutches and strawbossed. A couple of guys who'd been with me in Mogadishu—guys who'd seen life and death with me in the most extreme circumstances—were toting my lamps, chairs, and dishes into the truck. Talk about taking one for the team.

Getting back to the hospital was the only thing on my mind. The new baby, our third, had given me something positive to look forward to in that bleak time for my career, my family, and my soul. My future with the Teams was unclear after what my body had been through, and as I watched these elite warriors fill a truck with my shabby belongings, I wondered if I would ever join them on the battle-field again. I hoped so, but only time and my right leg would tell.

One of the guys slammed the big door shut, and I didn't waste any time hitting the highway with Ricky, my travel partner. My mind was already down South. I should have let Ricky drive, but I was stubborn about getting back to normal. I used my left foot for both pedals. The loaded Ryder truck felt agonizingly slow—full of beds and knick-knacks I wasn't even sure I would recognize when we unpacked them. I almost wished I could park it on the side of the road, rent a sports car, and get to Georgia a lot faster.

"What do you think it'll be?" Ricky asked as we rumbled down the interstate, my cast to the side and my "good" foot mashed on the accelerator.

"I don't know and I don't really care," I said. "Whatever it is, boy or girl, I'll be happy."

I pondered whether the arrival of this child would indeed bring Katherine and me into a new season of love. Things had been so dis-tant and difficult since I'd been back. Like many warriors, I had been trained for success in battle, but I was losing the home front. As a stub-born optimist, I thought we could turn things around. All we needed was a fresh start and a fresh commitment to each other and our family.

Halfway through the eight-and-a-half-hour drive, the phone rang. They were called "car phones" back then and they cost about two dollars a minute to operate, but any news from the delivery room was priceless to me.

"Hello?" I said quickly. "It's Howard. I'm here."

It was one of my wife's cousins. She sighed.

"Hi, Howard. I wanted to tell you that Katherine had the baby. It's a girl."

The words were right, but she sounded strangely unenthusiastic. Highly attuned to nuance, and trying to discern if the birth had been healthy, I could barely get my words out in the right order.

"Oh my gosh, is she healthy? Is she doing good?" I asked.

"Yeah, she's doing fine," the cousin said.

I hung on the line, waiting for a great big "Howard, congratulations! Your daughter was born and she's beautiful. Get down here quick." Instead, her words were few and suspiciously flat.

"What color are her hair and her eyes?" I prodded.

"Um, it was hard to tell. I think brown."

"Is something wrong?" I asked. "Is Katherine okay?"

"No, she's fine."

"Well, can I talk to her?"

Maybe I'll get better responses from the mother.

There was a quiet moment while she passed the phone. Ricky tried to read my eyes for information. I kept my left foot pressed on the pedal, trying to will the truck to move faster. Katherine came on sounding exhausted and maybe a bit happier than her cousin. At least I tried to read her tone that way.

"How'd it go?" I asked her. "You doing okay?"

"I'm fine," she said.

"How's the baby girl?"

"She's fine too."

"Everything look good? Ten fingers, ten toes?"

There was a moment before she responded, "Everything looks okay. She's with the nurses right now."

"Why? Is something wrong?"

"No, they're just cleaning her up."

"Well, does she have my big ears?"

That was always the important question because my first daughter, Rachel, had inherited my ears and was always pulling her hair back and saying, "See? I'm my daddy's child." Luckily, she also had long, beautiful hair to hide them with.

"No, I don't think so. I couldn't tell," Katherine said.

I was getting frustrated with the non-answers, so I decided to wrap it up and just see them when I got there.

"I'll be there in a few hours. I'm four hundred miles away," I told her. "Are you sure everything's okay?"

"Yeah, everything's fine. Listen, I'm tired. Talk to my cousin again."

Her cousin came back on the phone.

"Just tell me everything's okay," I said. "What's the baby like? Does she look like me?"

The cousin didn't give any answer at all. I tried again.

"Okay, does she look like her mama?"

"Yes, you can see a little of her mama in her," she said.

"Well, we're coming straight there. See you soon," I said and hung up, perplexed.

"Everything okay?" Ricky asked, my concern written on his face.

"I don't know. I guess so. That's what they told me," I said and drove in silence for a while wondering if there was some physical complication the doctors were still investigating. I braced myself for bad news but comforted myself with the thought that if it really was bad, they would have sounded even worse. *Maybe I was just reading them wrong. Maybe I'm the nervous new daddy.* I couldn't help smiling: my third child, and second daughter, had been born. I was a father again. I couldn't wait to hold her in my arms and reconnect with the miracle of life.

*

Having kids gave me a chance at redemption. My childhood had been so painful that I swore I would protect my own kids and parent them completely differently from how I had been raised. My mom, Millie, was just sixteen when I was born, and my first sister was born less than a year later. I have no memory of my biological father, Ben Wilbanks. I do remember his parents, Grandma and Grandpa Wilbanks, who lived on the dairy with us in West Palm Beach, Florida. Dad worked in the dairy, I was told. Early in the morning I would walk down the road to my grandparents' cottage. I loved Florida's mild weather, the sound and smell of the surf, the easy life.

At some point the details of our family history go dim. We know that my mother met another man, Leon Wasdin, while she was working as a waitress in a truck stop. Leon was six years older than she was. Some kind of relationship sprang up. I remember one day in winter getting in the car and arriving in Screven, Georgia, at a house I had never seen. It was the coldest weather I had yet experienced. I didn't realize that Screven had just become our new home; we were not going back to Florida, the dairy, my grandparents, the beach. I was seven or eight years old. Sometime later Millie drove me to the courthouse and drilled me on the way there: "When the judge asks you if you want Leon to be your daddy, you say yes."

I did what she told me, but in the back of my mind I was thinking, *Oh no. Now we're stuck with him*. Leon did not seem kind, and every memory of my biological father was squelched. I never saw a photograph of him, never heard a positive word about him. Stories passed among my relatives about how he had abandoned us and how Leon had saved us in some way. Millie once told me that my dad had kidnapped us and run off, then landed in jail. While he was there she grabbed us and ran off with Leon. I wasn't sure which story to believe, but I accepted that my "real" dad was a bad guy. Over the years I built up resentment against this phantom figure, not least because his apparent abandonment had left me in a new and painful family situation.

Leon was a watermelon farmer, and I found myself working in his watermelon business performing more manual labor than I thought possible for a child. I learned to hoe watermelon fields, removing less-productive vines so the more robust ones could yield better. The watermelons were enormous: long and fat, unlike the diminutive round ones in stores today. Thousands of vines crawled across the fields that Leon leased from local landowners. It was labor-intensive farming. Often all eight of us Wasdins, including Leon and Millie, would be out hoeing and breaking up the soil at the same time. The dark, sandy loam was crumbly and forgiving, but the wonderful life next to the ocean had given way to hot, muggy days, deep forests, and constant backbreaking work.

Once the watermelons were ripe, we had to get them out of the field quickly. On a Saturday we would work our way across the field in a line, cutting watermelons where they lay, throwing the twenty- and thirty-pound melons down a line of people to the edge of the field, placing them into a pile row, then loading them onto a small field truck and taking them to an eighteen-wheeler parked in the shade. There we packed them in by the hundreds, and if you did it right you could pack watermelons as high as your head without their splitting underneath the weight. The watermelons were so heavy and the work so arduous that we had to rotate positions often, especially when throwing them onto the field truck. You couldn't last long tossing those melons to the person in the truck bed so we would toss fifteen or twenty, then rotate, toss fifteen or twenty, then rotate. A week later we did the whole process again and got a second crop, then a third crop, and even a fourth crop from the same field.

When I hit fifteen years old, I was already driving like a grown man. I would wake up early and take Leon's truck to pick up field workers on the other side of the tracks in what was called the "quarter," short for the "colored quarter." Men living in lean-tos and homes without running water would come out their front doors and jump in the back of the truck. By the time I was sixteen, I was driving eighteen-wheelers laden with watermelons from Florida to South Carolina, unloading them, taking a two-hour nap, and driving all the way back to Florida or Screven. It's a wonder I didn't die falling asleep at the wheel.

The work was hard and it might have been fun, but the pervasive atmosphere of fear in our household sapped any joy out of it. Leon was a hard man. I don't remember ever feeling love from him or seeing him demonstrate affection. He would drink and go into a rage at the slightest provocation. When he gave me an order, I soon learned I wasn't supposed to ask for specific direction or I would be in big trouble. I had to figure it out on my own and hope I did it the way he wanted. He didn't like to talk, and this fact alone drove away nearly all the people closest to him. He seemed to work constantly and expected me to as well. When I didn't do something up to his standard, he beat me badly.

One of my jobs was to collect all the pecans that fell from the trees around our house. We sold or ate every nut that fell, and if we missed any, Leon became furious. He would park his truck next to the house in the evening, and if he heard any pecans popping under his tires, that was my butt. How well I remember the sickening *pop-pop-pop* those pecans made as he pulled in, and I knew each time I was in for a belt whipping.

Another one of my jobs was to go fishing with him in the inky black creeks near our home to catch jackfish, mudfish, and gar. There, surrounded by thickets and dense undergrowth with almost intolerable populations of gnats, we cast our lures into the water where poisonous water moccasins also resided. The lures cost three or four dollars each, and when Leon would get one stuck, he would make me take off my clothes, jump in the water, and detach the hook from whatever it had caught.

I remember one time being up to my chest in murky water, holding the line and getting ready to dive down and wriggle the hook free when I saw a water moccasin five feet away. Leon saw the snake and said, "Boy, you'd better go ahead. That snake's more afraid of you than you are of him." I dived down and found the hook. While tugging it I felt something underwater bump my arm. Snakes can't bite underwater, so I just thought, *I hope whatever bumped me is more scared of me than I am of it.*

Years later, when doing a dive at SEAL Team Two in Norfolk, Virginia, I was underwater when a sea creature bumped my arm. The very same words went through my mind: *I hope whatever bumped me is more scared of me than I am of it.*

As a father now, I can't imagine sending my son into black waters full of poisonous snakes to retrieve a hook, but that's the way Leon was. After a couple of years living under his roof, I concluded, sorrow-fully, that he had probably adopted me for the free labor. I did more work before I was twenty than some kids do their entire lives, and my body is still paying the toll.

The Wasdin house sat within a block of two churches, includ-ing our home congregation, First Baptist Church of Screven. Leon added a small, windowless bedroom to the tiny white house and this was my bedroom. The girls (my mom had given birth to my second sister) lived in the main house in larger, sunlit rooms. I spent so much time outside hunting and fishing that it didn't much matter. I sold possums and raccoons to a black man across the tracks for five dollars each. I shot raccoons out of pecan trees, cut off their tails and sold them to be made into fishing flies, then skinned out the carcasses and sold the meat. I tried raccoon meat one time. It was a little too greasy for me. The same man bought mudfish and gar I caught in local "runs" or creeks.

But those pleasant times exploring and hunting were outweighed by the punishments. I was beaten often to the point of having physical wounds. Beatings came for all sorts of reasons—basically, whatever made Leon angry. I remember one time in third grade when my friends and I decided to fight back against a bully who had been taking our lunch money and marbles and had given one of my friends a bloody lip. We had just gotten Daisy Red Ryder BB guns for Christmas. We plotted to bring them to school and wait up in the oak tree along the pathway for this bully to arrive. Then we would pepper him with BBs so he wouldn't shove us around anymore.

Sure enough, the bully came down the sidewalk, and we waited quietly in the tree with our guns. When he got underneath, we opened up on him: *pow, ch-ching, pow, ch-ching, pow*. Instead of running away, the bully did something I didn't expect: he stopped and stood there in stunned confusion while we shot him. Every time we landed a shot he grabbed the spot with a hand. His hands were flying all over his body as we volleyed BBs at him again and again.

The state patrol showed up and the school called our parents. The bully, now pockmarked from the BBs, seemed like an innocent victim. Interestingly, he never bullied us again, and in fact became a friend and part of our family's watermelon field crew. He was a loyal and good worker. Years later, when I was home from the navy on leave and helping Leon on the watermelon truck, the former bully said to me, "Feel right here on my shoulder." I felt a bulge beneath the skin. "Is that what I think it is?" I asked. He nodded and said, "Every once in a while a BB will work its way to the surface." It was my first sniper op, but unlike most targets, this one became a good friend.

When Leon heard I had shot the kid, he took me home and beat me half to death. The routine was always the same: he would take me into my room, lean me over the bed, remove his leather belt, and start waling. He was right-handed, so he stood on my left side, meaning that the belt landed more frequently on my right bottom cheek. My whole backside would become a patchwork of welts that scabbed and took days to heal. I often had to peel the underwear away from my bottom because the wounds wept fluids.

This kind of beating took place every couple of weeks until I was a teenager. Leon quit drinking when I was ten and some of the rage seemed to go out of the beatings, but he still delivered them with brutality. During the beatings Millie would sit in her chair in the living room. She and Leon each had their own chairs, and we were forbidden to sit in them. The house was small, and I have no doubt that the sound of the belt hitting me could be heard outside. I was forbidden from making sounds when being whipped, and I learned to endure it without making noise, apart from a muffled grunt or an occasional sob. But when they were particularly bad, such as the time we shot the bully with the BB guns, there was no amount of restraint that could keep me from crying out in pain, so ferocious was the beating. My tears infuriated Leon and he would say, "You'd better dry it up or I will give you something to cry about." Millie would often remark to me afterward, "He does this because he loves you."

Nobody knows how many times I lay in bed and cried myself to sleep from the time I was adopted to the time I graduated high school. I prayed sometimes, "God, please kill them. Let them die in a car wreck. I don't care what happens, just put me in another situation." I couldn't tell my friends what was happening. They knew our home was strict, but I was embarrassed to tell them the details. I never had any ideas of revenge because I took my mom's word: Leon must love me or he wouldn't care enough to beat me. My only solace came in work. The harder I worked after a beating session, the better I felt. I knew that Leon would not be angry with me if I was working hard. Work became my escape.

The belt whippings lasted until I was a senior in high school, though they became less frequent because I learned to do exactly what Leon wanted done, in the way he wanted it done. I was also bigger by then, and more often he punished me with his hands instead of with whippings. One of the last times he shoved me around, we had just arrived in Florida with a load of watermelons. We parked the truck. I got out on the passenger's side and walked into my Uncle Koi's house thinking that was where Leon was going.

Leon didn't come in, so I used the bathroom and came out to see him standing in the living room with his hands on his hips. He was livid. I was trying to figure out what was going on when he came at me and gave me a hard shove with both hands right in my chest. Apparently he had started emptying out the utility box of an old, rusty chain and expected me to help him do it immediately. I had done wrong by walking inside when there was work to do. From that point on, if I was anywhere near the truck and heard the hood come up, I ran there because Leon was going to need help checking the oil or whatever needed done. He expected me essentially to read his mind and be ready.

Leon did not give me advice on being a man, and I didn't ask him for any. It was unthinkable to have that kind of conversation with him. Instead, I went to my uncle Carol, Leon's brother, one of the kindest men in my life and a completely different kind of man than Leon. When I went through puberty, I asked Uncle Carol all my questions about the things that were happening to my body. Sometimes my naïve questions struck him funny, and he would start laughing and have to spit out his Red Man chewing tobacco juice so he wouldn't swallow it. I loved Uncle Carol. He taught me to drive an eighteen-wheeler because Leon didn't have the patience. Uncle Carol showed me what a man and a father could be. He gave me a glimpse into the kind of life I wished I could have had with my real dad, if my real dad hadn't been the bad person everyone said he was.

The other wonderful influence on me was Colonel Parker, the Air Force Junior ROTC commandant. I joined the Junior ROTC in high school and under his guidance rose quickly through the ranks. The discipline I learned at home helped, and so did my eagerness to please Colonel Parker. I always won the Best-Dressed Cadet award. My pant creases would cut you, my shoes were shined to a mirrored finish, my hair was cut exactly right, and I always had three creases in the front of my shirt. But Parker's influence went deeper than telling me how to tie a tie. He taught me to lead people.

I was the commander of the honor guard with a little squad under my command. I taught them to march in the Christmas and homecoming parades. Colonel Parker showed me how to lead by love, not fear. His structure and discipline had a positive purpose and wasn't about asserting his dominance. Colonel Parker commanded my respect just by his example and inspired in me a genuine desire to impress and please him. If I messed up it wasn't the end of the world, and he didn't rain hell down on me as happened at home. He would simply say, "Have you thought about trying it this way?" If it weren't for Colonel Parker, I wouldn't have known how to have a conversation with a superior.

As I grew into a young man, I also had to acknowledge that as painful as the beatings and lack of love were, being raised under Leon Wasdin's iron hand built some good things into me: a strong work ethic, organization, determination, attention to detail. It probably spared me the fate of my childhood friends, most of whom served time in prison. His way of raising me also helped when I joined the military. At boot camp at age twenty-one, I couldn't understand how other guys were getting in trouble all the time. They found it difficult to say "yes sir" and "no sir," couldn't keep their clothes folded and their A and B drawers straight, couldn't even make a bed. They would nearly cry when forced to do ten push-ups.

I thought, *Are you kidding? This is the least work I've done in my entire life. They're giving us three hot meals a day, a place to sleep, and you guys are acting like we're in prison. This is Shangri-La!* At night guys would lie in bed actually calling for their mommies. "Where's my mom? What have I done?" they would moan. A couple of days later those guys were gone. To me, boot camp was a breeze. At the end of each day I was like, *Is that all? What else are we doing?* To top it off, they gave me a big check at the end. I thought, *No way. They gave me training, food, a place to live, and they're paying me too? This is incredible.*

Right before going to boot camp I had my last big blowup with Leon. It happened when I told him I was marrying Katherine. When he and Millie heard that their Baptist-raised son was marrying a Mormon, he told me, "Pack your stuff, get out of my house, and don't come back." I remember standing face-to-face with him. I wasn't backing down this time. He saw me looking in his eyes and he said, "Go ahead, bow up to me," meaning he was daring me to arch my back in defiance, daring me to challenge him. "I'll go through you like a dose of salts," he threatened. That's a Southern phrase referring to the way Epsom salts clean out your insides as a laxative.

There was no talking to Leon. If I tried to have a conversation with him or look him in the eye, he said I was "talking back" and giving him "that look." The "look" meant any eye contact at all. As his child, you had to keep your head down to show submission. The truth is I needed guidance, a listening ear, and direction. I didn't get that from Leon like I did from Colonel Parker and Uncle Carol. I could have used it especially when making the decision to marry. Instead, I got the typical "my way or the highway" choice. Thank God it didn't come to blows that day, but I did leave the house I had grown up in one last time, went to the corner store, called Katherine's house on a pay phone, and at her mom's invitation lived in her parents' spare bedroom until Katherine and I were married. That was how I left home.

The pain of that childhood would last a lifetime. Thoughts about my "real" dad came to mind sometimes, but mostly I dismissed them, believing the stories of how he had abandoned us. In a strange way

I felt loyal to Leon for taking us in as kids, feeding us and raising us as best he knew how. But that didn't keep me from wishing that my childhood had been different, and wishing that I had been raised in a loving home with both my parents.

The issue of my parentage reared its head years later when I was ready to join SEAL Team Six and had to get top-secret clearance. As part of the adoption process, my birth certificate had been sealed in the records in Wayne County, and Leon Wasdin's name had been listed as my father. The FBI began digging through my past in preparation for granting top-secret clearance, and they did a thorough job. I heard from grade-school teachers and relatives that FBI agents were calling them to ask about my past. Then one day three FBI agents showed up in the ready room at SEAL Team Six red team, where we planned ops and prepped gear, and greeted me skeptically.

"You got something you want to tell us?" they asked.

My first thought was, *Uh-oh, they found out I shot up the bully. I should have disclosed that.*

But they weren't there about a BB prank. They were there to inform me that Leon Wasdin was not my real father. They pulled out my birth certificate and thrust it at me like I was some scam artist being exposed.

"We know for a fact that Leon Wasdin is not your biological father," they said.

"I know he's not," I said.

"So why did you put down Leon Wasdin as your biological father?"

I explained that when I was adopted, my original records were sealed by a superior court judge who ordered a mock-up birth certificate showing Leon as my father. That's how they did it in Georgia. I couldn't even see my original birth certificate without filing a petition with a superior court judge to unseal it. I'm told they do this to protect the adoptive parents and child from the biological parents.

I think they barely bought it.

When the agents left, I wondered, *Am I really going to be kicked out of SEAL Team Six over this?* I wasn't kicked out, though the process dragged on a few more months. It brought to mind again the painful fact that my biological father hadn't cared enough about me or Millie or my sister to stick with us, or so I thought. I longed for a man to treat me like a beloved son, not a hired hand or a whipping boy.

Given my experience of childhood, I was determined to give my kids a very different kind of upbringing.

*

I managed not to kill Ricky and myself driving that full truck at top speed, and we arrived at the hospital before sundown. I parked the behemoth way out in the parking lot and tottered across the expanse on my crutches, Ricky beside me. The hospital was the same one I'd been to many times for physical therapy, so it was like a second home to me. I couldn't go five steps inside the building without people stopping to shake my hand. They treated me like the rock star I still hoped I was. My physical therapist saw me through a window and came out. Others were hugging me.

"Hey, how is the leg doing?" he asked, running his eyes over the visible part of my cast, which he had not yet seen.

"Terrific," I said. "No more whirlpool."

He grinned.

"Listen," I said. "My wife just had a new daughter so I'd better get up there."

"Cool, come back down and we'll have a cigar," he said.

Ricky and I boarded the elevator, me in my Polo shirt and baggy sweats, the only pants that would fit over my leg cast. I looked like someone who'd rolled out of bed and gone to Costco in his jammies, but it couldn't be helped. In the stillness of that small journey, I replayed the conversations I'd had in the car. The flat voices, the impassive assurances. I so badly wanted to hear, "The baby's great! She looks just like you. She's got your ears!"

Instead, I'd gotten toneless assurances: "The baby's fine. Katherine's fine. Don't worry."

Ricky looked over at me. He knew I'd be a little tense until we surveyed things with our own eyes.

Katherine and her family were in the recovery room, and when we walked in, nobody moved. It was like they were waiting for the judge to arrive. Nobody rushed to greet me or Ricky, but acknowledged us with sober nods. Katherine looked up and tried to smile but seemed apprehensive. Her mother sat to the side, almost grimly quiet. I walked over to Katherine's bed.

"Hey, baby," I said.

We'd done this twice before, and those moments with Blake and Rachel had been flooded with happiness. Blake was my first child, and the son of my love. I remembered holding his little frame and realizing I had become a father for the first time and that life would never be the same. Memories of Rachel as a newborn rushed over me as well. She had arrived when I was doing land-warfare training in Virginia for Desert Storm. I got a call from SEAL Team Two command, the Team I was with at that time, and they cut me loose to go see her.

Those experiences had been pure excitement on all sides. Relatives had rushed down the hallway to greet me: "Have you seen her? She looks just like you!" The nurses had brought Rachel down, laid her on her mom's chest, and let me hold her as well. Holding that baby girl for the first time was one of the best experiences of my life. Girls are so different from boys, and you can tell from the start there is a special bond of protection, love, and care between a father and daughter.

This time, the mood hung as low as the sun setting outside the window. Maybe I would find that this had been a harder birth than the others. Maybe the problem was with Katherine, not the baby. Maybe the novelty had just worn off after the first two.

"Are you okay?" I asked Katherine. "You were making me worried on the telephone."

She summoned a smile that went more over my shoulder than into my eyes. "I'm fine. It's okay," she said.

"Well, where's the baby now?"

"She's in the room where they keep all the babies."

"Can I go see her?"

Katherine nodded and closed her eyes, leaning back against the pillow. Her mother watched as Ricky and I walked out. A simple "How was the drive?" or "Congratulations" would have been nice, but wasn't forthcoming.

Ricky and I walked down the hall until we found the big glass wall. On the other side were clear bassinets holding all the newborn babies, and there near the window was mine. Ricky looked at her, then looked at me, then looked at her again, his eyes widening just a touch.

All I could do was fill my eyes with her. She was beautiful. Not much of her was visible, but to me she already seemed perfect. Ricky watched for my reaction. Something seemed to unsettle him.

"Oh my gosh," I said. "Look at that."

"Look at what?" he said quickly.

"That little girl," I said.

"Yeah," he said after a moment. "She is beautiful. Now you've got two girls."

"I can't wait to hold her. Maybe they'll bring her down soon."

Ricky looked closely at her.

"She sure is pretty," he said. "I think she favors her mother."

With the little cap on her head, I couldn't tell, and it didn't much matter. The toes and fingers were all there; she was breathing and sleeping peacefully. I decided if everyone else was worn out or just plain not excited, that was their problem. Maybe they'd gotten into some sort of argument about the name. But I was a father again. Happiness bloomed in my heart. At that moment I saw a better future for all of us together.

Thank you, God, I said in my heart. *Maybe this is where we get to start over.*

We named her Heather, and she did not have my ears. In fact, a couple of months after she came home, I was cradling her in my lap and couldn't help noticing her dark complexion.

"This baby's dark," I said to Katherine through the kitchen door. It was a casual, almost offhanded comment, but Katherine's response seemed well rehearsed.

"Our family has a lot of American Indian in it," she said. "My mother's mother was full-blooded Cherokee. That's what manifested."

Her family was pasty white, to a person. I had never seen any manifestation of dark skin, so my curiosity was piqued, but I didn't let the thought linger. My mind was on a million other things: *Would I return to the Teams? Why had I survived while great men like Daniel Busch had died that day in Mogadishu? What would I do if my military career was over? Would my right leg ever really recover?*

As tough as my recovery had been, I was enjoying my time with Rachel and Blake immensely. I had been gone so much during Blake's childhood that, to use his words, he had "gotten used to the spaces in between." I never could tell the family I was leaving because ops came without warning. The only way Blake knew I was leaving was that in the middle of the night, when orders usually came, I would pick him up out of bed and put him in my bed next to Katherine. If he woke up in my spot in the morning, he knew I was somewhere fighting bad guys. When they picked me up after the op, often late at night, he was usually asleep in the back of the car.

I'd always tried to have adventures with Blake as well. We would run together for fun. One day we were jogging on the beach and saw Jet Skis for rent. I gave the rental guys my work pager and told them, "If this pager goes off, I don't care what you do. Flag me down, come get me. I've got to know." Then Blake and I rode like wild men in the surf for an hour. When we were done, I said half jokingly, "Don't tell your mama we did this. She'll get mad at me for endangering her little baby."

When we got home, Blake took a bath, came out, and said something about what we'd done. I gave him a mock-serious look and his face dropped like, "Oops!" I told him later that I was just kidding and that it's always better to tell on yourself than carry around a secret. I had already told his mom about our Jet Ski adventure.

I didn't realize, though, that Blake was also going through strange situations when I was away, before Mogadishu. One night at around eleven, his mother called a cab to the house, put Blake in it, and had him ride aimlessly around town until around 1:00 a.m., just Blake and this cab driver. The driver then delivered Blake back to our trailer and nothing else was said. Blake also saw a number of strangers come and go from the house, though he never witnessed anything that upset him. Naturally, as he got older, he connected the dots and had a lot of questions.

Those questions included some about his new baby sister. As Heather grew older and more beautiful, her unusual features stood out more: dark skin, kinky hair, a nose that looked different from either of our families. Adults were too polite to mention it publicly, but Blake and Rachel started to hear rumors at school.

"You've got a n***** sister," kids told Blake.

"Do not. Shut up," he responded. He came home more than once having been in a fight over his family's honor. He wouldn't tell us why at the time.

I heard the slur for the first time one day at Walmart when Heather was just six months old, but wasn't convinced it was aimed at me, so I let it pass. I came home to find Katherine straightening Heather's hair again, as if on some crusade to keep it from curling up as it naturally wanted to. She treated Heather differently in other ways as well. Whenever the kids went outside, Blake and Rachel were allowed to play in the sun unprotected, but Katherine and her mom were almost manic about keeping Heather covered in sunblock. One time we were out on a boat on the lake pulling the kids on an inner tube, and for some reason we didn't have any sunblock. Heather got so dark I almost couldn't believe it.

Blake in particular was starting to notice. "Dad, why is Heather so dark? Why does she look so different from us?" he asked. I gave him the safe explanation, the one Katherine and her family had given me: "That's just the way genetics are. Things pop up. You can't always see what's there."

After a while, as her appearance grew even more different, a new story surfaced. Katherine told me, "The reason our family came to Georgia from South Carolina is because one of them had an affair with a slave. So we have an African American in our bloodline. It shows up now and then."

Never mind that it had never shown up before, or that I'd never heard about their Cherokee or slave blood until now. On went the sunblock, out came the hair straightening iron, and louder grew the murmurs around town and within our family. It even got back to me through the grapevine that one family member was saying, "Oh my gosh, I cannot believe Howard has fallen for this."

The more I heard those suggestions, the more entrenched I became against them. I had a powerful incentive: my own guilt. While I was away on ops, I didn't have a girl in every port, but I had one in most of them. Those passing encounters could be dismissed by some as trivial physical encounters, but my heart knew they were infidelity, plain and simple. My conscience couldn't shake it. Guilt before God drove me to try to atone for that by sticking with Katherine now, over an entire community's increasing doubts.

I had another motivation: to be a different kind of father than Leon had been to me. Instead of driving my kids hard and getting after them with a belt, I wanted to parent with open arms and an open heart. I'm not saying I was good at it, but that goal was becoming more important to me as I got older. Having pushed my family away for so many years while serving on the Teams, there was no way I was going to do anything but embrace them now that I was home.

One day Blake was watching his cousins play a baseball game at the recreation center when a player from the other team came over and stood in front of him. "You're the brother of that little n***** girl, huh?" the kid said. Blake's cousin heard it and came flying out of the dugout with a bat in his hand. "You want to say that again?" he said. The kid backed off, but by now we couldn't ignore that Heather was different. The kids around town were just repeating what they heard their parents say. I didn't know much about genetics. I wanted to believe the slave story, the Indian story—anything to balance out my own infidelities. I had gone into stubbornness mode because I felt my life, family, and future depended on it.

We took a trip to visit my best friend in the Teams back in Virginia Beach in late 1994, when Heather was approaching a year old. He was living on the beach with his girlfriend, and we arrived one weekend to stay at their house. During the visit he invited me to take a walk on the beach with him, and there he laid into me.

"You have got to wake up," he said. "That is not your child. Look at her! She did not come from you."

Up to then I had been more curious than angry about the situation. My love for Heather and my natural delight in children had helped me keep unwanted thoughts at bay. So had my desire to start over and be the kind of father I never had. Now my temper flashed and my defenses went way up.

"You'd better figure out when to shut up, 'cause I'm not hearing any of this," I said.

"Anyone can look at that child and tell it's not yours," he pressed, motioning back to the house where Heather was. "You are letting yourself believe the most ridiculous thing."

I trusted this guy, and his words wounded me. The Teams are the best group of guys in the world, in part because nothing is sacred and the answer to nearly everything is: "Man up." He was coming at me direct and hard, like we always did to each other. But I was in a different place now, and that wasn't going to work this time.

"I don't think this is a discussion," I said. "I believe my wife. Enough said."

"Are you joking, man? Are you kidding?" he said, turning to me as we walked. "Open your eyes!"

I thought back to the hospital room the day Heather had been born. Nobody was glowing with joy except me. Katherine's mother's face had been drawn, almost mournful. Seeing it now in my mind, I realized it told me everything I had needed to know, if I hadn't been so focused on myself at the time.

"Listen, I'm here to have a good time, not talk about some ridiculous suggestion about my daughter," I said. "I suggest you leave that where it lies."

He made a noise of disgust. In truth, I might have listened if he'd approached it gently and offered some support. It wasn't, "Hey, can we talk about this?" It was, "Your wife slept around on you—deal with it." I was reflexively protective of my family and my honor, especially around the people I admired the most, my Team members. I'd already lost some of my tactical superiority because of my leg injury. To admit that my family and honor were gone was to lose the rest of who I was.

"You can think what you want, but everyone on the Team knows what was going on," he said. That hurt. Bad. It felt like these guys, my brothers in arms, were turning their backs on me. I'd given up my career and almost my life in service of my country. What did I get in return? My closest colleagues insisting that my new child wasn't mine. How could they betray me that way?

Another complicating fact was that I had been in a war and most of them hadn't. That changed my relationship with the Team members. I suspected there was some jealousy there, particularly among guys senior to me. This was a peaceful time for the United States. Most of the guys on the Team had never seen live combat. I was brand new to SEAL Team Six and happened to be on standby when the balloon went up. It was luck of the draw, and we all knew that. Whoever's in the box when the Shinola hits the fan, that's who gets the call. I was one of the lucky ones, if you can call it luck.

Getting trigger time ahead of a lot of other guys who had gone through the same training and served longer probably didn't sit well with them. I felt that might be feeding the rumors.

I had discovered at the memorial service for Dan Busch and others that the bond of war transcends all service. As close as I was to my buddies in SEAL Team Six, I now felt closer to the guys who'd gone through Mogadishu with me, whether they were SEALs, Delta Force, Air Force PJs, or whatever. Other guys had tried to explain that bond to me before, but you don't know until you've been in combat. Before then I had arrogantly thought that if you weren't in SEAL Team Six, you weren't on the A-team. Even my assessment of Dan Busch, when I first met him, was: *Okay, you're a good sniper, but you're Delta.* Now I knew there were guys in the SEAL Teams who I would never be in combat with, and would never develop such a strong bond with. I think they knew it too.

I couldn't help telling myself now, *Dan Busch wouldn't have treated me the way my SEAL buddy is treating me. He really cared. This guy is just getting in my face.* My bond with Dan, and my grief over his loss, felt stronger. Whether all that represented reality or just my perception, I don't know, but it drove the wedge deeper at that moment.

"Howard, are you crazy? Have you gone nuts?" my friend continued. "Look at that child. You're deluding yourself if you think that came from you."

I didn't have any more words, so I gave him a fist. He wasn't expecting it, but I could only catch him off guard once. We squared off and scuffled for a moment, two elite warriors, one with a crushed leg and no perceptible future, fighting pathetically in the sand over what they both knew was the truth.

It was stupid; there was nothing epic about it. Lashing out at my friend was one of the worst decisions I have made, and I regret it to this day. After a while we got up, went back to his house without speaking, and I packed up my family and left.

It was a quiet drive back to Georgia. Heather slept between us the whole way.

FOUR

REALITY CHECK

Bullets sound like a whip cracking when they fly over your head near enough to touch. In urban warfare, bullets ricochet all over the place, hitting the streets and bouncing into guys or striking concrete walls and "tumbling" down with the sound of a high-speed wasp until they come to rest in the ground or in somebody's flesh. In urban battles, ricocheting bullets cause more lower extremity injuries as soldiers get caught in a fast-motion, deadly pinball game.

I heard those sonic cracks and buzzes as I lay in the ditch in Mogadishu, looking up at the blue sky and wondering how things had gone so wrong. My mind was remarkably clear and calm in that moment. I had a good grasp on the facts: I knew we were running low on bullets. I knew I was down to my last magazine. I knew I was in real danger of dying. I could hear the enemy talking nearby, and I could even tell where the greatest threat was coming from. Blood loss had caused a little bit of systemic shock, and blood continued to flow out of my leg at a rate that would soon end my life, but in spite of that my mind was lucid. I was surprised at how I was still processing the data around me without any kind of panic. No blanking out, no losing track of time. I was very much in the moment and in control of whatever faculties were left to me.

Even when I realized I was going to die in this ditch and that my biggest regret was not telling my family and friends enough that I loved them—even then I didn't break down and come unglued. It just seemed the most rational thought, an epiphany perhaps, but not one that brought a flood of emotions. It was like having my eyes opened to see the true value of things. But it didn't change the situation at hand.

What bothered me as I reflected on that pivotal moment was what had not happened when I was lying there waiting to die. No bright lights. No tunnel. No relatives coming to welcome me home. No angel choir. No sense of timelessness. People who report having near-death experiences seem to say they experienced similar things: a bright light, a flood of peace and love, the presence of angels and deceased relatives, and often the sense that everything has slowed down so they can see and think with remarkable clarity and speed. I tasted a bit of that later with the staph infection, but when I was lying in the ditch in Somalia bleeding out, none of that happened to me. And the fact that it hadn't was starting to scare me.

Why didn't I get the same experiences other people did who were going to heaven? I thought. *Is there something wrong with me? Am I destined for hell instead?*

As I lay there waiting to be overwhelmed by enemy forces, all I heard was the piston-like sound of gunfire and fighters shouting in a strange language. The hair on the back of my neck stood up because they were so close. It would have been a lot more comforting to start fading into the next realm or at least peek over the edge to see what awaited me. That would have told me I was going in the right direction. But I got nothing. No assurance. No glimpse. No heavenly preview.

I never entertained those thoughts aloud. They lurked deep down, and I kept them there, hoping they would resolve on their own and go away. As you can imagine, they didn't.

On a more day-to-day level, the doubts about our daughter's paternity did not go away either but became harder to ignore. Katherine and I became so disconnected that to call it a relationship would have been stretching the definition beyond the breaking point. We went through what so many couples go through: distance, lack of caring or basic concern, never looking each other square in the face even when fighting like badgers.

Those months were a blur, and by the time Heather was eighteen months old, Katherine and I had separated. It had nothing to do with Heather but with a job that took me three hours away to Atlanta. If anything, Heather's presence still gave us a rallying point, a redoubt from which to fight against outsiders. No, the disintegration of our marriage had begun long before I arrived home on a gurney. The only thing that had held us together so long was my near-constant absence, which allowed us to lead separate lives. As Katherine reminded me on our worst days together, "I liked our marriage a whole lot better when you weren't around."

The truth is, I was the one to blame for the pathetic condition of our marriage. I was home for a hundred days a year. This was before e-mail, cell phones, Skype, and everything we have now. Going to battle was like going to the moon—total separation, a completely different life from the one you left behind. There was hardly any communication with family from the battlefield. I couldn't even tell Katherine and the kids where I was going most of the time or when I'd be back. As one example, we talked twice in six months during Operation Desert Storm. After a typical op I'd show up at home with a bag full of dirty laundry and a pretty intense need for marital intimacy. That lifestyle works for Old Spice commercials but not in reality.

My delusion was that serving the country at such a high level would cause this woman to stick with me through long absences and neglect. That was selfish and way out of line. I had blinders on as to what was happening in my own home. Add to that the simple fact that I'd never seen a good marriage in action, and there was nothing to interpret my own experience by. For me, "good" was the fact that nobody was shooting at me, or kicking the stuffing out of me after school, like Leon did. I had developed a pretty warped definition of normal. By those standards, my marriage was positively healthy. But by any other standard, it was sick unto death.

It was hard for me to think of letting go of Katherine and the life we had tried to build together. In choosing to marry Katherine, I had left behind my own family. In Katherine's family I had found much of what I was searching for: family life, love, acceptance. They had breakfast together every day and her parents had actual conversations with their kids. At my house we never conversed with our parents other than to ask permission to leave the table once we had eaten whatever was put in front of us without complaint.

Katherine's family did me a lot of good in those years. They showed me what family could be like. They gave me something to aspire to. They welcomed me into their community. But I had blown the opportunity at happiness with them. We were married young, and I had spent zero time building a relationship, so it really shouldn't have surprised me that there wasn't one there when I came back in tatters from Mogadishu. I did so many things to destroy my marriage out of blind selfishness. I was trying to fill a hole in my heart that had been there since the days of my childhood when I got whipped bloody a hundred times for no good reason. Now I had wrecked my own marriage in pursuit of that same elusive happiness.

The strange truth is that if I hadn't been injured in Mogadishu, we might still be faking our way through life together. The Black Hawk Down battle not only changed my life, career, and spiritual trajectory, but also sped the demise of our relationship. My coming home brought everything to a head.

We stayed together for more than a year while I went bodyguarding in the Philippines in 1995 to try to extend my career and make money. But when I came home, Blake—who was around ten years old—began telling me how Katherine had met some guy at a football game and was starting to hang out with him. When I brought it up with Katherine, she replied icily, "You ought to spend more time at home."

From that point on she dated other men more or less openly, and I saw that there was no salvaging what we had. I remain in her debt for the two beautiful children she gave me, but at that time I continued to blame her instead of realizing that I needed to finally reckon with God about things in my life. I think of Katherine now and say God bless her for staying with me as long as she did.

*

I was working in Atlanta, training the Olympic security forces for the 1996 games. Being away from Katherine gave both of us a much-needed break to consider the future. You can only take so much constant arguing followed by days of silence and stewing anger. The break also allowed my mind to focus on what had happened over the previous eighteen months. I would lie in my hotel bed at the Holiday Inn and hear in my mind the murmurings from back home: *That child isn't his. . . . She doesn't look like anyone in his family. . . . She fooled him good.*

Soon we decided to make our separation official and permanent. As divorce papers were drawn up, my attorneys, a husband and wife team, brought up the question I had been avoiding: "We're going to have to discuss child support," they said. "We need to know how many children you have."

At that moment the choice crystallized for me. Knowing that Katherine had been willing to date in front of my very eyes, and that Blake had observed and related a number of suspicious things that happened while I was gone, added to the doubts springing from the obvious physical differences between Heather and me. I decided, finally, that I would get her tested to see if she was mine.

It wasn't difficult to do. I was visiting the kids frequently, driving three hours to Jesup to spend weekends with them. On one of those weekends, I told them I was taking them clothes shopping at the Macon Mall, which was true, but first I headed to a clinic to get their cheeks swabbed. Blake was about to turn eleven, Rachel was five, and Heather was not yet two. I didn't make it a big deal and didn't even tell them to keep it a secret. As far as they knew, we just went by the doctor's office and that was it. I was amazed how quick the procedure was. The doctor swabbed their cheeks and mine and we were done. I didn't have Blake checked, and the only reason I swabbed Rachel was to have a control in the results. I knew she was mine because she was cursed with my looks, especially my ears.

After that we had a fun day together shopping for school clothes, riding the carousel at the mall, and having dinner at TGI Friday's. By the time I took them back to Jesup, the clinic visit was a distant, boring memory.

It took a week for the results to come back, and I endured the wait as best I could. Day in and day out as I was training the Olympic security forces, the impending response from the clinic lurked in the back of my mind. Now that the question was out in the open, I felt more vulnerable than before. My heart seemed to beat at an elevated rate the whole time and wouldn't calm down until finally the call came from my attorneys. The results had been sent directly to them.

"Are you ready? Are you sitting down?" they said.

"Cut out the funny business and tell me," I said, sitting in my hotel room, my stomach tightening with anticipation.

"There is a 99.987 possibility that Rachel is yours," they said.

"Great. We all knew that," I said, almost sweating with nerves. "How about Heather?"

"There is a .00017 chance that Heather could be yours," they said, and then there was silence. What do you say after that? How do you comfort someone?

It was true, then. There were no Cherokees or slaves in the family line. Just me, Katherine, and a guy who'd taken his life into his own hands by bedding a Teams guy's wife while I was away.

"Thanks," was all I could think to say. "Thanks for telling me what I already knew in my heart."

We hung up, and I reflected on the new reality. So it was true. I had conveniently ignored the math of Heather's conception and birth. I had been born two months premature so I didn't think in those terms. Now it seemed obvious that between going out on workups and deployments, it was impossible for her to be mine. More than anything else, I was hurt that Katherine hadn't told me outright and saved me the time, confusion, and public humiliation.

Though the news stung, I also knew that if Katherine and I had wanted to, we could have kept the relationship together in spite of our infidelities. Instead of pretending nothing was wrong, we could have faced the situation squarely, forgiven each other, and moved on. If I had been a stronger person and more generous of heart, I believe it's possible that I could have stayed and actually made the marriage work. I could have assessed the situation and led our family to a better place. I could have stepped up to the plate and been a husband and father to Blake, Rachel, and Heather. Reconciliation was always possible.

I called Katherine a few days after the results came in to talk about the divorce and how our possessions would be divided between us. I basically gave her everything, including our house. When we came to the subject of child support, I sprung the test results on her.

"By the way, I had a DNA test done," I said. "The documentation is being sent to your attorney. Heather's not my child."

Katherine didn't even try to deny it, and I appreciated that. Three years earlier I probably would have hunted down the guy who slept with my wife and done some serious damage. Now I was too wounded and defeated to mount any revenge. It wouldn't have made sense, anyway. She hadn't done anything worse than I had done. She just got caught. Now it was all out in the open. As with any op, the "humint"—the human intelligence—had now arrived. Once you have that, you can move on to what's next.

Within a few weeks our marriage was officially over.

*

My marriage wasn't the only thing collapsing. So was my spiritual community. I had left the Baptist church I'd grown up in when I met Katherine and had jumped into the Church of Jesus Christ of Latter Day Saints with both feet. They had everything I wanted: strong families, order, clarity as to family and community roles, and the promise of great rewards in the afterlife. I went for years thinking the Mormon church was the only true church. Other Christians had it partially correct, I thought, but the LDS had it perfectly figured out. We were a cut above, just where I liked to be.

Of course, as a certified hypocrite, I was not living the moral life I espoused, but I still became an Aaronic priest in the Mormon church and upheld their values in word if not in deed. But as soon as our local congregation found out that Katherine and I were divorcing, they started the process of excommunicating me. I have spoken with many Mormons since who say I got a raw deal and that the decision was personal. One friend, a Mormon himself, even called the Mormons in my community "the redneck brotherhood" for the way they handled my situation.

I do think it came down to a few misguided leaders. The people of the congregation continued to be good to me, but the leaders were bent on kicking me out of fellowship. I was so insulted by their efforts that I did what I normally did in such cases: disengaged from the process. I ignored their invitation to drive three and a half hours away to defend myself against their accusations, which probably would have done me some good.

The final result was that one day I got a letter telling me I was no longer part of the LDS church. Ironically, the letter arrived around the same time as the DNA results. Would their decision have been different if they had known about those results? Maybe. Or was God putting me on a new path by way of this circumstance? Was this his way of bringing me back to true faith instead of a works-based approach to spirituality? Years later I would conclude that the break was to my benefit; it brought me back to the most simple concepts we have as Christians: faith in Christ and his grace alone making us whole.

But at the time the excommunication hurt. Everything that had supported my life was crumbling, and now my own spiritual community had rejected me. On the outside I was an impressive ex-SEAL and wounded veteran plying his trade for dollars with security forces throughout the South. But in reality I woke up each day feeling completely broken.

So I did what any fool would do: I climbed into the bottle. My pain and troubles had mounted so high that I felt overshadowed by them, with no one to help me through. My massive guilt for surviving, when guys like Dan Busch had not, still made no sense to me. And what had I survived for? My marriage had just failed; I was off the Teams and had no real job satisfaction. Now I couldn't even go to church. I began drinking just so I wouldn't hurt. Soon I was drinking every night to the point of numbness. It became the dismal anchor of my daily routine.

This was a different kind of drinking than we had done in the Teams. Going out with the guys to party and drink and womanize always brought with it certain codes of conduct. Everybody knew their boundaries. I saw guys drink until 2:00 a.m., then bench press 315 pounds the next morning. The code said that drinking and womanizing should never interfere with our work, so we kept ourselves in check.

My new habit was different. I started going out every night with the squads I was training, and I usually didn't have to buy the drinks.

Getting liquored up didn't make me feel happy, but it kept my problems just far enough at bay that I could sleep. This went on for the better part of a year and would have continued until I'd drunk myself into oblivion if someone hadn't intervened and proven himself a true friend.

Tom McMillan and I had met right before I got out of the Teams. He was the Team commander for the State of Georgia Special Operation Response Team (SORT), meaning he ran the special ops units for the Georgia Department of Corrections. While on leave one time from the Teams, as a favor I did some training for federal prison guys and demonstrated how to clear a building at a maximum security prison in Reidsville. Tom came up to me afterward.

"I'm impressed," he said. "Maybe you could help our guys out. We don't have funding, but they're a good bunch of guys."

"It's not all about the money," I said.

We shook hands, and there began one of the best friendships I've ever had. Tom is an upbeat, teddy bear of a guy, and more loyal than anybody I have ever met. If you have a flat tire in South Carolina and call him at 2:00 a.m., he's on his way before you hang up the phone. Because of him I began working with Georgia SORT and spending a lot of time with Tom on the shooting range and in various other training scenarios. He then hired me to help with security for the Olympics, and together we trained his officers for nearly a year leading up to the games.

After the Olympics were over, Tom called on me to do hostage training for one of his units, and I stayed at his house for a few months, parking my old white Toyota pickup with Virginia plates in his driveway. His kids called me Uncle Howard and I felt at home. I was enjoying the job—six days a week of intense training—and enjoying living with Tom and his wife, Susan. I was still in great shape. You wouldn't have known what had happened to me in Mogadishu unless I was in a pair of shorts and you saw my calf, which looked like a handful of hamburger. I could hide my injuries with a pair of long pants, but I couldn't hide my nightly drinking habit.

One night Tom and Susan and I were playing cards and having some drinks. Tom knew when to stop, but I always drained the bottle until I'd reached that place where I could fall into bed and go unconscious for a while. At some point that night I hauled myself upstairs and did just that. Maybe it was a combination of the long week and the liquor, but the next morning I didn't wake up for a long time. After a while Tom and Susan worried that I might have died, so Tom came up to make sure I was still breathing. I didn't stir until 1:00 p.m.

When I finally came downstairs, I felt like someone had taken me out with the trash. Light hurt my eyes and every step sent a throb up my legs and into my head. Tom and Susan were looking chipper by comparison, having spent half a day being useful and productive people while I was sawing logs and sleeping off a hangover in their upstairs bedroom. My head was still pounding and thick with cotton.

After I'd grabbed something to eat, Tom invited me out front.

"I've got something to show you," was all he said.

I followed him into the harsh light and there I saw my old Toyota, but now it wasn't dirty. It was sparkling, the sun glinting off the mirrors and windows. Tom had spent the morning washing and waxing it, applying Armor All, and making it look like a dream. Here I had treated these people like some sort of hotel-and-saloon and yet Tom had done me a huge favor. I felt like a slug.

"When's the last time you saw your truck looking this good?" he said, patting the fender.

"Not for a while," I said and ran my hand over the shiny exterior. Tom walked from the truck to the front step and sat down. I joined him. The step felt cool, a welcome refreshment.

"Howard, you've looked a lot better yourself in times past," he said.

Not many people could say that to me and keep me as a friend. Tom was already like an older brother to me. We are both Scottish and both have the same kind of calling on our lives. Tom is quick to tell you that his coat of arms is to defend the oppressed and downtrodden. He even has that motto tattooed on his right forearm, as does his son. At some deep level we are called to the same work. We are brothers in arms.

"Howard, we've got to stop this drinking," he said. "It won't get anybody anywhere."

He was so gracious to include himself in my mistake.

"You don't need to fall back on this," he continued. "It's a crutch for feeling sorry for yourself. A lot of people fall into that hole and it's hard to get out. Listen, that ain't the way to go. Drinking every now and then is no problem. But take a close look at yourself and realize what you're doing. There's a lot more to life than jumping out of an airplane or swimming four miles underwater. There's more ahead for us. We've got too much to do to let something like this get in the way."

His words pierced my heart, and in spite of myself I broke down sobbing. It wasn't just the hangover either. We talked for an hour, and I poured my heart out to Tom in a way I hadn't with anyone in a long time. He's a great listener, and he nodded as I dragged my woes out into the open. I didn't even care about my reputation anymore. Tom gave some advice but mostly listened, and when I finished, he put his hand on my shoulder.

"I believe in you, Howard," he said. "You're going to get through this, and I'll be with you every step of the way."

Then he stood and gave me a hug. I had never felt so loved in all my life. Even the fact that he didn't try to nitpick the details of my life or offer instant solutions showed me that Tom was reality based and really did believe I could pull it together. His actions that day gave me dignity and showed me a better way. The choice of paths was clear.

When I went inside, I looked in the mirror and didn't recognize myself. Sunken eyes, a shriveled face—I'd aged myself badly in those few months.

"This can't go on," I said to my reflection. "Tom's right. It's time to crawl out of the bottle."

There aren't many times when the words of a friend are obviously the voice of God, but that was one of them. Tom McMillan not only proved he was my best friend, but his bold intervention saved my life. Maybe by some chance I could have pulled myself out of that tailspin on my own, but I doubt it. When you hurt on so many levels, alcohol-induced numbness becomes addictive. It takes a friend to rescue you, as it says in the Bible: "Two people are better off than one, for they can help each other succeed. If one person falls, the other can reach out and help. But someone who falls alone is in real trouble" (Eccl. 4:9–10 NLT).

I quit drinking nightly from that day forward and put my focus on the job at hand, training the younger guys and passing on what I knew to the next generation. It felt good to be clean, to break that dark routine, not to feel rotten every morning. But giving up the bottle didn't answer my soul's deeper questions. Clear-eyed and sober, I now had to face God on my own—no hiding behind a buzz anymore, and no hiding behind my previous reputation. All had been stripped away.

I had been raised Baptist and switched to Mormonism, but since I joined the Teams, the truth was that I was my own religion. The god at the center of my life was always me.

It's funny how we live happily for ourselves until things go south, and then we shake our fists at God. That's exactly what I did, first from a wheelchair and then from the emptiness of a life alone. I was angry that I'd been injured, angry that my wife had cheated on me, angry that my church had rejected me, angry that I had survived instead of giving my life for the other guys. I didn't feel worthy to be alive, and I now believed that God was punishing me with an extended life of misery.

It felt like when I was a boy, praying for God to kill my parents. I thought it was the only way I would ever be happy because I was so angry at the beatings I had to endure. I wished so badly that somebody, maybe my real dad, would come and be a loving father to me, rescuing me and giving me the kind of happiness other kids had. Now that same kind of anger rose up and consumed me. Darkness engulfed my personality. Vindictiveness tainted my thoughts and words. I was a mess.

I thought a lot about Dan Busch who was not just a great friend but also the most intriguing mystery to me. Here we were in a tier-one organization made up of a bunch of alpha males, guys beating their chests and competing on every level from shooting to running to swimming to chasing women. Dan had all that physical and mental ability (though he never chased women), but his demeanor was completely different. Unlike the rest of us, he was easygoing and never seemed rattled. He could rise above anything thrown at him and keep his equilibrium. At twenty-eight years old, he was awfully young to have such mature qualities. At least I'd never seen them in someone that age.

Dan and I had met before Somalia at the compound in North Carolina where we did workups in preparation for the mission. I started hanging around with him and was impressed. But people are always different at home than on the field. The family man at home often has a girl in every harbor. The laid-back guy at home gets aggressive and crazy when deployed.

Except for Dan. Dan was the same home and away. He talked calmly, and when you came near him, it was as if you entered a zone of peace and clarity. It's hard to explain.

Dan was a solid Christian. He didn't shove it in your face and try to get you to say a prayer right after meeting you. He also didn't talk about his faith as if he were trying to convince himself it was true. He was just the kind of guy you talk to once and walk away saying to yourself, "I could talk to him about anything." During our time in Mogadishu, I would watch people seek out Dan to talk about their family issues, problems back home, personal troubles, whatever it was.

Twice in Somalia, guys had an AD—accidental discharge of their weapons—in a hangar. That's a really big deal and basically means your military career is over. When both ADs happened, the first guy the offenders went to for comfort and counsel was Dan, who was sitting in his normal place in the corner where he often read the Bible and prayed. He had a gift for making you relax and realize a situation wasn't as bad as you thought. That was how Dan manifested his faith to us in Mogadishu: by having peace, by being there for us, and by listening.

Whenever tension rose up among the guys, Dan usually had a joke or anecdote to calm everybody down. One time Delta Force guys were getting ready to scout our safe house at Pasha in Lido. Just as they were getting on helicopters, frag orders came from a general that said SEALs should supersede the Delta guys and do the mission instead. The Delta guys literally had to get off the helicopters and make room for the SEALs. One Delta guy was miffed, and as he was stepping off, he said, "God forbid we get in the way of SEALs doing a real-world job." I was just about to offer my snotty reply when Dan stepped in to defuse the situation: "At least it's not a pretend op," he said, and everyone laughed.

Even in an environment where testosterone levels were peaking at 100 psi per man, he was able to bring peace. I saw him do it many times. I always wished I could stay as calm as Dan did. My nature was to get spun up physically and emotionally by what was happening around me and then have to de-escalate. That's still true of me. I often pop off with wrong words at home and ten minutes later I regret it and see that I could have handled it better. I do a lot of apologizing.

When we weren't on ops, Dan and I spent a lot of time sitting on top of conex boxes, baking in the sun getting our tans on. Sometimes we went hunting. Dan loved to hunt and fish. We would get helicopter pilots to fly us out from camp so we could hunt hogs from the air. It was good training for snipers like us, and it had the added benefit of shaking up the menu. We would bring those hogs back and cook them up for everyone. The movie *Black Hawk Down* shows us roasting one of the hogs Dan and I shot. It was great food, but even better, being away from the city let us forget about the world for a while.

One time we shot this big hog from a helicopter, landed the bird, and pulled the carcass in with us. Dinner was looking mighty nice, but suddenly, when we were a thousand feet up, the hog started kicking. We had neglected to put some safety rounds into him. I looked at Dan, he looked at me, and without a word he grabbed the hog's front legs, I grabbed the back legs, I reached behind me to open the door, and we pushed the hog out into a free fall. Then we shook our heads and laughed.

There really was no other option in that situation. I might have tried to go Rambo on the hog and stab it with my knife, but at a thousand feet up you don't take those kinds of chances. The animal could have gotten up and started charging around the helicopter in a mad rampage while I stabbed at it trying to find an artery so it could bleed out. We went back home empty-handed but with cheerful hearts. We had lost a good meal, but we were alive.

Faith came up in our conversations, and we spoke about Mormonism and Christianity and all sorts of other things. At the time I was a committed member of the LDS church and pretty defensive about it. Dan was an evangelical Christian. Most people of that stripe are hostile to Mormons, but not Dan. He never condescended or dismissed me or my faith. He actually asked insightful questions about it. I opened up to him because I knew he wasn't out to change my mind or convert me to his way of thinking.

Why had a scoundrel like me lived while a saint like Dan died? I couldn't resolve the question. At that point, wandering and alone, I needed the truth. I was haunted by guilt for surviving. I felt like the guy up a tree with a wild cat in that old comedy routine. His friend is on the ground with a gun but doesn't want to shoot because he might hit his buddy instead of the wild cat. Finally the guy in the tree says, "Shoot up here anyway. One of us needs some relief." That's how I felt. Something had to give. I wasn't afraid of the truth or what the verdict of my life was so far, I just needed some relief. I needed certainty about my status with God and the meaning of my life.

The only man I knew who would give me a straight answer was my childhood pastor, Ron Wilcox.

✳

Say "Ron Wilcox" anywhere in Wayne County and people's faces brighten. Ron is a hero to all sorts of people. He's a pilot, a musician, a pastor, an auctioneer, a businessman, a salesman, and much more. Ron was my pastor when I was growing up and the guy I trusted most. In some key situations he parented me. Back then Pastor Ron drove a red four-wheel-drive pickup with a gun rack in the back, which we kids all thought was cool, especially for a pastor. He had his hand in so many things that it was hard to keep track of them all: he played piano (and occasionally guitar and pedal steel) in a Southern gospel band, bought and sold farm equipment, flew a crop duster airplane, and earned his doctor of ministry degree while pastoring our church, First Baptist Church of Screven.

Ron had left a good-paying job and benefits to go into ministry. During the week he supported himself by driving a truck full of corn and soybeans to market for farmers during the harvest. While on those country roads with a full load of fresh crops in his truck, he wrote sermons in his head that he preached on Sundays. He was a straight shooter in person and from the pulpit. He didn't try to hurt anybody's feelings, but he wouldn't sugarcoat the truth. Under his leadership our church grew from two hundred or so members to more than eight hundred. People wanted the truth.

I knew that Pastor Ron would tell me the truth now, even if it hurt me. So I made an appointment and headed down highway 301 to meet him at the car dealership where he now worked during the week. He had been successful there, and they had given him an office with a door. When I arrived, I could see people bustling around the showroom and new cars gleaming. I felt as distant from them and the world around me as if I were observing it all from outer space.

Ron was pretty busy that day—even as we talked he was fielding pages and e-mails from dealers wanting to sell him cars. A big stack of papers sat on his desk, mostly contracts waiting to be finalized. He did a lot of trading for vehicles between dealerships. Still, he was so ambidextrous and at ease with this stuff that he made me feel totally relaxed talking about deep matters of the heart in the midst of his daily duties. For Ron, the sacred and the mundane always lived side by side. He could hear and understand my concerns in a busy car dealership as easily as a church. I loved Ron and knew I was in good hands.

"How's your mom and them?" he said first, shaking my hand in his leathery old mitt.

"Everyone's fine," I said. I hadn't seen Ron since my last deployment, and I could tell from the look in his eye that he was expecting something more from me than catching up on life. He knew I was there with a purpose but waited for me to come to it. After a little chit-chat I dove in.

"Pastor Ron, let me cut to why I'm here," I said. "You know what kind of life I've lived and the career I've had. My job for a lot of years involved doing things the average person never has to think about— shooting people, blowing things up, taking guys down. I've done a lot of killing, and it says right in the Ten Commandments that it's wrong to kill. Maybe I even overdid it sometimes, I don't know. I'm wondering how much wiggle room does that commandment leave? Is it 'Thou shalt not kill without exception'? Or 'unless someone has a knife to your wife's throat'? Or 'unless someone is a threat to national security'?"

A big misconception people have about warriors is that they enjoy killing. The truth is, the only guys who glorify killing are those who've never come close to doing it. I never considered taking a human life a normal thing or something to be taken lightly. I would see civilian guys around Georgia wearing T-shirts with slogans like, "Kill 'em all and let God sort 'em out." Nobody in uniform, at least nobody I knew and especially nobody in elite forces, would have worn such a slogan or expressed that sentiment in private or public. Anyone with that kind of attitude has never aimed a scope at someone or tossed a grenade at a group of enemy fighters. People who glorify killing have no idea what the reality of killing is like.

"Add to that my infidelity and the fact that my ego has been about as big as the Goodyear blimp and I'm a pretty natural target for God right now," I continued. "I feel like I'm going through hell and it must be God taking retribution on me, punishing me for all that stuff I did, and rightly so."

One thing I like about Ron is that he often answers questions with questions.

"I understand you did those things, but why do you think God would be punishing you for them?" he asked.

"Because that's how life works," I said. "When I was a kid I got whipped for doing something wrong, and sometimes for doing something right. That's the way it is, and it's the same in the SEAL Teams. You pay for your errors and mistakes, sometimes with your life. I've started to think I'm going to hell because of what I've done. In fact, I feel like I'm there right now."

Ron seemed a little surprised. At one point he even gave a little chuckle.

"There's something wrong with a person who doesn't ask these questions, especially after you find yourself lying wounded and naked on a tarmac in a foreign country," he said. "But given how forgiving God is with us, do you think you've done something so bad that he has a vendetta against you? Did he decide to stop forgiving you because your sins are somehow worse than others'?"

That kind of response works with me. He made me think about it instead of launching into some answer.

"I don't know how he deals with other people," I said. "But it just makes sense that there are consequences for what I've done. I've lived a pretty wild life. I've killed people in battle. Then my experience in Mogadishu was so horrifying, and I came home and lost most everything that matters to me, except my life. It feels like God is keeping me alive to punish me for killing others and for doing so much wrong. I feel like I'm going straight to hell. It must be some kind of payback. I can't explain it any other way."

Ron's eyes grew steely, and I knew he was about to bring a contrary word. He was never afraid to hit a charging bull on the nose.

"You know, I've never cut you any slack or given you special privileges, even when you were younger and not so open to advice," he said. "Sometimes you've taken my counsel and sometimes you haven't, and that's fine. It's up to you what you believe. But I can tell you with some certainty that you are not going to hell or suffering right now because of what you did on the battlefield. Jesus said that the greatest love a man can have is to lay his life down for a friend, and you put yourself in situations where you might have had to do that.

"You were defending your country, doing what you were supposed to. That's right in the sight of God. He is not like parents who whip a boy for the least thing. With him, you can keep screwing up and as long as you keep asking for forgiveness, he's not going to hold a grudge. God is omnipotent, and he doesn't have the constraints or faults we do. He's perfect, and he is love. I know you've been through some tough stuff in your short life. But if you let it, that can bring you back to a closer relationship with the Lord.

"A lot of times people get afar off from him in all their chasing. The thing to do is turn back to him and start majoring on forgiveness. Forgive yourself for what you've done, then forgive others for what they've done to you. Once you learn that, it lightens that load on your shoulders. Get good at forgiving, just like God is. It's the only way."

I rolled those ideas around for a moment while he fielded a call, and then I realized I hadn't shared one of my main fears with him.

"Pastor Ron, I know it sounds stupid to say, but I guess what I realized through all this is that I could die," I said. "It's ridiculous, but I really believed I was superhuman at one time. Not anymore. Now I see how fragile and short life can be."

Ron smiled. He'd been through that realization himself. I remember hearing how he survived two airplane crashes. Once he lost the engine of a Cessna after takeoff when the sun was already down. He landed on a county-maintained highway he knew was there, even in the dark. His wings hit the pine trees lining the road but he walked away without injury.

The second crash was in his crop duster. He came in to land on a dirt strip in a field that was too muddy. The wheels bogged down and the plane flipped over at more than forty miles per hour. Ron broke four teeth and his neck and had to be dragged away to safety. When I saw him after that, he told me, "For the first fifty-five years of my life I thought I was indestructible. Now I just feel irreparable."

He looked at me now with a depth of experience in his eyes.

"We're not exempt from the troubles and atrocities of life by being

Christians," he said. "We all live out this existence. It's true that God can put a hedge of protection around us, and he certainly put one around you many times, I'm sure. It's unthinkable what you went through. But let me assure you that though we all walk the same road, there is nothing we can do to make God love us more or less. It doesn't matter if we commit ten sins or ten thousand sins. It won't make God love us any less. If we ask his forgiveness and love him back, nothing can get in the way."

He paused a moment and let me ponder that.

"And by the way," he added, "I'm proud of you and proud to have had an influence on your life. I didn't realize at the time the impact I was having. I was just doing my ministry, which is somewhat scary. You never really know what people are thinking of the guy standing in the pulpit or if you're doing any good. Maybe that's the case with you too. Maybe God has more for you than you can presently imagine. The impact of your life may be a lot more than you can see right now."

I stood up, shook his hand, and let Ron get back to work. As I exited through the showroom to my car, I decided to quit crucifying myself and quit characterizing God as a vengeful deity raining judgment down on me. That was a big victory, to see God as more or less neutral. Not until later, in a different time of life and with the help of people with professional training in counseling, did I further straighten out my thoughts. And even though Ron had convinced me that I wasn't eternally condemned, I still felt survivor's guilt, though I didn't know that term yet.

Nevertheless, God stabilized my life that day. I felt more hopeful about my eternal prospects, if not my shorter-term ones. Without Ron's timely advice, I think I would have sunk lower and come to an early end one way or another. Now I saw that maybe the events of my life weren't tailor-made punishment so much as my Creator molding me into something different. Even though I couldn't see past my nose at that point, maybe I did have a future. Maybe I was like a sword being forged in the fire. I remember watching old Japanese sword makers fold the hot metal over repeatedly to make it stronger. It made sense that God was refining me so I would become stronger as well. He hadn't forgotten me. His discipline burned, but it was leading somewhere. At least I hoped so.

A slow healing of my relationship with God began—the key word being *slow*. Instead of getting sicker in my heart, now I was at least coming back to zero. The ability to receive and give love was still a long way off, but I had this nagging feeling that maybe love did exist somewhere, and maybe someday I would be allowed to find it.

As Tom told me one night as we sat around his house talking without drinking, "When you find yourself in a bad place, it's not the light that moved." From that point on I started looking for the light again.

It took awhile to locate it.

FIVE

TENNESSEE

The SEAL Teams are good about keeping guys on after their glory days, and I had an open door to work as an instructor in Coronado or write manuals or evaluate training runs if I wanted to. It's like being on the practice squad for an NFL team: once you got cut, you could stick around training camp to help players get better. A lot of Teams guys did go to Coronado to be BUD/S instructors or to the language institute to be interpreters, but I didn't take those options seriously. I was still young.

In my arrogance I wanted to be a door-kicker, not an instructor. If I couldn't suit up and play on the A-team, I wasn't interested. That was a character flaw, I'm sure, but also a natural reaction to pain. It hurt to be around the thing I wanted so badly. Imagine losing your girlfriend but still working for her father. Imagine seeing what you can't have day after day. My peers and guys even older than I were still going out on ops. Being that close made my heart sick.

So I cut loose of that community and tried to build my freelance career, training security units like I did with Tom in Georgia. But that plan wasn't paying as much as I had expected. To my genuine surprise, nobody was waiting around to throw money at a former member of SEAL Team Six just for being awesome. I seriously over-estimated the demand for a guy like me, and when I saw how little work was coming in and looked at my actual skills and professional assets, the facts before me were frightening. I hadn't held many other jobs and had no college degree. I was a one-trick pony who'd gone lame. Earning enough to live on was going to be a challenge.

My attempts to regain past glory took me to the Miami area where, of all things, I decided to attend a police academy. There, for a while, I found what I was looking for. When the other cadets learned about my history and high-level training, they treated me like the celebrity I wanted to be. After nine months in the academy, I took a job with the Hallandale County Police Department. I was a star before I even did anything, and I thrived on the feeling of adulation from those around me. Everyone wanted to hear what it was like being a Navy SEAL. I set about rebuilding my confidence and pride on those stories and that reputation.

I also had some perspective-altering experiences that deepened my sympathy for people I otherwise would have written off. One time I was running down a black kid who had helped steal a Cadillac. In what must have been the longest foot chase in the state of Florida that year, I finally tackled him in the middle of a residential street. The only reason he didn't outrun me was because his pants were so baggy that he was holding them up the entire time.

I gently flexi-cuffed him, and after a few moments his words shocked me: "You ain't going to beat me, Officer Wasdin?"

I assured him I was not.

"I just thought that's what you cops did," he said. "Beat us. That's why I was running."

I came to find out when I took this kid to the hospital to get stitches for the cuts on his hands that he was stealing and running drugs as a drug mule simply because he was hungry. He and his younger sister ate soup for dinner, and he felt the same kinds of hunger pangs I had known at times as a child. I bought him a big hamburger from McDonald's, and later when I would see him on the streets, he always waved at me.

That incident changed me. In my own mind I had characterized him as a street thug the moment I first saw him. When I learned that he and his family were surviving on soup, it invited me to see his situation differently. *I could be that kid but for God's grace. He doesn't need rough treatment; he needs love and support and better role models.* Because of that kid and other things I saw on the job I became less of a hardcore enforcer and more understanding of why people behaved the way they did in those poor neighborhoods. A certain amount of crime is driven by basic human needs. It's still wrong, but the last thing people need is discouragement and hopelessness, even when they get caught.

I was enduring pain of my own, though of a different sort. My Mogadishu injury had left me with a leg length difference that threw my entire body out of whack. My back and neck were a wreck. For years I couldn't sleep through the night, whereas before that I could fall asleep at the drop of a hat. Seeing that I was struggling, one guy on the police force kept pushing me, "Go see a chiropractor. It will help you out." I was skeptical because I had seen a chiropractor once before heading to Somalia and hadn't felt that it did much for me. But I was desperate enough to try again.

I made an appointment and went to see a local chiropractor. When I left that office, it was as if someone had flipped a switch. The pain in my lower back and neck was gone. I began sleeping through the night, which made a huge difference in my quality of life. I'm a show-me guy. If you demonstrate that it works and explain why, I'm all in. And it did work for me. What surprised me most was the positive effect it had after all those years of physical therapy, surgeries, and massages, which had not taken away the pain. From that point on, I went regularly to chiropractors wherever I lived. I had no idea that chiropractic care would one day play a major role in my career.

While on the police force I met a woman named Raquel. Her father and brothers were in law enforcement, and I hit it off with them immediately. Raquel and I started dating and became the hot couple in our little circles. We fed off the attention we got for being together, and I fed off the admiration from her and my colleagues. Though I was maturing in my view of the world, I was still a sad man who wanted his ego stroked almost as much as he wanted food and water.

Raquel and I were dating, but my attraction was actually to her family. Her brothers had me over for barbecues and invited me to join the social organizations they belonged to. I really liked those guys. After a while it seemed like the right thing to marry Raquel, to show my commitment to all of them. Raquel and I didn't have a lot in common, but I was drawn to the stability of the built-in community she had around her. Tom and Susan came down for the wedding, as did Blake and Rachel, and for a while it looked like I had found a new direction.

Broward County was a nice place to live, and I matured as a public servant while in the police force. But police officers don't make a lot of money, and after two years a better-paying job offer came up with a body-armor company in Tennessee. They wanted to send me around the country demonstrating their body armor to potential buyers, and they offered to pay me two or three times what I was making as a police officer.

Raquel was not thrilled with the idea of moving to Tennessee, but I finally convinced her that we should give it a try for the experience, if nothing else. We packed up and moved to a pretty house on the side of a mountain overlooking Norris Lake. Between my marriage, my nice home, and my newly expanded paycheck, I felt as if life was finally going my way.

*

In the meantime, Blake was living with his mom back in Jesup and coming into his teenage years. I had always encouraged Blake to build a relationship with his mom no matter who he lived with, but lately they weren't seeing eye to eye. Katherine and I both wanted custody of Blake, and when he turned fourteen he had the legal right to decide who he wanted to live with. He decided he wanted to come live with me, and I picked him up after a long drive from Tennessee. Without a hearing and without any delay, I suddenly became a full-time father again. That had been a major goal for me as I got my life back together. Still, I didn't realize how much it meant to have custody of Blake until we were driving through Baxley, thirty minutes away from the courthouse in Jesup.

With Blake in the front seat and me behind the wheel, I experienced total emotional release, the kind that has only happened twice in my life. It came out of nowhere. Suddenly the magnitude of what had just happened fell in on me and I broke down crying. Not only did tears flow, but my whole body seemed to lose strength. My muscles involuntarily relaxed, and I began losing control of the car. I pulled into a parking lot, draped myself over the steering wheel, and sobbed right in front of my son who had never seen me shed a single tear.

So many things washed over me—exhaustion, euphoria, relief, and victory. I had held all that tension inside for years. Now my son was with me and the battle was over. Somehow I had stormed the hill in the face of every kind of law giving preference to the mother for custody. I had planted my flag on the top—and won. *Are you kidding me?* I thought. *This is finally over? My son is with me for good? Is this a dream?* I felt as if a cement truck were lifted off my back: winning had become so rare for me, and so had affirmations as a father. Now a judge had given me custody of my only son. When you haven't been on top in a while, it can be overwhelming.

In that parked car, the flood of peace and the release of anxiety left me totally drained.

Thank you, God. Thank you for giving my son back to me.

Resonating within me were emotions I had forgotten I had. One of the deepest yearnings of my life was to connect with the father's heart I had never known. Perhaps my biological dad could have supplied that fatherly love and unconditional acceptance every boy wants. Lacking those, I always sought the approval of people around me, particularly men I respected. Now I had the opportunity to be a loving father to Blake, to guard and nurture him the way I had so desperately wanted to be guarded and nurtured. Bringing Blake home was like rescuing myself.

His coming to live with me also felt like part of a larger restoration of the life God wanted me to have all along. Though I couldn't put words to it, it felt as if piece by piece God was putting the things

I had wrecked back together. But what would that new life look like? And would I get where God wanted me to go or would I blow it again?

I didn't know. All I knew at that moment was that if we had been under physical attack I couldn't have lifted a finger to defend us. I was that exhausted, mind and body. After a while Blake helped me into a little country restaurant. I hadn't planned on stopping so soon, but I had no choice but to wait this out. Blake was clearly concerned. He had never seen his dad break down. Real men, I was told, don't cry or even talk about their feelings. They don't say I love you or show affection.

I always wondered who I got my affectionate side from; my mom is like granite, only granite is warmer, and Leon didn't seem to have the capacity to demonstrate love or even say the word. For now, Blake held my hand while we were eating and watched me intently. By the time dinner was over, I was composed and our resolve was strong. He hugged me as we stood up. We got in the truck and drove to Tennessee to start a new life together.

Blake had gained some extra weight and was self-conscious about it. As soon as we got to Tennessee, on the day before school started, he joined the football team and started working out. When he wasn't in the gym or on the playing field, he was out climbing cliffs and running around the woods near our house. He also joined Junior ROTC and was always doing physical fitness courses, map reading, or leadership training.

Junior ROTC teaches kids about the army and its various duties and ranks. Blake learned basic things like how to get from one spot to another quietly, how to do a hundred sit-ups without blinking, how to get through obstacle courses quickly, and how to dress in uniform every Thursday with boots shined, brass polished, and pants pressed. He wore a beret and lined up for inspection, then marched around with his battalion. By his sophomore year he was a squad leader with six or seven people under him. Blake was at the head of the line, marching them around and barking commands.

I remember one weekend watching him go through a course that involved setting a rope across a river and climbing across as a squad. They also had rifle practice and went down to ranges and shot from prone, kneeling, and standing positions. Blake was one of two kids in his Junior ROTC program to win a Presidential Fitness Medal. What put him over the top was the mile run: he ran it in five minutes and twelve seconds.

Blake's Junior ROTC involvement was inspiring, but it concerned me that he might enjoy the military experience a little too much. One day he mentioned that he was considering a career in the military, and I knew it was time for a father-son talk. I sat him down and said, "I know you're interested in the military as a possible career, but if I have my way Junior ROTC is as close to the military as you will ever get. I've bled enough for both of us. If there's anything else you want to do with your life, I'd prefer you did that. If the pull is so strong that you have to serve your country in uniform, I'll understand. But if you do, don't go anywhere near the SEALs. It's a lot better to choose a profession where you don't feel you have to sacrifice your family like I did in the Teams. Find something that pays enough money, and then come home and take care of your family."

I have had a similar talk with twenty-five or thirty guys over the years who wanted to try out for the SEALs. I've successfully dissuaded all but two. I figure if I can talk you out of it, I've saved you a trip to Coronado. If it's burning in your heart, you'll do it anyway. If you waver in your commitment when we're sitting in a warm room over cups of coffee, what will you do when you're out in the Pacific Ocean freezing your buns off? Blake took my advice and put the idea aside. God had a different path for him.

On the home front, he and Raquel were getting along well. Raquel had welcomed him to our home when I received custody. Even before we were married, when Blake came to visit me in Miami, Raquel had gone out of her way to take care of him and establish a relationship. Now she took primary responsibility for driving him between school and home and his various activities. Blake admired her compassion, especially for animals. If she saw an injured animal on the side of the road, she would pull over to help it. She also began mothering him a bit, putting boundaries on his time and telling him to go to bed earlier so he wouldn't fall asleep during the day.

We had been living in Tennessee for just a few months when Raquel started complaining about the weather. She had been in a couple of car crashes as an officer and had hurt her knees. Now when it got cold, her knees ached, and soon I was hearing all about it.

"My knees hurt," she said one evening. "We need to move. I can't take any more winters like this."

"We're not moving," I responded. "This is a great place and a great lifestyle for us."

"It's kind of slow up here," she said. "There's not much to do."

"There's plenty to do. It just depends on what you like."

What started out as gentle discussions began escalating. Raquel insisted that her knees couldn't handle the Tennessee weather, that we lived in a boring area, and so on. At times we would settle ourselves down by watching a movie and things would be fine for a while. Then the complaints would start up again.

I should have paid more attention to Raquel's discomfort. As much as I talked about putting family first, I was still the top guy in my own mind and when work called, I went. We had a saying in the SEALs: when you're good, you're gone. It's the same in corporate America. It felt good to be in demand. I told people that my biggest priority was putting biscuits on the table for my family, but I was hiding my ambitions and ego behind my role as provider.

Then came the surprise.

A year after our move to Tennessee, I was at the annual Utah Sheriffs' Association golf outing, sponsored by DuPont, maker of Kevlar. It was all about glad-handing. We had gotten the body-armor contract and were trying to keep it. My job was to show up, contribute to their outing, sponsor holes, talk to the people who were there, and keep establishing relationships with potential clients.

One evening after the day's events I got a call from Blake. It was after midnight his time.

"Dad, she's gone. Raquel is gone."

"What do you mean, she's gone?" I asked from my helpless vantage point in a hotel room in Utah, a thousand miles away.

That's when I knew. We talked it through for a few moments and then I said, "Blake, just stay with the neighbors. We'll figure this out when I get home."

It was too early to file a missing person report, and by the looks of it Raquel was missing on purpose. Blake spent that and subsequent nights with his good friend and our great neighbor, who took him in like a son. I soon found out that Raquel had gone back to the life she previously had. She had never wanted to leave law enforcement or

Miami. She was miserable in Tennessee in all the ways she had told me about, and probably many more. Not only that, but the bloom was off the rose of Howard Wasdin. People smell bad up close, and once we were married she discovered I was a normal human being like everyone else. Plus, nobody in Tennessee cared who I was. I had no cache with the locals.

When I got home Blake was upset, though he tried not to show it. He had started to relate to Raquel, not as a mom, but as a respected authority figure and member of the family. He summed up his feelings to me one day: "If being in Miami and not dealing with cold weather is more important to her, then I guess we're better off without her anyway." In that statement and others I saw a reflection of what I had become: cynical and unable or unwilling to build relationships with people for fear of being burned by them. My defensive side came out, and I made a vow to myself, quietly: *Nobody's going to hurt him again. You can hurt me, but nobody will have access to the inner sanctum of our family. He won't grow up like I did.*

Raquel had taken my truck, my only means of transportation, which put me in a bind. I couldn't get to work and had to borrow a truck from a friend so I could go emergency car shopping. At the local Ford dealership, because of my haste, I was overcharged not only on the cost of a new truck but also on the financing. I would later hear it lovingly referred to in the car business as "taking someone's head off." The salesman that day got my head and a big chunk of my wallet too.

Then, without explanation, Raquel came back from Miami. She called out of the blue: "I'm coming to Tennessee. Pick me up at the airport. I want to talk."

I didn't know what to think. Apparently things weren't working out in Miami the way she had hoped. Her parents had moved to a vacation home in another state. Miami hadn't welcomed her back the way she expected. When I arrived at the airport, I felt more or less neutral. She had not left on any terms. No words had been exchanged. She came off the airplane, ran to me, and hugged me as if nothing had happened. I was so confused that I didn't even know how to physically behave around her. Blake gave her a chilly reception. He had become protective of me and didn't know how to receive her sudden reappearance.

Raquel stayed for two weeks and then realized it wasn't going to work. We filed for divorce and my second marriage ended. She moved back to Miami.

Blake and I became bachelors, doing our own laundry, cooking our own food, and taking care of our own dishes and lawn. The house ran like a well-oiled machine, I'm proud to say. We went to his Junior ROTC competitions and football games together. I picked him up at practice, and when we could find the time, we would go fishing and hiking. I taught him to set trotlines and passed on a bunch of survival skills. Some of the best memories I have are of sitting around the fire with some of his buddies, seeing coyotes circle us curiously, and teaching them how to take on nature with little more than a pocketknife.

One of the most fun things we did during that time was attend Blake's military ball, the annual formal event that every ROTC program participates in. Students dressed up in uniforms and formal gowns or dresses. They served punch and hors d'oeuvres. Everybody was standing around looking at each other the way awkward teenagers do. Guys were on one side of the room and girls on the other. Both were scared to ask the other to dance. Three brave couples took to the floor, but only on slow songs.

Finally I said, "Enough of this. Blake, we've got to liven this place up." He and I had a routine we'd done for years called the monkey flip. You've probably seen it done. Blake hunched down and stuck his hand between his legs, and I yanked his hand so hard that it flipped him over. It was a party trick that got people excited, one we had been doing since Blake was just a little boy. We went onto the dance floor, did a couple of dance moves, and then did the monkey flip. People went crazy and flooded the dance floor. The ice was broken, and I'm proud to say I got more offers to dance than Blake did.

Around that same time, Blake decided to test his toughness on me. He and the neighbor boy, Lyle, were on the football team together. Lyle liked eating dinner with us because of my cooking. One day I was in the kitchen cooking when Blake and Lyle came home. I was standing there in my apron, stirring a sauce on the stove. They rounded the corner and announced to me that they had just finished working out and were feeling pretty buff.

"Dad, we think the two of us can take you," Blake said.

I thought he might be joking, but he and Lyle kept standing there.

"Take me, like fighting?" I asked.

"Not full-blown fighting," Blake said. "Just a match of strength."

I had mixed emotions. Part of my heart swelled with pride because my son had become a man. He wanted to try his strength against the old man, and he approached it without disrespecting me. I was impressed by how he brought it up. On the other hand, I knew I was going to win and didn't want to hurt or humiliate him or Lyle too badly.

"All right," I said.

"There's one stipulation," Blake added quickly. "You have to let me get you in the position I want before we start wrestling. I get to put you in a hold. Then I'll say go and you can start."

"Fine," I said, turning off the stove burners, wiping my hands on my apron, and walking into the living room.

We cleared a space on the floor, shoving the couches and coffee table aside by the player piano.

"Give me a second with Lyle," Blake said, and they huddled up to hatch their plan. I heard them snickering and talking and then saw them high-five each other in anticipation of their victory. Now the whole thing was getting on my nerves. *Those ungrateful so-and-sos. I cook dinner and this is how they repay me?*

Blake came over.

"Ready?" he said.

"Ready," I said.

He put me facedown on the floor, reached under my left arm, and put his hand over my left shoulder. When you're in that position and you push your arm forward, the pain is excruciating for the guy you're sitting on because you're lifting against his shoulder joint. He then put his right knee in my neck. The move is called an arm bar, and he had seen me do it a hundred times in my training class. It was a way of controlling somebody while putting on handcuffs. Blake and Lyle's strategy was to start with the arm bar, and if I got to a point where I could slip out of it, Lyle was going to jump on me and help secure me. *This is what their little huddle was about?* I thought. *This'll be over fast. I should have left the food cooking.*

Blake took a few seconds to get his hold on me nice and snug. My face was flat against the floor, but that was about to change.

"Okay, son, let me know when you're ready," I said.

"You got him, Blake?" Lyle chimed in from a few feet away. Blake cranked my arm even more.

"I got him. All right, Dad. Go," he said.

Blake had seen the arm bar hold many times but had never seen the way to get out of it. As soon as he said, "Go," I rolled back toward him, taking my right arm and sliding it quickly under my body. That moved all the pressure off my neck and arm, and now I was using his arm in mine to push him back onto the floor. I leaned back on him and his head bumped the floor, which dazed him for a brief second, in which time I rolled over, grabbed him, and wrapped my left arm around his neck, putting my bicep on his left carotid and my forearm on his other carotid. Lyle was in the corner saying, "Should I go? Should I go?" But by that time it was too late. I held Blake's neck just tight and long enough to make him start to black out, and then I laid him gently on the floor, went back into the kitchen, put the apron on, and flipped on the burners. Blake hardly knew what hit him. Lyle scurried over and hunched over him while Blake roused himself from the floor.

"Why didn't you jump on?" Blake said, looking at Lyle woundedly.

"Your dad was on top of you so quick, there was no need getting both our butts kicked," Lyle said.

I have to say the hot wings tasted especially good that night. The encounter became legendary, and Blake has told the story a hundred times to his buddies. To this day he's never even joked about taking the old man down again. I guess he's cured.

Blake and I also did actual productive work together at the company I worked for. At the work site was a small factory for manufacturing the body armor. I was working on creating a body armor plate that could stop an armor-piercing round. That was a big deal in law enforcement technology at the time. Blake and I would go in on Saturdays, stack the right amount of fiber and resin into the plate trays to make the correct polymer mixture, seal it with plastic, suck the air out with vacuum hoses, wait for a while, then pull them out and put them in the drying room. When they were dry, we took them out and sanded all the edges off, painted them, and put a strike face on the front.

We always talked as we worked, and I saw that Blake picked up easily on instructions. He was a hard and willing worker. It reminded me of the best times I had with Leon while working in the watermelon fields. Within two months Blake and I had perfected the plate and sent it to the National Institute of Justice, where they shot it and gave it a Level IV certification, meaning it was strong enough to stop armor-piercing rounds. Not only was it strong, it was light and thin. The company sold a ton of them.

But life got tricky because the company was sending me out so much to demonstrate and sell its products. My increasing time away left Blake in the care of our neighbors, Lyle's family, who were an absolute godsend as we scrambled to make my absences work. Lyle's mom taught at their high school. Sometimes Blake would stay with them for a week while I was out showing off our company's life-saving vests. I felt the tension and guilt from being away. I knew I wasn't being the father I wanted to be but didn't know how to bring life into balance.

For the first time since leaving the Teams, I was truly enjoying my work. I was the top tactical operations representative for the company. We did business with police forces in the United States and around the world. My job was to show the effectiveness of the vests by doing a live demonstration, firing a bullet at the vest and showing the results. The vests could be made to stop various types of bullets, with a special plate for each caliber, all the way up to plates impervious to armor-piercing rounds.

Tactical vests, which offered more coverage around the body and greater protection from high-power bullets, were worn outside the uniform. Conventional vests were concealable and for use in local security forces where high-power bullets were less common. Some vests could carry gas masks, spare magazines, and other necessary equipment. I had worn the armor in the field, too, and could testify to how it worked in real-life situations.

After being convinced the vests would protect them, potential buyers wanted to know about wearability and care: Would it get hot under a police uniform? Would it bunch up in places? How should they care for it over time? How long would it last? Each one of our vests was tailor-made to the individuals in that particular security force. Once the order was placed, I went with a measuring tape and measured each individual from chin to clavicle, including chest circumference and so on.

One of my most memorable customers, and probably my biggest catch while I was at the company, was the New York City Emergency Service Unit, which is what they call their SWAT team. I went to New York to demonstrate the vests, and as a result they placed a huge order. Off I went to each station in each borough and measured each emergency services officer for a vest. I then fitted, sized, and designed a vest for each one. I had so many great conversations with those guys, developing relationships and talking about our different experiences in the field. Just two years later, the city was hit by terrorist-piloted planes on 9/11, and I'm almost afraid to know which guys were lost that day. I had served and befriended so many of them in more peaceful times.

My professional ambitions went beyond selling ballistics vests. I wanted to build a name for myself as a tactical expert. I felt a driving need to prove I was the best at whatever I was doing. That goal was bolstered when a reality television host from Japan, Kane Kosugi, contacted me about going through my tactical training course in one of his episodes. Part of the reason I did it was to promote the body-armor company I was working for and to get our name out there. We shot the episodes, and I was depicted as the hard-driving, no-excuses trainer getting a SWAT team ready to clear buildings, rescue people from vehicles, rappel down cliff faces, and shoot bad guys. I played up that persona, sometimes turning up the heat on Kane when he made a mistake.

At one point we were rappelling down a cliff and I attached Kane's harness to my own. Then, without warning, I took out a knife and cut his rope. He fell several feet before the fall was arrested by my own harness. It made for great television. Kane's reaction was real, and it simulated what can happen in volatile situations. My buddy Tom McMillan got to be in the episodes as well. It was my first experience with television, and I learned a lot watching the film crews get the footage they needed, set up shots, and tell the story visually. Kane was a good guy, too, and a fast learner. At the end of the series I stood there on camera with Blake and said I would be proud if my son grew up to share Kane's qualities of teachability and hard work. It was a good experience all around.

*

Still, I was throwing myself into my work the same way I had thrown myself into the Teams, at the expense of everything else—often including Blake. I felt satisfied but selfish. In the back of my mind I knew I was doing it all to distract myself from how miserable I was.

In the face of my own emptiness, I was still trying to prove myself through achievements, to overcome the doubts placed deep inside of me during my train wreck of a childhood. It was easy to justify being gone all the time. I had to make money somehow.

Few companies were looking to hire a sniper. Few jobs required you to mount big demonstrations where you fire a bullet at a vest in front of potential customers. It was a good fit for me in all sorts of ways, from the social aspect to the tactical. But I still went back to the hotel each night and walked into a pit of loneliness and pain. I was professionally happy for the first time since the Teams, but personally I was floundering. Nobody would have known by the way I carried myself with swagger and outward confidence.

God obviously saw my heart. He knew that the soul wounds I had incurred in battle and in childhood had not healed. In fact, because they had not been properly treated, they continued to fester inside me. I still wondered if I was worth anything, why I had been raised under such a hard hand, why my biological father apparently had abandoned our family, why God had spared me when death had come so near in Mogadishu.

Thoughts of the wounded boy we had treated next to our safe house surfaced frequently in my mind. I wondered how his leg had healed up, if the wheelchair had worked well for him, and what he was doing now—even what his scars looked like compared to mine. I hated my scars. I wouldn't wear shorts because people might see the knotted tissue on my leg, an ugly reminder of how human I was and how my life had been shattered. I knew that some people I admired, people in the Bible, boasted in their scars—people like the apostles Paul and Peter. When they were beaten and imprisoned, they were thankful and pointed to it as evidence of God's calling and favor.

Even Jesus retained the scars in his hands, feet, and side after his resurrection. It made no sense to me. How could people boast in their failures, their weaknesses? My scars, on body and soul, were sources of shame to me. In the cold isolation of a dozen hotel rooms, my inner wounds continued to bleed.

One night my professional ambitions and personal responsibility came into sharp conflict. I was overseas demonstrating our vests at a big meeting with the president of a large company when I got the call no parent wants to receive.

"This is the emergency room," a voice said. "Your son, Blake, has been in a four-wheeler accident."

Talk about coming out of a dead sleep. It was 1:00 a.m., my time. I bolted upright and began thinking what it would cost to fly back immediately. I started throwing things at my suitcase as I listened to the voice on the other end of the line.

"He and another rider went over the handlebars onto the gravel of a steep road near your home," the voice said. In the background I heard another voice, the voice of our neighbor. She was saying, "He's okay, Howard! Blake is fine."

She was there with him being the parent I had decided not to be. Pain shot through my heart. What kind of father was I, halfway around the world serving my own interests and not even there for the basic care of my child?

I found out that Blake's only injuries were road rash and skinned palms. He and his friend had come skidding down the driveway and gone over the handlebars. They could have been hurt much worse.

It felt like a shot across the bow: *Keep going this way, Howard, and someday something truly serious will happen and you won't be there. I gave you your son back—and you're about to blow this chance too.*

I don't remember praying at that point for a career change, but God must have known I needed one, even if I wasn't strong enough to initiate it. At the top level of the company, changes were made that let me know it was time to move on. I had been working directly with the guy who hired me, the godfather of body armor, Lenny Rosen. He was one of the first people to sell ballistic nylon vests. He was in his seventies when he hired me, mentored me, and brought me under his wing. He was the one who encouraged me to patent the plate to stop armor-piercing rounds. But the new company management let Lenny go and things started going south right away.

Some other promising job possibilities presented themselves, and when those firmed up, I quit the body-armor company and Blake and I moved back to south Georgia. It was 2001. I had solid commitments from customers from different countries who wanted me to train their security forces. I was looking to make a very good living. Then 9/11 came and everything in my field of tactical training changed. My plans evaporated and I was left high and dry, without work, without love, just Blake and me hoping something would come along and save us.

That something was right around the corner.

SIX

AMBUSHED

DEBBIE

I had signed my divorce papers less than twenty-four hours earlier. It was January 2002, and I was starting over. The last thing I wanted in my life was another man.

I'm a CPA and was at my office on a Saturday preparing for the onslaught of tax season. Software had to be installed, W-2s prepared, and all my systems test run for the sprint to April 15. I've always been the kind of person who gets things done, a bit of a perfectionist, which is an advantage when you're in my field. I like predictability and stability and controlling my environment. To me it was an extension of the home I had grown up in—stable, loving, and strict. I liked to think I provided that same peace and stability to people through my work with their taxes and businesses.

I was jarred, then, by the unexpected sound of a knock on the front door of my empty office, rare for a Saturday morning. I had never been scared to be at the office after hours, but this was an unusual time for company.

"Debbie, it's Connie," came the voice. Connie and her husband, Philip, were casual friends of mine. Connie is an interior designer and has a business in Jesup. We had become friends over the years because I was constantly remodeling and redecorating the house—not because the house needed it but because I was so bored with my marriage that I threw myself into this creative outlet. Connie has a beautiful singing voice and a beautiful soul. I always felt upbeat after visiting with her. We would often chat while looking through fabric swatches and wallpaper books at her store. That store had become an escape for me from the home life I dreaded.

Over the holidays I had seen Connie and Philip at an open house given by a local doctor and his wife. This couple always put on a great party and took pride in making sure everyone had a good time. I had attended with another couple, also in the medical profession, with whom I had become close over the previous couple of years. Connie and Philip were there, too, and we fell into such enjoyable conversation that we carried the laughter to the Waffle House for breakfast when the party was over. That was really the only time I had been socially active with Connie and Philip. We didn't run in the same social circles. In the previous ten years, my only social circle had been Eryn's friends and their parents.

Now Connie was hatching a plan.

"Listen, I have an idea," she said, walking back with me to my office and bubbling like a teenager. "How about you and your friends go out with us tonight? Philip and I are going out to dinner and thought it'd be fun if you all came along."

Third wheel, I thought. *That sounds like a blast.*

"Aw, thanks for thinking of me, but my friends are out of town this weekend and I'd feel like I'm just tagging along," I said. "I'm kind of busy today anyway. I do have good news, though. I signed my divorce papers yesterday."

"You did? Then you have to go, and we'll get you a date!" she said.

I groaned inwardly. *Why did I say that?*

"Oh, no no no," I said. "That's not going to work. I don't want to be set up. Besides, I don't know how long I will be here today. I've got a lot to do."

I often worked until 2:00 or 3:00 a.m. during tax season, a habit I had started years before so I could spend more time with Eryn during the day and evening. I would go home, eat with her, spend time with her, put her to bed, and then go to the office and work into the wee hours, only to get her up and dressed and drive her to school in the morning. Then I would go back home to rest for another hour before getting myself dressed and going to work. I had learned by trial and error that 3:00 a.m. was my limit. As long as I was in bed before then, I had no problem functioning the next day. Later than that and I was in a fog. Eryn was with her father this weekend, so I saw it as the perfect time to get ahead on whatever work needed to be done without staying up so late.

Connie continued, "I'll get Philip to find someone to go with us. Oh, we've got to do it, Debbie. It'll be fun!"

"Please, Connie, don't bother. I'm working anyway," I said, hoping that would be the end of it.

"Just wait," she said, determined. "I'll talk to Philip, then I'll call you back."

She walked out with a mission. Connie was being so sweet. She had an idea how miserable I had been for so long. I didn't share a lot about my personal life, but she had been in my home and knew my husband at the time. She had a general idea of the life I had mostly hidden so well from others. I had always been a fun and bubbly person, but this man had stolen my joy for so long that I had forgotten how to laugh out loud and just have fun.

Post-divorce freedom was hitting me like fresh air rushing into a stale room, like taking a breath for the first time in my life. I think Connie could sense I needed to spread my wings and recover. She was determined that day to get me out there. Part of me was hesitating and complaining inwardly about going. Another part of me had been so lonely for so long that any company was welcome. If I could have just met a friend to have dinner with occasionally, I would have been happy. But going out with a total stranger was not my idea of celebrating new freedom.

A couple of hours later Connie called.

"We found someone," she said, her voice practically glowing. "He's Philip's cousin, Howard Wasdin."

She said the name as if it should mean something to me.

"Okay," I said blankly.

"Howard Wasdin, former Navy SEAL," she repeated. "Do you know him?"

"No."

"He's been in the newspaper a lot recently."

"Okay," I said. "That's nice."

"You haven't heard of him? He lives in Screven. He just moved back to town. He's coming out with us tonight! I can't believe you don't know him. He's so handsome!"

I would learn later that Howard had turned down Philip about eight times before Connie succeeded in begging him to go as a favor to her. It was like they were dragging two stubborn mules toward each other. I wasn't enthusiastic about it. I had grown cynical toward men, thinking they were all the same. I was still assessing my scars from the last twelve years. An unfortunate lesson I had learned from my previous marriage was that people are not always who you think they are. You must look closely and listen intently.

Connie insisted, "You're really going to like him. He's a fun guy. It's going to be a blast!"

Then my mind went back to an encounter I'd had at the BMW dealership in Jacksonville. When I was at my lowest point, three days after my then-husband Randy had left and two days before my thirty-fifth birthday, I was rear-ended by a jacked-up shiny pickup truck. While I was at the light waiting to turn left, the kid behind me was so interested in eating his Powerbar that he didn't notice I hadn't turned yet. *Whack!* I had only owned that car for about eight weeks; it was my first attempt at regaining control of my life. Now it was wrecked. Concerned about having it repaired properly with authentic parts and not voiding the warranty, I called the dealership in Jacksonville and had it towed to the body shop there.

At that point the fight had gone out of me. I was tired of having to defend myself. I asked the manager, "Can you please fight the other driver's insurance company for me? They are awful to deal with and want to skimp on fixing my brand-new car."

"Absolutely," he said.

Thank God—one less fight.

The people at the body shop were wonderful, friendly people. One afternoon in Jacksonville I received an unexpected compliment from one of the younger guys at the dealership. He invited me to dinner. I was there late, it was around dinnertime, and there was a place across the street. I was sure he was just being nice, but I declined; at the time I was separated but had not yet filed for divorce.

Nonetheless, his invitation made me feel attractive for the first time in more than a decade. *If that guy found me attractive enough to ask me to dinner, maybe there is someone else out there who would*, I thought. I had tucked the experience away, pulling it back out when I needed self-assurance.

Now, trying to get off the phone with Connie, I reflected back on that day.

Maybe I should just say yes, I thought.

"Okay," I told her, sighing and realizing that her begging probably wasn't going to end until I gave in anyway. "I'll go. I'll consider it a celebration of signing my divorce papers. See you in a few."

Connie was so excited about the night that her words came out at 180 miles per hour.

"Oh, that's so great! I'll tell Philip. We'll pick you up around seven, okay? This is going to be so fun."

I had socialized with Connie and Philip just the one time before, and after they set me up with Howard we never really did anything socially again. It was a one-time event, packed with such urgency for them that neither Howard nor I could resist. Why I said yes, I still don't fully know. Why Howard caved in to Connie's request, Howard doesn't really know. We were both resisting relationships like the plague. Everyone's behavior was so unusual that I came to see it as divine intervention, guiding each of us to act out of character so the objective could be fulfilled.

Had Howard or I known how the night would progress, I'm not sure if we would have dived right in or run for cover.

In the meantime, I had to turn from tax papers to making myself look decent. I didn't give it a lot of time. I would touch up my makeup and throw on nicer clothes. Who was I trying to impress anyway? I just wanted to have a fun night—nothing memorable, nothing serious. With Eryn at her daddy's, my apartment felt empty and lonely.

As I went home to get ready for the big date, my mood bounced back and forth between resignation and curiosity about what the night might bring. On the one hand, I'd had more than my share of bad male behavior and wasn't sure I could stomach any more. If the guy was a loser, I might end up walking out of the restaurant, leaving him to be the third wheel. As I tried to picture what he might be like, I couldn't imagine him or any guy I would want to spend time with. But I'd promised Connie, and I was stubborn about keeping my word, which is why I'd stayed in my bad marriage for so long. I wasn't going to back out on her.

Still, the warning signs were there. I especially didn't like how she had spoken so admiringly of Howard Wasdin. *Who was this guy? What's a SEAL?* I had my ideas, but I really didn't know. *If he's so great, why is he back in Wayne County?*

"He's in the paper a lot," she had said. "He was shot a couple of years ago. Have you seen *Black Hawk Down*? He was in that battle."

I did vaguely recall sitting in my office going through the local paper one day and seeing a photo of this injured navy man lying in a bed in Germany. His leg was lifted up in a sling and he was holding a little triangular metal brace for support. All I remembered was that he was the most broken and sad-looking person I had ever seen. I thought he had lost his leg and pictured him with a prosthetic limb. I just wanted to give him a hug and tell him it was going to be okay. *Was that the guy?*

What Howard or any potential date didn't know was that I had been broken too. I was like that guy lying in a bed trying to heal. Connie had done a good job of building my expectations for the night, but this poor guy on the other end didn't realize that my self-esteem had been squashed. I longed for someone to talk to about my grief and loss, my lack of self-confidence, my distrust of men. I didn't need a relationship; I just wanted a friend. I'd gone out with just one guy in the past few weeks, and he was such a bore that I ended up buying my own dinner so he wouldn't expect any kind of commitment or future expectations from me. He was a nice guy, just not the right guy for me.

Connie, Philip, and Howard picked me up at my apartment. When I answered the door, Connie was as effervescent as she had been on the phone. Philip stood with the confident satisfaction of having bagged a trophy date for me. My mood was calibrated to be the opposite of theirs. They wanted me to be impressed, so I was fully prepared not to be. They were proud of themselves and just knew it was going to be a fun night. I had serious doubts and gave it only a slim chance of being worth my time.

Suddenly a guy in dress pants and a freshly pressed shirt walked in behind them as if he owned the room. He radiated charm, confidence, and good looks. I looked this so-called trophy date up and down, scrutinizing him quickly and looking for a reason not to like him, wanting to reinforce the wall I had built so carefully around my heart. Instead, my heart did a half somersault in spite of myself. *Wow, he is gorgeous,* I thought. Then immediately, *Crap! Tonight's going to suck. I bet he'll be full of himself.*

He caught sight of me and smiled, easing my mind a little. He didn't stop a beat, didn't run, didn't seem disappointed. He just stood there smiling openly and shaking my hand. That smile raised my self-confidence a few notches. Still, my walls were up and a stubborn feeling rose within me. I would continue looking for flaws in this pressed and dressed gentleman with the beautiful smile and cowboy boots. *There must be something wrong, and if there is, I'll find it.*

Another feeling rose up in me too.

I don't care what happens tonight. I signed my divorce papers yesterday. I'm going to celebrate and have a good time, regardless of what happens with this pretty boy.

"Howard Wasdin," he said, putting his name out there like an impressive new automobile.

"Debbie," I said, not even bothering to use my last name. I hated my last name. It was all that remained of a broken marriage, broken promises, and twelve years of emotional pain.

Even if this date is a colossal failure, at least we can go down in a blaze of glory, I thought. *At least I know Philip and Connie will keep it lively, and in the worst-case scenario, Connie and I can talk all night. We are never at a loss for words around each other.*

We headed out the door. My evening was about to get very interesting.

We decided to take Howard's car to the restaurant. He was driving a Lexus SUV, which made him look like a hotshot, but was borrowed from the car dealership where he worked. You couldn't hide those dealer plates. He opened the passenger door for me and made some ironic comment.

"I guess it's all about chivalry," he said.

I fired a response right back at him.

"I expect a man to be respectful, and in my book, chivalry isn't dead."

A look of surprise passed over his face as he closed the door for me. He walked around to the driver's side, seeming to reassess me in those few seconds.

Howard had a lot going on at the time. He was working with a reality show called *Combat Missions*, and the movie version of *Black Hawk Down* had come out, so that battle and his role in it were in the news. Philip was drawing those topics out of him from the backseat, and Howard seemed to have an ego-boosting answer for everything. It seemed his life was more interesting than anyone else's. His sense of superiority emanated onto the rest of us.

Oh yes, I've seen this before, I thought. The flaw I was looking for had emerged. Now I could relax a little bit. The pathway to my heart was closed.

Philip and Connie sat in the back and were smiling and laughing, entertained and maybe a little alarmed by the conversational pattern that Howard and I fell into. It was like sparring. When Howard would fire off some impressive fact or observation, he would glance at me to see if I was amused. I would quickly fire a response back and more often than not my expression was unimpressed. I think this bewildered him. *Who is this guy? He speaks as if his opinion is the last word on any topic,* I thought. He was visibly surprised and perturbed whenever I threw a smart remark back at him or gave my own opinion, especially if it contrasted with his.

It must have been like watching a tennis match or two boxing opponents circling each other and taking occasional jabs. I had been through the ringer and could give as good as I got. Howard clearly didn't realize that I was in no mood to be on a date in the first place, much less with someone who wanted me to bow to his ego.

We continued bantering back and forth, testing the waters, pushing against each other's resolve.

"Hey, Howard," Philip chimed in from the backseat, probably to break the aggressive cycle of conversation he was observing. "How about signing up for that upcoming Iron Man–type competition? Are you interested?"

"I don't know," Howard said. "I just turned forty. They'd move me up to the next age group."

"Well, at least you'd have a better chance of winning against older people," I said.

He went silent for a moment. It wasn't meant to be an insult, just a fact. I had no idea who Howard was, what he had done in his life, what physical shape he had been in—and how his physically demanding career had come crashing down so hard. Howard shook his head. Nervous laughter rang from the backseat. A stern look crossed Howard's face and he raised his eyebrows.

"Tell you what," he said, sort of playfully but also not. "How about I pull over and let you out on the side of the road?"

"That's fine with me," I said.

Game on, big boy.

He smiled and kind of laughed, but I could see he was flustered. He didn't know what to do with me. I liked it that way.

After that initial verbal jousting, which felt rough but was mostly in play, the atmosphere somehow gave way to fun and laughter once we sat down at the restaurant. Howard was a truly charming and fun guy. The place was loud and we all laughed freely. After a while I almost forgot Philip and Connie were there because I kept falling into long conversations with Howard. We seemed to mesh perfectly. I understood him and he, me at some level I had not experienced before.

What is this? I thought. *What's happening here? Am I being suckered or is this real?* I almost wished the egocentric guy would emerge again so I wouldn't feel so taken in.

On the drive back to Philip and Connie's place, Howard put in a CD Blake had made him that day. A song called "Drowning" by the Backstreet Boys came on. We all sat there listening, easing through the Southern night. I didn't know at the time that the ocean and water were a big part of Howard's life. I just knew it was a beautiful, romantic song that seemed to capture our mood.

Howard's hand left the gearshift and gently touched mine. My eyes closed, and little by little the bricks I had used to build my wall of protection came down. When the song ended, Howard played it again. Then again. We probably listened to that song five times during the thirty-minute drive back to Jesup.

"I think he's playing that song for you," Connie whispered to me after the second time. I shushed her, and we all settled into a sweet and peaceful drive home.

We relaxed at Philip and Connie's house for a while and watched a funny sports bloopers video. I was sitting in a chair and Howard was on an ottoman leaning back on me, touching my hand lightly and rubbing his fingers against it. I had never felt such energy shoot through my body from such a gentle touch. It was as if I'd been living in a shell and didn't remember what it felt like to receive physical affection. My heart thumped faster. I hadn't realized how much I had missed being touched or feeling genuine affection toward me.

We left Philip and Connie to go back to my apartment. As soon as we left the driveway, Howard looked at me sort of mischievously.

"CPA, huh?"

"Yep."

"Own your own business?"

"Yep."

He grinned. "Not impressed."

Okay, now it's my turn.

"Navy SEAL, huh?"

"Yep."

"Best of the best?"

"Yep."

"Not impressed."

He laughed and that was that. We never felt the need to impress each other with accomplishments from that point on. We had established common ground.

Howard drove me back to my apartment, and I invited him in for a while. He sat on a chair, and I sat in front of him on the floor. Looking back on it, I see that my tendency was to sit in the lowest point of a room because I felt so beaten down by my previous experience. We talked for a while, and right in the middle of conversation I leaned up and kissed him. I don't know why I did it or how I got so bold. It was almost like someone pushed me. We kissed for a long time, and the energy between us was just outrageous. I like to think I'm a fairly controlled, content person, but something about Howard took me outside of myself. I felt as if we could have powered the state of Georgia with all the energy flowing between us.

After a while, Howard abruptly pulled back and said, "I've got to go. Blake should be home by now." He seemed uncomfortable for the first time, but I respected him for being a dad and a man of honor toward me. I walked him to the door and we kissed again, passionately but gently. Not even our shoes had come off and it was still the best "sex" I'd ever had.

I leaned out the door to watch him go. He turned to me at the stairs to say something again. I thought it might be, "I had such a wonderful time. I'd love to see you again." Instead, a hard look came into his eyes and he said, "Hey, I'm in the book. Give me a call some-time." A lump jumped into my throat.

He did not just say that! I thought. *Who does this jerk think he is?*

My night went instantly from high up in the clouds to the bottom of the basement. If a man doesn't have enough respect for a woman to call her, he doesn't respect her enough to deserve her. His words caught me completely off guard. I took a breath, gained my compo-sure, and steadied my voice.

"I don't know how your parents raised you, but my mother raised me not to call boys," I said. "So if you want to talk to me, you'll have to call me."

He looked like he'd been punched in the face. His countenance dropped and his smile faded.

"Good night," I said flatly.

"Good night," he replied.

I closed the door with the worst case of mixed emotions I'd ever had. The wonderful man I'd spent the evening with had transformed into a disrespectful, unmannered jerk. Me call him? My heart was torn right down the middle. I went to bed wondering, *Who is Howard Wasdin? An ex-hotshot who put on the manners just long enough to bag his date? Or the intelligent, tender gentlemen whose passion swept me off my feet? Is this how dating will be?* I had forgotten how first dates could be—like one-hit wonders, great but never heard from again. I didn't know what to expect next, or if I would ever hear from him again. Perhaps it was the result I had half expected: a memorable night that went down in flames.

The next morning I woke up with a bruise on my lip, and it took me awhile to figure out why. I had never kissed someone so passionately.

SEVEN

THE NEW GUY

HOWARD

I kicked myself all the way back to Screven.

How could you make such a stupid comment, Howard Wasdin? You had a wonderful night with the kind of woman you didn't know was out there—funny, disarming, gentle, strong, playful—and you ruined it by giving her a line straight out of a singles bar: "I'm in the book. Look me up sometime." Give me a break! It's a wonder she didn't just slam the door in your face and tell you to get lost forever.

I loathed myself and what I had become for every second of that drive. Debbie was right: How had I fallen so far, treating women like objects created to adore and admire me? Would I treat one of my sisters that way? When had I gotten so disrespectful?

Part of the reason was my approach to dating since Raquel had left me. As the self-appointed protector of Blake's heart, nobody was going to be good enough, ever. While we were in Tennessee, I had dated a lot of really good people, several of whom I'd met in other parts of the country. But I had developed a built-in auto-reject mechanism that kicked in about four weeks into the relationship. At that point, no matter how well it was going, I began looking for the least little excuse to justify ending it. Any longer than that and I felt they were chipping away at my defenses and might soon gain access to Blake's trust.

One of the women in particular was a really nice professor from a university in the Midwest. She seemed perfect—too perfect. One day she showed up unannounced at the Knoxville, Tennessee, airport and called me. "Surprise, I'm at the airport to visit you!" she said. My response was basically, "Surprise! That's my excuse for cutting you loose."

Others were good to my son, but the first time they said, "Blake needs to clean his room," they were gone. "Blake is spoiled." Gone.

In defense of my son I had become a class-A jerk.

Now, in one night, Debbie had touched my heart more than any woman had, and my defense mechanism kicked in more or less immediately. With Debbie it wasn't the four-week rule, it was the four-hour rule. That's how quickly I felt vulnerable to her.

I also was looking for anything to pump up my ego and signal that I was the hot commodity, the man of the hour again. My confidence had taken a hit when I left the body-armor company, not because I left the job, but because of what happened next: the crash and burn of my plan to be a well-paid, world-renowned tactical expert hosting groups of international security forces in my own backyard and potentially making millions.

I had brokered a deal with the United Arab Emirates to train security forces for Abu Dabi. I went to Dubai and Abu Dabi to meet with the chiefs of police there. It was a really big deal.

"We know of you and have seen what you can do," they said. "We will send our teams there to Georgia so you can help us build viable SWAT teams for our cities. The teams will need three levels of training: beginning, intermediate, and advanced."

The police forces in many United Arab Emirates cities are made up of Pakistanis because UAE citizens have so much money they literally don't have to work. I had had a good rapport with Pakistanis in Somalia, where they served as our allies. I began setting up a range near where I lived in preparation for the teams arriving in Georgia. I would make fifteen hundred dollars a day. With that kind of money I thought I could retire to Costa Rica after a couple of years. Life was going to be good.

Then, on September 11, 2001, the airplanes hit the Pentagon and the Twin Towers. As you would expect, all military training for foreign nationals was suddenly outlawed. The Pakistanis I was going to train couldn't even get into the United States anymore. Just like that, my plans of interesting work and great money disappeared. Not only that, but now my entire line of work was jeopardized.

I only had so much saved up for Blake and me. I began scraping around for some kind of paycheck and finally found a job selling cars at a General Motors dealership in Jesup. This paragon of manliness and tactical brilliance spent Saturday afternoons describing the good qualities of family sedans to couples looking for their first car. I'm almost embarrassed to say I was good at it too. I have an outgoing personality and throw myself into whatever I'm doing. People picked up on that energy. Most sales guys were laid back, but I enjoyed people so much that I crossed the lot to shake their hands and help them find what they were looking for.

Still, it wasn't the career I was dreaming about: Howard Wasdin, car salesman.

That put me at a low point the night I met Debbie. I was casting about for some shred of pride and was willing to burn those around me in my blind pursuit of confidence. In the end, I was the one thrown for a loop by the whole experience. Going out on a blind date with Philip and Connie was the last thing on my agenda. Blake and I had made plans to eat fried chicken from Sybil's and watch a movie at home. I already had the chicken in the truck when Philip called and started hounding me.

"Hey, buddy, what're you doing?" he said ingratiatingly. "I have a favor to ask. A girlfriend of Connie's went through a terrible divorce and we're going out with her tonight. Do me a favor and go out with us. Otherwise she'll feel like a third wheel."

It took me about .05 seconds to form an opinion.

"Uh, let me think. No," I said as firmly as I could.

"Come on," he wheedled, "it'll be good for you. She's really nice."

"Next you'll be telling me she has a great personality," I said.

"She does!" he said.

"No thanks," I said. "I'm not taking one for the team tonight. See you later."

I hung up. A moment later a call from a different number came in. I answered suspiciously.

"Howard, it's Connie," said the voice.

Great, I thought. *Now it's time for the soft sell.*

"Listen, I know you don't want to go out, but this would be really good for you," she said. "You've been through a tough time, and my friend Debbie has too."

"Connie, I'm really not interested in meeting this person," I said. "I won't be good company. Let's not and say we did."

But Connie wouldn't let it go.

"Howard, I've never asked you for anything," she said, "and I promise if you do this one thing for me, I'll never ask you to do anything else. Please, please, please. She's a sweetheart. Go to dinner with us."

Connie had appealed to my loyalty and that was hard for me to resist. It was true that she had never asked me for anything, never placed a claim on our friendship. But now she had. As a man of honor, those words had power. I said yes for that reason alone.

I went home, grudgingly changed into other clothes, and left the chicken with Blake and a buddy of his. My attitude was bad from the start because I just didn't want to be there. My plan for this op was to get through my obligation to Connie as painlessly as possible and get back home where I could sleep and maybe have some cold leftover chicken.

Then I walked into their apartment and saw Debbie. *Okay, she's kind of cute*, I admitted to myself. *Whatever.* My defenses jumped up, but I kept stealing glances at her. She was really good looking. No matter. Surely there were plenty of objectionable qualities I would find and use as an excuse to push her away.

We headed to Mudcat Charlie's restaurant, and as we talked on the way I couldn't help but notice that unlike most other local girls, she had no idea who I was. When I introduced myself, she acted like I was the checker at a grocery store or something. "Hi, I'm Howard Wasdin" wasn't working the magic it usually did.

Then, to my annoyance, she started zinging me back whenever I said something funny. I was used to people laughing at what I said. She would actually supply her own retorts. Soon we were tossing barbs back and forth in a friendly way, but some of hers were even sharper than mine. It caught me off guard. At one point Philip and Connie became visibly concerned because I said, "I've had enough of you. What if I pull over and put you out?"

Debbie responded, "Fine by me."

Who is this woman? I thought. But I was intrigued.

The next thing I knew we were at the restaurant and I was in the middle of a long conversation with Debbie, who was sitting beside me. I even forgot that Philip and Connie were there. They had started their own conversation and were nibbling at the fries, looking left out and a little regretful that we were getting along so well without them.

For me a new world had opened up, and I found myself enthralled by Debbie's intelligence, wit, and warmth. The last woman I'd been out with had told me her life consisted of listening to police scanners, cheering for wrestler Stone Cold Steve Austin, and avoiding books because she was no longer in high school and wasn't forced to read. *Duh!*

Debbie had the best sense of humor I'd ever seen in a woman. Her words could cut like a knife and then offer the cure. Everything about her was refreshing and invigorating.

I was only too happy when we dropped off Philip and Connie. *Who are the third wheels now?* I thought. The next hour with Debbie was magical. I'd never been so attracted to someone before. It wasn't just a physical need, it was a pull of the soul that made me want to be near her.

That's when I snatched defeat from the jaws of victory as I stood outside her door. Without knowing exactly how to say good-bye to someone who already had such a powerful hold on me, I reverted to form: *When in doubt, act like the great Howard Wasdin. Then let people grovel for your attention.*

But Debbie didn't grovel. Hurt passed over her face as I said my regrettable words, but she kept her dignity, rebuked me gently yet powerfully, then closed the door and left me alone with my despicable self. My heart hit the floor. I'd never felt like such a horse's patootie in all my life. Debbie will probably never know how much I beat myself up about that moment.

Part of me hoped she had been bluffing about not calling boys. The next morning I knew I would find out how strong this woman really was. Did she mean what she had said, or would she break down and call me first? I didn't know which I preferred. One would prop up my ego. The other would mean Debbie was unlike anyone I had ever met.

All day I waited. She didn't call. The phone sat there like a stone. The suspense was killing me and now I knew, she did mean it. She was going to write me off just like that. So on Monday morning I did something I had never done before: I made the first move. I didn't even know Debbie's last name, so I called Philip and got her number, then dialed and waited.

"Hello?" she said in her sweet voice.

"Good morning, sunshine," I said, trying to hearken back to what we had felt before I stuck my feet in my mouth.

"Good morning," she said with genuine feeling, and I knew we were back on solid ground if I could keep myself from ruining things.

"I was wondering if you'd like to come over and have breakfast with me," I said politely.

"That sounds wonderful," she said, so we spent a terrific, relaxing morning together before work, eating take-out at the dealership. Over the next few weeks we became virtually inseparable. We would often spend breakfast or lunch together at my office or sitting on a bench in the service department if I was too busy to leave work. I was in love and even enjoyed relearning how to be a gentleman.

Debbie taught me not with words but by the way she responded to what I did. If she had chased me the way so many women chase men today, constantly calling and texting, I would have run a country mile to get away. But Debbie knew that if she was worth having, then she was worth wooing. Every woman is. I experienced the thrill of the chase and the dignity of respect. It felt amazing.

I didn't know then that Debbie was starting over as well and setting new ground rules. She wasn't going to sell herself short or go begging. It was a fresh beginning for both of us, and this time we were committed to doing it right.

For a month we kept our relationship private, even from our kids. We couldn't be certain it would last, but it also felt too special to share. We would drive around the countryside in Debbie's black convertible BMW listening to music. "Drowning" by the Backstreet Boys became our song. We'd put the top down and ride for hours, enjoying each other and relaxing. She would lay her head on my shoulder. Never had I experienced a sweeter, more peaceful time.

I noticed little things about Debbie, like the shape of her lips. They are heart-shaped, and when we were kissing, sometimes I would gently push her away just to look at them. They were beautiful, and I told her that often. We both felt like we were in a dream because we were so comfortable with each other from day one.

Most guys have that moment when they introduce their new girlfriend to their best friend to see how they get along. In my case, that best friend was the ocean. My love for the ocean ran deep. It had developed when I was young, growing up in West Palm Beach. The sound of the beach became the sound of a soul at peace to me. To truly relax I had to hear the waves crash and see the surf and smell the salty air. Those were the best memories from my childhood.

When I was ten years old, my family moved to Screven, which is landlocked, but the beach never left my heart. Mom and Dad would take us all to Jekyll Island several times a year, which was the biggest thing in the world to me. I would look forward to it for months. Some people enjoy the mountains. They want to see the trees and rocks and streams and snow. They want to hear the wind rustling through the leaves and gaze upon vistas of forests and peaks. They want to smell pine needles. That isn't me. I feel like I was born to live where the water meets the land. It's where my heart rests.

The Atlantic Ocean was always the place I felt most comfortable. When you jump into the Atlantic, you feel great because it's warm and inviting. When I got into BUD/S, I was looking forward to getting to know the Pacific Ocean as well. I had dreams of perfect sand, warm water, and Beach Boys songs running through my head. I pictured a sunny oasis for good-looking girls and ripped guys who surfed, played volleyball, and generally spent life having a good time.

Little did I know that the Pacific Ocean is cold even in July. I got to San Diego in January for BUD/S and ran from the compound directly into the ocean because I just couldn't wait. To my shock, the water was cold. I waded out a little farther and ran my hand through the surf: still cold. The winds only made it worse. Nobody was cavorting in the water or even playing sand volleyball. *Are you joking me?* I thought. *Where's the "wish they all could be California girls" Pacific Ocean? Is this an off day? How much time are we going to have to spend in this stuff?*

I soon learned that what makes Hell Week at BUD/S so difficult is mainly the cold water of the Pacific. It sucks the desire to continue right out of you. Yes, the sleeplessness is hard—being awake constantly from Sunday to Wednesday. When they finally gave us a meal in the cafeteria on Day 4, guys literally fell asleep while eating, heads drooped on their chests or facedown in their plates. Yes, the physical exertion is exhausting. Your muscles start giving out, your skin chafes as the sand rubs you raw, and the salt causes those wounds to sting.

Yes, the mental game is tough. You see guys break down and cry like children. You see them run to ring the bell to indicate they quit and will never be a SEAL. But even if you can manage all that, the cold can still get you. You can be a superior physical specimen—a top weight lifter, a triathlete, an elite football or basketball player, a runner, anything. You may have the best stamina and skills a person could ask for, but that continuous bone-numbing cold is the final judge of whether or not you really want that Trident on your chest. If you can conquer the cold, or rather your body's response to the cold, you can go the whole way.

I remember being half-frozen one night during Hell Week, lying on a metal plate on the pier and experiencing stage 2 hypothermia. When they allowed us to sleep, it was on metal plates in the open air, lined up together like cordwood. Guys would literally shiver like leaves in the wind while sleeping, their bodies trying desperately to create heat even as their minds cast about for comfort in dreams. I was one of them, and the misery was nearly complete.

Then a BUD/S instructor, who, like them all, was notorious for his lack of sympathy, came up and put a warm cup of hot chocolate in my hand. He used soothing words to invite me to quit. A warm shower awaited me, he said, and a big thick towel, a nice dinner, and as many warm drinks like this one as I wanted. All I had to do was ring the bell signaling that I was done and say good-bye to my possible SEAL career.

The warmth of that cup felt otherworldly. It did not seem possible that such comfort existed in the world of sand, salt, and surf I was inhabiting.

Anyone who has been through BUD/S and says he never thought about quitting is either lying or is not mentally stable. I would not want that guy on my team because he is out of touch with reality. Misery is misery. Pain is pain. It hurts. It does not have to control you, but you cannot deny that it is there.

That moment when I was shivering uncontrollably, half-delirious from lack of sleep, and holding that cup of warmth in my hand was the moment I came closest to quitting. It took all my resolve to shove it away, knowing that in doing so I was embracing more hours, more days of continuous, almost unbearable cold. That would include two-mile timed swims and then a seven-mile swim around the island wearing only a wet suit top. The Pacific was merciless without a full wet suit, and we felt her icy teeth in every single stroke.

Still, even in those conditions my connection to the ocean strengthened. Out in the water you realize how finite you are in the grand scheme of things. My thoughts run wide and deep when I'm bobbing in the open ocean. I think of the ocean's permanence compared to the tiny lifespan of a man. I think of how relentlessly the tide has been hitting the shore for ages past. I think of how God set the boundaries of the oceans and how the waves carve different shapes on the land in a perpetual creative process, then erase them to start over again.

Several times I've gone deep-sea fishing with friends and cousins. One time Rachel and I went fishing for red snapper thirty miles off the coast of Jacksonville. My cousin Greg and friend Chris were with us. As soon as the boat stopped, I jumped in. Greg and Chris peered over the boat and looked at me like I was crazy. Two seconds later Rachel plunged in with me. Like father, like daughter. At that moment I had to consider that my love of the ocean was genetic. We swam around the boat and enjoyed the freedom while Greg and Chris said things like, "There are orcas down there, and great whites. I'm never getting out of this boat." They didn't know the freedom we experienced out there.

Another time I was diving for lobster in Key West. The lobster there back themselves into the coral so you have to reach in and grab them. You find them by looking for their antennae sticking out from the reef. One thing we do on the Teams is "subdue your mask" by putting tape on the shiny parts. The rigger's tape on my mask had worn off and the chrome finish was showing through.

I had six good bugs, which is what they call lobsters in Key West, when I saw a set of antennae sticking out from the coral. I swam over to look in the hole and suddenly saw the wide-open mouth of a moray eel coming at me and biting my mask. Moray eels are nearsighted, but when they see the sun glint off a fish's scales, they lunge at it. This eel got a mouthful of plastic mask, which it pulled away from my face and then spit out before retreating into its hole. I was so startled that I dropped my lobster bag and had to go find it. I kept the mask because of the teeth imprints on it.

Incidents like that aside, the ocean also promised safety. On the Teams we knew the ocean would protect us in times of danger. Things going bad? Need cover? Just get to the ocean. We could handle anything from there. It was our home. For years I even used a wave clock that played sounds of the surf while I fell asleep.

Those things were on my mind when I took Debbie to St. Simons. I didn't make it a big deal. I just wanted to share that part of me and relax with her in my place of comfort. It was my dream to live near the ocean one day, so we talked about that as we sat on the balcony at Brogen's and looked over the ocean. The pier was always a busy place with people fishing, people walking, kids playing on the playground, and adults bustling around the shops and restaurants. I told Debbie about my love of the ocean, how I always feel at ease near the ocean even if I am only close enough to smell it. I don't know if she understood at the time that it was much more than casual conversation, but she eventually came to understand it more fully.

After dinner we took a drive to Jekyll Island, which is more romantic and quiet. There we strolled for a long time on the beach, admiring the moon and the stars, still talking and getting to know each other. Our relationship had turned into a comforting friendship. On the drive home, she laid her head on my shoulder and her hand touched mine. We listened to "Drowning" again and again. I knew the message of the song was coming true for me because I was already drowning in her love. That night was an important turning point, and we began seeing each other exclusively. Our doubts began to ebb away like the tide.

At one point back at Debbie's townhouse, we happened to look at cheerleading pictures of Eryn from the previous football season. There in the photo, on the same squad, was my stepdaughter, Heather. Debbie gasped.

"Oh my gosh," she said. "I remember your family now. I saw you drop off Heather and pick her up from practice a couple of times. Why didn't I recognize you?"

I, of course, had been so focused on myself that I didn't remember any of the other parents, but we were amazed at how God seemed to have kept our paths separate until the right time.

Something wonderful, even miraculous was happening, but it didn't come without a fight.

*

A month or so after Debbie and I started dating I was at the car dealership early on a Saturday morning, blowing up balloons from a helium tank and affixing them to the windshield wipers of vehicles on the lot. We hated the task, but our boss made us do it to bring in buyers. Two colleagues, a man and a woman, were with me when a big diesel Mercedes-Benz pulled up.

First customer of the day, I thought optimistically.

I'd never seen the guy at the wheel before, but he got out and slammed his door, and then I noticed something: Debbie's daughter, Eryn, was sitting in the passenger seat. I recognized her from photos.

That must be her daddy, I thought. *I wonder what this is about.*

The guy walked right over to me. I felt a little silly holding a balloon. My colleague graciously took it and tied it to a nearby windshield wiper.

"Are you Howard Wasdin?" the guy said.

"I sure am," I said. "How can I help you?"

Eryn peered at me from just above the level of the dashboard.

"I'm Debbie's husband, and I want you to know we're still trying to make things work," he said. "Why don't you leave our family alone? Don't you see this will be bad for my daughter?"

He motioned back to Eryn. I was respectful.

"Maybe you and Debbie need to talk because she's telling me her marriage is over. It was my understanding that papers have been finalized and signed," I said.

"That's not true," he said. "I refuse to sign them. I don't believe in divorce. We're sorting things out. You're trying to be a home wrecker. You don't even care about our family."

He started yelling and getting closer, pointing his finger at me, but kept far enough away that he wouldn't get hit. Part of me hoped he would get into my personal space so I could lean into his finger, then break off his arm and beat him with it. But I looked over and saw the little girl. I couldn't do anything with her there. I didn't want her seeing her daddy ranting like this. Yes, I could have put the guy down on the hood of his car in just a few seconds, but it didn't seem fair and it didn't seem right—not for me and not for Eryn. That wasn't how I wanted to start our relationship.

For ten minutes or so this guy followed me around, keeping safely back but yelling and blaming me for the state of his failed marriage. I was incredulous at first and didn't know how to respond. My colleagues quietly drifted away to a more peaceful part of the lot. For my part, I was having a hard time keeping my right hand uncocked.

Finally I'd had enough of his mouth.

"You're saying a lot of unpleasant things," I said. "If you really want to push this, let's go behind the dealership and settle this man-to-man. You've got your daughter in the car, so you don't want to mess with me here, but if you want to walk around the corner, we can definitely talk."

He knew what I meant, and he quickly refused.

"We can talk right here," he said.

Then he swung on his heel, got in his car, and drove off.

My colleagues came back over. The woman was the first to say, "I can't believe you didn't knock him on his can."

"He was begging for it," the man said.

But I was proud of myself for holding back. In retrospect, I think he showed up wanting to provoke an altercation, to alienate me from Eryn. I was mad enough by the time he left that it could have become physical. Angels must have been holding me back and giving me unnatural tolerance.

I was so upset the rest of the day that I don't remember selling any cars. I called Debbie and told her this guy had shown up with Eryn in the car, and she groaned.

"That's Randy," she said.

Debbie hadn't told Eryn she was seeing anybody. Like me, she wanted to protect her child from relational attachments to people who might not hang around. We were careful to speak by phone at night after Eryn went to bed. Debbie would come by the dealership for coffee in the morning after she had dropped Eryn off at school. We often had lunch together. On the weekends that Eryn was with her dad, I would try to leave Debbie's house before 5:00 p.m. on Sundays so Eryn wouldn't see me there when her dad dropped her off.

Now that Eryn knew who I was, Debbie and I started seeing each other more openly, though we didn't date like normal people do. We didn't like hitting the town, but preferred staying in with our kids, cooking meals and having movie nights together. We started bringing our kids together on Friday nights at one of our places. It became everyone's favorite thing to do. That family feeling was so powerful to me. Debbie was a much more stable person than I was. She had held the same job all the way through high school and college, and had run the same CPA practice for years. She had never lived far from Jesup. Being with her gave me a feeling of being home and safe.

My kids felt it too. Blake and Rachel loved their new friend Eryn, and Eryn loved playing with them. They were instant buddies. Unfortunately, Eryn chose to treat me like an ax murderer on parole. She wasn't just cold; she was actively hostile.

Part of me understood. Eryn had never shared Debbie before.

By the time Eryn was old enough to remember, Debbie and Eryn's dad were estranged within their own home, and then he left and was living in another apartment altogether. Debbie and Eryn had done everything together and now I was interrupting that closeness. The first night Eryn and I officially met—not counting the unfortunate episode at the car lot—was for dinner at a Mexican restaurant along with some of Eryn's other friends. From the moment Blake and I walked in, Eryn's behavior was atrocious. She started kicking and jostling Debbie under the table to the point I felt that if I didn't leave, she was going to cause a scene. I hadn't even taken my coat off when I said to Debbie, "I'm not doing this to her. I'll see you later."

Debbie was embarrassed and appalled. She assured me repeatedly that Eryn had never given her any trouble before. "I don't know who this child is," Debbie said in exasperation. Eryn even had a sign hanging in her room that she had made with markers and crayons. It read, "I hate Howard." She wore her attitude like a bad dress and avoided anything we were doing.

Debbie finally took her to a therapist who helped kids get through complicated life transitions. The therapist even talked with me. His conclusion: "I can tell you, the problem is not Howard. It's anybody you date. Eryn has never had to share you. She's very selfish with you. I don't know how you feel about Howard, but you can deal with it now or later. At some point you have to face it."

Hearing that, Debbie was ready to put her foot down. But the next Friday night Eryn was so rude that my kids and I talked the whole way home about it. I decided it was time to make a choice. When I got home, I called Debbie as I usually did before bedtime and asked, "Is it worth it, what we're doing here? Do we want to stick it out or break up so she'll be happy?"

Debbie's response was firm: "There's no child in my family telling her mama what she can and cannot do. Let's hunker down and stick it out. Things'll change. I hope."

In battle you know you're in the right place because people are shooting at you. As our relationship absorbed some of these blows, we just kept our heads down and tried to do what we felt was right.

I had been attending First Baptist Church of Screven because I had realized that no man is an island and that I wouldn't heal of the wounds of the past alone. I needed a team. I enjoyed the Sunday school and church services and was starting to give God more room in my life, now that I knew he hadn't pronounced eternal judgment on me. I also wanted Blake to be in church. We felt a sense of camaraderie with the people there. With Debbie we tried a Church of God church because the music was so good. Even church hunting with her felt like an adventure.

One of our main prayers was that Eryn would finally see me not as an interloper but as someone who truly loved her mother—and loved her.

Then the decisive moment came.

One day while riding bikes, Eryn went sprawling on the asphalt and skinned up her hands and knees pretty badly. By the time I saw her, her hands and knees were red and puffy. The scrapes still had asphalt in them. Pus pockets were developing. I took one look at them and said, "We have got to clean this out." Debbie has no medical background so she said, "I can't. I don't know how and I'm not sure I could stomach it."

I've treated a lot worse things on the battlefield, so Debbie brought me peroxide, a bowl, a washcloth, and a brush. We sat on the floor of the den, with Eryn trying to hide her hands from me, squalling and making a scene. I began scrubbing the wounds, just as I had done with the boy in Mogadishu, though his were much more serious. The scrubbing and peroxide hurt Eryn and I kept telling her, "I'm so sorry, but it'll get worse if I don't."

"You enjoy hurting me!" she yelled, and she meant it more broadly than a couple of scraped palms.

"No, baby, I'm trying to make you feel better," I said. "I'm sorry, but I've got to do it. If we don't clean it out, it's going to get infected and hurt worse."

Eryn cried harder as I applied the peroxide and brushed the asphalt and debris from her wounds. Pretty soon Debbie was crying, and before I knew it, I was crying, too, even as I did the delicate work. Finally we got past the painful part, I bandaged her up, and Debbie put her to bed. We could only wait and see what happened next.

Our prayers were answered literally overnight. Blake and I walked in the door the next day for dinner and I got the surprise of my life: Eryn came running down the stairs of Debbie's townhouse and from the fifth stair took a flying leap into my arms.

"Hey, Air-bear," I said, and she gave me the biggest hug. Debbie watched with wide eyes as her daughter, who had never shown me one ounce of affection, thanked me for helping her heal. Her hands were no longer swollen but had formed little innocuous scabs—just as we wanted them to.

From that moment on we were like family. The animosity and possessiveness evaporated. Years later I walked her down the aisle when she got married. Through multiple battles God was proving that Debbie and I, and our families, were meant for each other.

But the last and most hurtful battle for our relationship was yet to be fought.

EIGHT

COMBAT TESTED

DEBBIE

Howard and I were so in love, so attracted to each other body and soul, that marriage was on our minds almost from the start. It felt so right being together, and even the kids acted like siblings. But we also underestimated how fragile we still were, and how many wounds remained from the past. Those wounds were easily ripped open, and that's exactly what happened the day Howard planned to ask me to marry him. Out of nowhere came a malicious attack from an unexpected source that threatened to tear down the love we had so carefully built.

My kitchen had become the bustling base for both our families. Eryn and Howard's kids, including Heather, gravitated there as if drawn by the love Howard and I felt for each other. The atmosphere of fun and relaxation had a healing effect on all of us. Howard and I enjoyed coffee every morning, and we all watched TV or played games most nights until Howard & Co. went home. Weekends were full of slumber parties for the girls. Blake and his friends were always coming by. It was enough to make our heads spin—Howard and I had gone from being lonely single parents with few prospects to lives bursting with love, excitement, and a new sense of family. Everything was meshing together better than we could have planned.

HOWARD

The July after we met, Debbie and I decided to take all the kids on a family vacation. She had never been camping, and I was all about experiencing as many "firsts" as we could together. We rented an RV from a dealership in Jacksonville, grabbed a couple of tents and supplies, and hit the highway with Rachel, Eryn, Heather, Blake, and one of Blake's friends. We were headed to Bear Mountain, North Carolina, among other locations. The idea was to tool around, have fun, and see as much as we could in the time we had. The boys set up a tent at our first campsite and tried relentlessly to keep the girls out during the day. In spite of their efforts, they still slept in sandy sleeping bags that night. The girls slept in the bed at the back of the RV, three little angels all in a row.

On our second night on the road, I decided to make my famous campfire beans, which are one of the most important parts of a true camping experience. We had leftover honey-baked ham that we had bought for sandwiches. I sliced and scraped the last bits of ham off the bone and threw them in a pot along with onions, brown sugar, and baked beans. I then cooked it over the fire as the aroma filled the campground and the kids came over to watch it bubble. It was the first time Debbie, Eryn, or Rachel had eaten campfire beans, and this was no ordinary batch. The honey-baked ham turned it into five-star campfire beans. We gathered around a picnic table and everyone dug in.

The conversation that night was about the Old West and cowboy movies we had seen with characters eating this same dish. The kids especially enjoyed the campfire beans and helped themselves to more than one serving. I was pleased it had gone over so well. After dinner we played games for a while, watched some of *Gone with the Wind* on the DVD player in the RV, and then tucked the girls in for the night. One side of the RV had a couch that converted into a single bed. The other side had a table that folded down to make a separate single bed. As Debbie and I converted the kitchen into a sort of dorm room, Heather walked in from the girls' bedroom, yawning.

"Daddy, can I sleep with you?" she asked.

"Of course," I said.

She snuggled into my single bed with me, and I knew I wouldn't be able to sleep for a while. I was just waiting for her to drift off and I would gently place her in bed with the other girls. After a while the laughter and chatter from the back quieted down and Heather's breathing became regular. All the girls were asleep. I took Heather back and tucked her in. It was peaceful and still in the RV and throughout the campground. Debbie and I talked quietly, reminiscing about the day.

Then it all started.

The campfire beans we had eaten for dinner started having their effect. One by one, and sometimes in harmony, our little girls' bodies began sounding gassy notes from their multiple helpings of beans. Debbie and I tried to stifle our laughter as the noise grew and became a virtual symphony. Sound came from one side of their room, then another, and then all together. At one point I think we even heard sounds from the tent outside where Blake and his friend were certainly warming up their atmosphere.

"*Gone With the Wind* was sure the right movie to watch tonight," I said to Debbie as the "winds" kept sweeping through our RV. For some reason I had been so focused on the culinary excellence of the meal that I hadn't even considered what the result would be a few hours after we had eaten. We chuckled through the night as the kids kept us entertained, little knowing how loud and musical their bodies were as they slept.

We spent the next few days driving from one campsite to another, setting up camp and tearing it down. We inner-tubed, explored caves, and stopped at any place that looked touristy. It was way too much fun. As we drove we listened to books on tape we had picked up at Cracker Barrel. We had rented the RV for seven days but were having so much fun that we called the dealership to ask about keeping it a few more. We ended up staying out for ten days and still didn't want it to end.

Our last stop was at the Biltmore Estate, which I chose because Debbie had never seen it and she enjoys good architecture and design. As we toured the estate, we quickly realized that we needed to keep a close eye on the kids. The place was so massive that they could get lost behind a couch or in a closet and we might never find them. We toured the estate through the maze of rooms, always looking back to make sure the girls were not wandering away as they played.

One of the rooms we visited was a bathroom with a tank high on the wall and a brass pull to flush it. There was a sign reading, "Do not flush toilet." Leave it to our girls—before Debbie could stop them, one grabbed the brass pull and yanked it down. Water began to flow. Debbie snatched her by the hands and ran out, hoping the place wouldn't flood and that we wouldn't be kicked off the property. We're pretty sure no damage was done.

The bigger surprise was outside when we met up with Blake and his friend. They had been exploring the grounds alone. I guess I hadn't taken a good look at Blake since that morning, and now I saw something suspicious in his earlobe.

"What is that?" I asked.

"What is what?" Blake asked in typical teenager fashion.

"That thing in your ear?"

"Oh, that," he said. "My friend pierced my ear for me last night. We bought a kit at the Walmart you sent us to."

You have got to be kidding me.

I didn't know how to respond. Now that I looked at Blake I saw that he had developed a look on this vacation. They had bought playing cards and bandannas at Walmart as well and had been staying up late playing card games. Now the bandannas were wrapped around their heads, and each boy had an ace tucked under the bandanna and a huge fake diamond in one ear. On top of it all was a baseball cap holding the look together.

Ridiculous, I thought, but I held my opinion to myself.

"What are you guys hoping to accomplish with all this?" I said, swirling my finger to indicate all the fashion action going on around their heads.

"What?" Blake asked.

"The bandanna and the cards?"

"Oh, that. We just thought it'd look cool."

"Oh," I said. In that moment, maybe because I was having such a good time, I made a key parenting decision. Instead of climbing all over Blake's case, I just let it slide. Within a few weeks the whole bandanna-playing-card-earring phase passed. The fact that I didn't make a big deal of it helped the novelty wear off faster.

DEBBIE

Earrings aside, Blake blossomed in the new situation. No longer did he and Howard stay holed up in their bachelor pad. Now a family had gathered around him. I was especially sensitive about not forcing a change on Blake or trying to become his latest mother figure. He was a teenage boy who had felt the sting of rejection too early and too often. I felt it was a good thing that he treated me, his dad's latest girlfriend, warily at first. I was in no hurry to prove myself. Trust is built by consistency over time, and I was in it for the long haul with Howard. I decided to treat Blake as kindly as I would anybody else in my circle of family. That meant giving him plenty of space to get used to having me around. I also felt that the ideal outcome was for Blake to have a strong relationship with his mother and his father. I encouraged him to cultivate those relationships above anything.

As Blake and I and the rest of the children hung around one another day after day, we passed little milestones of trust, and most of the time you couldn't see them coming. One summer morning before the first day of school, I offered to take Blake clothes shopping, an annual routine for my family. He looked at me as if I had offered to fly him to the moon.

"You want to take me clothes shopping?" he said.

"Sure," I said. "It'll be a good start to your school year."

This was clearly new territory for him. He quietly accepted my invitation, and off we went to buy new shirts, pants, and supplies. At the end of our trip, as we were unloading bags of clothes and notebooks from the trunk, Blake cleared his throat.

"Thank you for taking me shopping, Miss Debbie," he said. "This was a lot of fun."

"Sure," I said, and before things could get awkward he disappeared into the house with his new stuff.

One time I called just to see how he was doing, which was normal in the family I grew up in. At first he didn't know how to take it.

"I guess I was wondering why you were calling," he asked me respectfully after we'd chatted for a few minutes.

"Just to see how you're doing," I said. "I thought I'd catch up on how things are going with you."

He was silent for a moment. "Really?" he said. "You just wanted to talk?"

"Why not?" I said.

After a moment he started to tell me what was happening at school. Then he mentioned the junior prom, which he wasn't planning to attend. I told him he might want to reconsider that one.

"You will look back and wish you had gone," I told him. "Just ask a friend. You don't have to go with someone you want as a girlfriend. Sometimes it's more fun to go with someone who is just a friend anyway. There's no pressure. You can just relax and have fun."

Blake thought about it for a minute and then said, "Okay. That does sound like it could be fun."

Since I had encouraged him to go, I made myself available to help make it a special night for Blake. I took him out again to select clothes, this time for a formal dance. I knew the owners of the local tuxedo rental shop, and they were more than happy to help outfit Blake. We looked through a book of options in their shop.

"Cool, a zoot suit!" Blake said, pointing to a big, baggy suit in the book.

"Yeah, it is cool, but I don't think you want to wear that to the prom," I said, thinking of him standing on the dance floor in those billowy pants and long, draping coat. "Here, how about this one?"

I pointed to a black tuxedo with a grey-striped silk ascot. The ascot had a black tack securing it that looked classy. Blake loved it. The owner took his measurements and went over his options, then we were off to the flower shop.

"What color dress is she wearing?" I asked Blake as we drove there.

"I don't know. Does it matter?" Blake said.

"Of course it does. We need to know for her corsage and for your boutonniere."

"What's that?"

"The flowers she wears on her wrist and the one you wear on your tux."

"Okay, I'll ask."

He called his date and got his answer.

"Her dress is yellow," he said.

"Good. Let's talk to Mary."

Mary, the flower shop owner, had been another bright light in my life, a sweet Christian lady who always offered a sympathetic ear or a positive word.

"Hey, Debbie, what are you up to?" she asked as she hugged my neck and then Blake's.

"We're trying to get Blake set up for prom. Can you help us with some flowers?"

Within fifteen minutes she had found perfectly matching flowers for our couple's outfits. But that wasn't all. I had this bright idea that instead of going out and spending a bunch of money on dinner at some loud, unromantic local place, Blake and his date could come to my apartment and we would create a romantic ambience for them. I had been planting spring and summer flowers around the back patio, and my many projects made it look like a cute little cottage.

"Blake, how about instead of you going out to dinner, we transform the back patio into a romantic wonderland, and your daddy and I treat you both to dinner?" I offered. "If you don't want to, that's fine. I just thought it might be a nice alternative."

"That sounds great!" Blake said.

And so our work began. I bought tiki torches to strategically place around the patio, candles for the table, and ferns to give a lush, full feeling. It began to look even better than I had envisioned. Howard planned the menu, of course. On the night of the prom he made steak and potatoes and we bought a cheesecake for dessert. The prom fell on a weekend when we had Blake's sisters, whom we recruited to be our servers and waitresses.

Blake went to pick up his date, and after having his photo taken a thousand times by his date's mother, he brought the young lady to my apartment. I couldn't resist taking a bunch of photos myself, and then Blake escorted his date to the quaint patio where the table had been set and was waiting. Blake pulled out the chair for her. Gentle music was playing from speakers his sisters had set up. Candles flickered, torches cast dancing light, and the sunset poured its own majestic beauty over everything. It was so romantic that I found myself stealing glances outside just to take it in. I half wished Howard and I were out there enjoying it.

The little girls had dressed in their nice clothes, fixed their hair, and practiced their brightest smiles. Howard even dug in his closet for a pair of dress pants and a dress shirt, also donning a white apron and placing a towel over his arm as he sought Blake's approval of the bottle of sparkling grape juice. He poured it into their fluted champagne glasses. The girls, proper and serious, started by bringing out some appetizers, then the salads and the main course. They took turns refilling glasses, removing salad plates, removing dinner plates, and serving dessert, all in perfect silence. It did our hearts good to see them taking so much joy in making Blake's prom special. I'm sure it felt good for big brother to be the center of attention for a change, since the girls more often occupied that spot.

After dinner Blake and his date headed off to the dance and had a great time. The next day we drove them to a Braves game in Atlanta, stopping off at a park on the way home where they raced go-carts, played in the batting cages, and climbed a rock wall. Howard and I both wanted to make Blake's high school years memorable, and Howard seemed especially appreciative of my efforts.

As we went through those life experiences together, Blake and I built a relationship. Once during the workweek, I had a mischievous itch to take the day off. Howard was busy, Eryn had something important going on, and playing hooky sounded fun. So that morning I told Blake, "I've got an idea. You skip school, I'll skip work, and we'll go to Savannah instead." He raised an eyebrow, giving me a look that said, "Are you just trying to win me over?" But I wasn't. We went to Savannah and had a great day seeing the sights.

After observing that I wasn't going to suddenly disappear and that my mood toward him didn't change from day to day, Blake's polite distance evaporated. Soon he was talking about anything and everything. He asked for counsel about dating and girls, subjects he was reluctant to talk about with Howard. He seemed to like the strategic advantage he gained from a woman's perspective. My advice was sound but pretty generic: "Don't commit too early. Date around and find out what you're looking for. See who will make you happy. Really get to know someone first."

Our conversations even touched on his relationship with Howard. They butted heads occasionally, as boys and dads do. I told him, "If you need to bring up something difficult, do it this way. It's all about how you approach subjects. He'll be more receptive if you come at it right."

Soon Blake didn't just tolerate my presence but grew protective of my feelings. One night I attempted to make a big dinner for the family, a doomed exercise for someone like me. The hamburger steak turned to charcoal. The potato dish came out beautiful on top but cold in the middle because I had sliced the potatoes too thick and used a deep dish, which kept it from cooking through. Only the fried okra turned out well.

Still, Blake and the rest of the family sat there courageously eating the dismal offering. Blake especially seemed to go overboard, making faces to indicate he was enjoying it and complimenting me on my cooking: "This is really good, Miss Debbie." Finally I couldn't stand him being brave for my sake anymore. I laughed, shook my head, and said, "Blake, you don't have to eat that, and neither does anyone else. It's almost inedible!"

"No, really, Miss Debbie, it's good," he insisted.

"Blake, you are so sweet, but it's not," I said.

I'm a realist. We all laughed as I took everyone's plates and relieved them of duty. We ended up having something Howard threw together, which tasted a lot better. After that, Howard and I agreed that from then on he would always cook and I would clean the kitchen. That was a win-win for everybody.

Perhaps my biggest sign of loyalty was allowing Blake's albino boa constrictor to live with me. I wasn't thrilled at the prospect of sharing my residence with this unusual roommate, but it was Blake's and he had no other place to keep her. Her name was Keri and she was the pet of his dreams. I winced when he lugged Keri into my home office with her fifty-gallon aquarium and thought, *This boy had better appreciate this.*

"Thanks, Miss Debbie!" Blake said cheerily, knowing he had successfully charmed me into snake-watching duty.

"Okay, but I'm not feeding that thing, and she is not running loose in this house," I reaffirmed.

"No problem," he said.

"Cool," said Eryn from behind me. She was excited. She loved pressing her nose up against the glass and watching Keri consume live mice. I found it disgusting.

Keri settled in. She had gotten larger since Blake bought her, and with increased size came increased strength. Snakes don't have a lot to do all day, and Keri had started exploring ways to escape. She had grown big enough and strong enough to ease up the side of the aquarium and push the lid up. In her previous house she had escaped several times, once becoming entangled in the springs under the couch. Blake's response was to put books on the lid and hope that would keep her inside. He didn't realize just how strong all those live mice had made Keri.

One Saturday night my house was empty for a while. Eryn was at her dad's house, Howard's girls were with their mother, and Blake was out with friends. Howard and I had been out all day and we got back to my house feeling famished. We hadn't had any dinner so we decided to order pizza. As we settled in for the evening, we noticed the fifty-gallon aquarium was empty. Keri was missing. She had done as we had feared: eased up the side of the aquarium, lifted the lid despite the books, and headed for freedom.

"You've got to be kidding me," I said, looking woefully at the empty tank. I had become accustomed to the massive snake being there, but I still refused to touch her. I had warned Blake many times, "I'd better not see her slithering around the house." Now she was doing just that, roaming the new environment and exploring the terrain. I was repulsed by the idea of this creature sliding into my warm bed, rubbing its scales all over my floors, or flicking its tongue in the shoes in my closet.

"Howard, this is a high-level emergency," I said. "We've got to find that thing."

As we waited for the pizza to arrive, Howard and I looked in all the typical hiding places: under couches and chairs, under beds and tables, inside cupboards, bathtubs, behind the toilet, inside closets. I had this creepy feeling that Keri was under my feet so I kept hopping up as if she had touched me. When the doorbell rang, we hadn't found her and were still a couple on a mission. Howard ran to the door.

"Come on in, man. Let me grab my wallet," he said to the pizza delivery driver. We were still looking in every possible hiding spot, and I shut the front door behind the delivery guy to make sure Keri didn't escape.

"Y'all looking for something?" the guy said, watching us with amusement.

"Yeah, my son's snake escaped from her aquarium," Howard said as he grabbed his wallet from the countertop. "We've been looking—"

Slam. Bang!

"What was that?" I said.

We looked to see the pizza box on the floor and the delivery man gone, the door slammed behind him. Apparently he didn't like snakes either. Howard chased him down the driveway to pay for our food. The guy made it perfectly clear he was willing to take the financial hit if he didn't have to get any nearer to Blake's boa.

We eventually found Keri and I gave her an eviction notice. Blake understood. Her new house was a better fit anyway.

But my closeness with Blake was making his mother uncomfortable, and that gathering storm would soon darken our skies. All summer Blake had trained for the football team. He was at the high point of his football career, and the school was putting together a special program featuring senior players with their parents. One day Blake came to me in the kitchen. "Miss Debbie, can I ask you something?"

"Sure," I said, wondering what would warrant such an introduction.

"I would like you to be in the photo with me and my dad for the football program."

I paused. Emotions collided inside of me. I loved that Blake thought enough of me to ask, but I didn't like the idea of possibly getting between him and his mother.

"Well, don't you want your mama to be in there with you?" I asked. His eyes steeled up.

"No, ma'am. I would like you to be in there with me."

Blake and I had built up a lot of trust, but any conversation about his mother was bound to be delicate. We never talked of her except when I encouraged him to keep making that relationship work. I didn't have a lot of room to maneuver now.

"That sounds like a lot of fun," I said. "Let me talk to your dad about it before I say yes."

"Thank you, ma'am," he said and walked out as if he'd crossed an important bridge.

Blake's request put me in an awkward spot, but Howard was convinced it was a step in the right direction.

"We want to get married someday anyway, so it's natural for him to treat you like someone important in his life," he said. "He's on such bad terms with his mama right now that if you don't go, it'll just be me and him. How lame is that?"

After some serious consideration, I felt I owed it to Blake to honor his wishes, so on the scheduled day I went with Howard to the school for photos for the program. At the homecoming game I accompanied Blake and Howard to the center of the field where parents were gathering with their senior players and cheerleaders. The pride in Blake's face told me I had done the right thing.

But it would lead to a painful encounter.

Howard and I had fantasized about getting married close to the one-year anniversary of our first meeting, so when fall arrived, I was half expecting a proposal. It must be my personality. I'm detail oriented and forward thinking, a planner by nature. I knew I wanted Howard in my future and I hoped he wanted me. In September, I noticed subtle signs that Howard was planning something. He's terrible at keeping secrets—you can read them all over his face. When Howard's giddy, there is no suppressing it. I can put on a poker face if I need to. Howard can't. He is just Howard.

Something was up; I just didn't know exactly what.

One Saturday morning in October, Eryn, Rachel, Heather, and I were taking it easy around my house. Lunchtime was approaching, and we were getting ready to drive up to McRae to meet Howard for a picnic at Lake Grace, a small, wooded location where people fished and rode inner tubes. It was a lovely place with mown grass and scattered farms nearby. Howard and I had driven there a number of times to enjoy the scenery, daydream, and see how much water was coming over the dam. The name seemed particularly appropriate to our situation: Grace, something we all needed.

I wasn't sure why Howard had invited us for a picnic on a Saturday, his busiest workday, but I was happy to go. We were ready to leave when there was a knock at the door. I answered it and saw it was Katherine, Howard's first wife. The tight smile on her face told me this wouldn't be a pleasant visit. With her was a female relative who promptly barged in and helped herself to the use of my bathroom.

"Can I talk to you outside, Debbie?" Katherine said sweetly.

"Sure," I said, hoping against hope that this would end well. Maybe Katherine would say she was happy about my relationship with Howard and hoped we would build the life we wanted. That would be so healthy for the kids and for all of us. I stepped onto my porch and waited.

She wasted no time with niceties but turned to me defiantly.

"I heard what happened with Blake," she said. I wasn't sure what she meant at first. She continued, "The photo in the program. The football game."

"Katherine, I meant no disrespect to you," I said. "Blake asked me to do those things, and I wanted to honor him by saying yes. I have encouraged him to build a relationship with you. I'm all about children having strong relationships with their parents. You are the only mother he'll ever have. I can never replace that."

She looked at me sideways, as if I hadn't responded as she had expected. She seemed annoyed, then speechless. Then she puffed herself up again and suddenly switched subjects.

"You know Howard calls me every morning," she said. The statement caught me off guard.

"I know he calls the girls every morning," I said. While driving to McRae for work, Howard would call Rachel and Heather before they went to school. He was a good dad that way.

"He's not just calling for them," Katherine said.

"Really," I said flatly, trying not to take the bait.

"We talk every morning," she said. "That's why he calls. He wants to talk to me. We're rebuilding our relationship."

I felt foolish for allowing it to hurt me. But she was just starting.

"You know he's been seeing a woman over in Blackshear," she said, growing confident and walking around my porch as if she'd rented it for the day. She paused and glanced at me for a response. I didn't know what to say. I had never been confronted like this, and something in her posture and the edge on her voice told me she wanted more than an argument—she wanted a physical fight. My skin bristled with animal anticipation. This was new to me.

Easy, I told myself. *Don't react. Be calm—calm is strong.*

"There's another woman in Baxley he's running around with too," she continued. "You're not the only one he's got. He's been going behind everybody's back. Same old Howard."

Her words struck me as strange and unbelievable, but also put me on guard. *Howard, running around with women in other cities? It couldn't be—or could it?*

"In case you didn't know," she continued, "we're still seeing each other. We have a good relationship. You ought to know we even sleep together. Right here in this house. In your bed."

My stomach froze, and I tried to will myself to reject the image. My poker face was firmly in place, but my guts spasmed.

"Really? In my bed?" I said calmly, telling myself it was a desperate lie. The weird claim almost made it easier to dismiss everything she had said up to that point.

Then I remembered the time when she had barged into my house dressed nicely, as if going to a formal event, when I wasn't there. She had found Howard changing clothes before he was supposed to meet Blake and me for the Senior Night Out. It had upset him, and he had told me about it later. *Is it possible something had gone on that night—beyond what he had admitted?*

Sensing that her attack was having an effect, she came toward me deliberately. I wondered if she would stop.

"All Howard wants is for his family to be together," she said with synthetic sweetness. "We're a fine Mormon family. We have cookouts."

Cookouts? I thought, almost laughing. *You mean like everyone else in America? Should I show you the grill I have out back?*

It was a strange comment, especially since she treated it like some master stroke. But I was still shaken by the conversation. She stopped short of me, and I knew this was the decisive moment. The unwanted encounter could either erupt into something very ugly or go an entirely new direction, if only I knew how to defuse it. I took a moment to quiet my heart and gather my response.

God, I prayed, *help me say the right thing—or at least not say the wrong thing.*

"Katherine," I said as she stared bullets at me. "I told you before, I'm all about family. If Howard wants to get back with you and repair your marriage, then I'll step aside and let you. Families should stay together—that's usually the best thing for everybody. If what you're saying is true and that's really what Howard wants, then I won't give you any trouble. You can get back together and be a family."

Her eyes widened and her mouth fell half open. The anger and aggression she had worked up had nowhere to go. She seemed to rock slightly backward. I had called her bluff. Lashing out at me made no sense now that I had given up.

Finally she blurted out, "No! No, I don't want him. I . . . I would never take him back. I don't have to be married again."

Whatever happened to "We're a fine Mormon family. We have cookouts"? I wondered.

She blustered and backed away. I was suddenly aware that behind me, the kids in the house knew what was happening. By keeping my cool I knew I had protected them from a nasty experience as well. Relief surged. *Thank you, God.* I stood there as Katherine's relative emerged from the house and walked nonchalantly down the porch steps, as if my house were a public restroom.

"Rachel! Heather!" Katherine hollered from the foot of the steps. The girls poked their heads out. "Gather your things. We're going."

I was still processing what had just happened—Katherine's strange, deliberate confrontation about my relationship with Howard, launched fearlessly at my own house—and forgot that Rachel and Heather were supposed to go with me to McRae. Before I knew it Katherine was gone, and so were the girls. The house became quiet. In the stillness I could hear my heart thumping.

God, what just happened?

Blake arrived and noticed immediately that I was shaken up.

"Are you okay, Miss Debbie?" he asked.

"I'm fine, Blake," I said. "I just had an unfortunate conversation and need some time to think about it."

Blake, Eryn, and I got in the car and drove to McRae to meet Howard for what was supposed to be our most important day together since we had met.

During that ninety-minute drive, my mind whirled like a carnival ride.

I tried to dismiss the doubts Katherine had sowed, but they found root in the soil of my previous pain. I drove quietly, in turmoil. Eryn occupied herself in the backseat, but Blake, who was older, resonated with my mood. I knew I had to find my own peace before explaining anything to him. He reached for my hand and held it as if he knew I needed comfort.

Meanwhile, my analytical mind jumped ahead of me and seized on every bit of what Katherine had said. Did Howard call Katherine's house every school day? Yes, I had to admit. That was the wonderful thing about him—he tried to keep good relationships with his children, even with Heather, who was not biologically his but called him Daddy. But could it also be true that he used those phone calls to talk to Katherine and perhaps rekindle a relationship? I guess it was possible, though whenever he spoke about his previous marriage it was with a wince.

How about the idea that Howard had been seeing women in Blackshear or Baxley? It didn't seem possible. He had no time and it was an incredible risk. I could have driven to his home or his work at any moment, and sometimes did. Having one affair, let alone two or three, would have meant putting on an elaborate act.

I also had very good evidence against this accusation: Howard's habit of calling me a dozen times a day. He was like a one-man GPS unit, always reporting where he was going and what he was doing. To be honest, it drove me crazy at first. By nature I'm not a constant communicator, and I especially dislike being on the phone all the time. Cell phones steal your peace, invading every last inch of your life. I talk enough on the phone at work, so when I get into the car, it's my safe zone to listen to music and let my mind come down off the day.

Not Howard. He stays in constant communication, even about little things. After dating for a few weeks, I would find my phone ringing at work.

"Howard, line one," my assistant would say.

When I got on the line, he would say, "I just wanted to let you know I'm heading to the dry cleaner's and then to the grocery store."

Okay . . .

Or, "I'm on a quick break. Just wanted to see how your day is going. You didn't answer your cell phone."

I wasn't used to giving updates on myself throughout the day and often cast about for something interesting to share. Usually my assurances were pretty standard: "Everything's going really well. I'm just, you know . . . working."

I did not feel the need to check in, especially when I was doing normal work or boring errands. I just wanted to finish them and get home. I learned something about myself, that I pretty much let people live their lives and am confident in their loyalty to me until they prove otherwise.

Howard's love language was different; he wanted frequent communication. Part of that was from his training on the Teams. He and his fellow SEALs were in close contact all the time, he told me. He knew every minute of the day that someone had his back. He missed that in civilian life. That's why if he was on a long drive, he would spend most of it on the phone with me, just to have the company. If I wasn't available, he would leave a message with the girls or with my office: "Let her know I'm here doing this or that." Even now he's got our entire family on FlightAware so when one of us travels by airplane, the rest can track the flight as it makes its way across the sky.

After getting used to it, it felt nice to have someone who wanted to know about my day or what I had for lunch or what was going on with the kids. I preferred that to someone who didn't even notice when I walked into the room. Now those countless phone calls from Howard were like gold. They proved to me that it was all but impossible for him to be carrying on other relationships. When we weren't on the phone with each other, we were together at my house until bedtime, and then on the phone until we fell asleep. There was just no way he had time to do all the things Katherine said he did.

Still, after I finished discounting everything she had said, my mind started all over again. I felt an urgent, almost irrational need to prove over and over that it wasn't possible. I hadn't realized how messed up my head was from my previous marriage until that moment. My heart wanted to recoil from possible pain. I almost had to will myself not to believe what I knew to be lies. I recalled too vividly my past experience of a man changing personalities the day I married him. That experience was branded into my mind—and I never wanted to repeat it.

Is Howard really who he seems to be? Or is he someone completely different? Are all men deceptive by nature? Do they all woo you, then turn into monsters?

Even if Howard was who he seemed to be, was it possible that our fairy-tale love was just that—a fairy tale?

I often marveled at how our lives were perfect opposites. Howard had traveled the world on daring missions, risking his life and living with near-constant uncertainty. As a SEAL he never knew when he would be called up for an op, or when that op would end, or where it would be. Even as a representative for the body-armor company he had traveled far and wide, working with people in every region of the United States and sometimes internationally. I rarely traveled farther than Atlanta and spent most of my time in the county I grew up in, keeping my head down and working as a CPA. I was always seeing people I'd gone to high school and college with around town. My life was very local.

The differences went further. Howard's childhood had been traumatic. Mine had been heavenly. Howard loved the outdoors. I spent most of my time indoors. Howard was a great cook. My cooking wouldn't kill people, at least not the first bite. So many contrasts, and yet our pairing felt so right. Howard was looking for a stable and consistent person to share his life with. I was glad to finally have someone who was wild about me. We filled the gaps in each other's lives almost perfectly.

But were we too different to make it work long term? What kinds of problems would we encounter down the road? Were we setting ourselves up for failure? Should we each find someone more like ourselves?

My heart was ragged and harassed when we arrived in McRae. The car dealership was busy—Howard had done well there. As the sales manager, he hustled to help customers and clean up a business that had been flagging. He'd gotten rid of a bunch of inventory that had been sitting on the lot forever. He drove an hour and a half each way every day and didn't take much of a break for lunch because lunch was when customers came in. I was proud of how hard he worked.

But today my eyes were full of hurt, and he knew something was wrong.

"Hey, how are you doing?" he asked and pulled me into an embrace.

"Not so well," I said. We had talked by phone and he knew Katherine had come over, but didn't know what she had said. I didn't even feel like telling him. Why ruin his day or revisit feelings that were still raw to the touch?

The truth was that for the first time in a long time, I just wanted to be alone to figure things out.

HOWARD

I could tell from fifty yards away that whatever had happened to Debbie had been bad—really bad. As a warrior you develop special skills, and one of them is how to read people's eyes and body language fast, especially in a combat situation. This was a combat situation of a different kind, and suddenly I knew I was fighting for the only relationship that had really mattered to me, outside of my children. The home team had been ambushed and the outcome was uncertain.

To make it worse, I had planned an elaborate proposal to Debbie that day. For weeks I had anticipated the moment she and the kids would arrive for our picnic at Lake Grace. Before leaving the dealership, an airplane I had hired would pull a banner asking Debbie to be my wife. I pictured her surprise as she looked up and saw the words in the sky professing my undying love. I imagined everyone around us—hundreds of customers and employees—cheering and applauding as I got down on one knee and presented her with a ring.

Of course I hoped she would say yes. I believed she wanted to be with me as much as I wanted to be with her, but there was always that uncertainty until you heard it with your own ears. For weeks my mind had gone over every detail of how it would play out, with happy anticipation.

Now war had broken out. Debbie's ring was burning a hole in my pocket, and for now that's where it would stay.

Debbie tells me I check in a lot by phone—I guess I like hearing her voice—and on a quick phone call that morning one of the kids told me Katherine was there and was talking to Debbie on the front porch.

Uh-oh, I thought as my stomach soured. *This can't be good. Watch out for incoming fire.*

When I finally reached Debbie later, she was her typical unflappable self. "Everything's okay. I'll tell you about it later," she said, but my heart was aching. I tried to keep my spirits up: *Maybe it wasn't so bad. Maybe they just had a friendly conversation. Maybe Katherine needed to bring something to one of the girls.*

The fast pace at the dealership helped me journey through the hours before they arrived. Being the sales manager had boosted my pocketbook and my confidence somewhat. It was hard work, but I was willing to bust my hump for it. I was in love with Debbie, and life was better than it had been in a long time.

But my mind kept going back to that knot in my stomach, the imagined conversation, the potential damage that had been done. Debbie knew my first marriage had been tough. Now it was as if someone had thrown open the door to a dark, old storage unit and said, "Here's some of Howard's baggage. If you marry him, you'll own all of this too." Was Debbie willing to put up with my past? Was I worth it to her?

I couldn't eat a thing.

My fairy-tale relationship with Debbie seemed ready to unravel. Friends would ask, "Are you guys as happy as you seem? There's no way. It's got to be an act. You hold hands in public. That's just crazy." But we were that happy. And I didn't want it to end. Ever.

When Debbie finally pulled onto the lot with Blake and Eryn in the car, her face said it all. This was a woman who had taken heavy fire.

"Hi, Howard," she said, and the usual cheer in her voice was gone. I hugged her tightly and immediately decided to scrap my big plans. There would be no ring that day, no picnic, no airplane banner, no surprise engagement. This was a triage situation now, a time for healing and repair, not celebration or major life changes. After a moment I excused myself briefly, stepped into my office, and called the pilot.

"Hey, Bruce, listen, no banner today."

"What, Howard? Are you kidding?"

"I've got a situation on the ground I'm dealing with," I said. "I'll pay you for the banner. Just don't take that thing up."

"Okay. Fine. No problem. Good thing you called."

Instead of a picnic, we had a simple lunch in town. Debbie shared a bit about the conversation, and my blood rose as I realized that I had become the target of bizarre accusations. It was one thing to deal with reality—a guy with a machine gun or an RPG on his shoulder. You can handle those problems pretty straightforwardly. But fighting against phantoms gives you nothing to aim at. It's a helpless feeling trying to disprove false information.

"I can't believe it," I kept saying. "None of it is true."

I knew my words could only take the healing so far. Doubts are hard to uproot, especially when they're about you. I took Debbie's hand in mine and held it. *If things had gone my way, she'd be wearing a ring right now,* I thought. I sensed that we were about to move to a level of greater trust—or fall apart altogether. It was in God's hands.

Deep in my heart, I knew Debbie had the character and the skills to overcome this unfortunate situation. She has a way of asking gentle questions in response to harsh words. She is thoughtful and analytical, able to pick things apart so thoroughly that you understand them from every angle. She would make a fearsome lawyer.

But what about in an area so fraught with personal pain? Would fears from the past rise up and drive a wedge between us? I couldn't know.

As we drove home in separate cars, I thought of the many dangerous situations I'd lived through with other warriors. You don't really know someone until you go through hard times together. My relationship with Dan Busch in Mogadishu had proven that. Some guys look great before the bullets start flying. Then they get this faraway look in their eyes or freeze up. Others, like Dan, rise to an even higher level of effectiveness and loyalty. In combat, everyone's character goes on full display.

Now a grenade had landed in our bunker. What would Debbie do?

Over the next few days, a distance came between us that hadn't been there before. Normally Debbie was talkative and gregarious. Now she was quieter and engrossed in her own thoughts. She also wanted to spend more time apart than usual. I had seen her every day for ten months. Now two days went by without us seeing each other   a seismic change for people who had grown so close.

"I need some time to sort things out," she told me. The words were like death to me.

I finally found someone I want to spend my life with, I thought. *Am I going to lose it over this bunch of lies?*

I found myself praying frequently and fervently. *God, help us through this. Help me say the right words. Help Debbie see the truth. Please.*

I had to leave it in his hands. I could reassure her and rebut false ideas as much as I wanted, but Debbie would have to choose to trust me again. She missed work on Monday, something I had never seen her do. She said something about staying home and sorting things out.

A week after the incident I was cooking one evening, and Debbie was keeping me company in the kitchen. I was just glad to have her around, even if she was more guarded. We chitchatted about work, but I could tell she was thinking of other things. Finally she came to her purpose.

"Howard, I know that what Katherine said was not true," she said, "but I'm having a hard time stopping my mind from going round and round with it. I need to hear it from your mouth. That will help me process it."

"What do you need to hear?" I asked, stirring the spaghetti sauce on the stovetop. I wasn't looking forward to the topic, but I would do anything to help Debbie get free and get us back on track.

"Loyalty is a big deal to me," she said.

I'm right there with you, I thought.

Over the next few minutes she laid out the questions that had been raised in her mind: Had I been seeing other women? Was I calling to talk with Katherine every morning? Had I ever been unfaithful to Debbie?

No. No. No.

Hearing the accusations come out of her mouth wounded me. How could Debbie give them any room? What kept her from sweeping them all aside? Didn't she know me any better? I knew her marriage hadn't been a bed of roses, so I tried to keep that in mind. But it was painful to hear the baseless charges coming from someone I loved so deeply.

"My biggest concern," she said, "is that you might want to get back together with Katherine and patch up your former family. Just tell me, do you want to be part of that family again? Because if you do, I won't stand in your way."

I couldn't believe what I was hearing. How many times could I say no? What would convince her?

"Where do you see us going, Howard?" she added, not knowing I had tried to propose to her the week before, or that the ring had been sitting in my drawer ever since. Anger rose up in me, and I tried to keep it in check. As the sauce boiled, I lowered the heat, stepped away from the stove, and took her hands in mine.

"Debbie," I said, speaking as evenly as I could, "I am with you for the long haul. I don't want anyone else on the planet but you. I don't know how to be any more clear about it with my words or my actions. I'm sorry this happened—you don't know how sorry I am—but my feelings toward you have not changed. I love you more deeply than I have loved another person before, and all my loyalty is to you—to us. I won't betray that."

She listened silently. I could see her mind working, and for the first time since the incident, she seemed to find a place of rest. She sighed as if releasing a heavy burden.

"Thank you," she said, and I knew she was saying, "Thank you for letting me ask questions that should never have come up between us. Thank you for being patient while I worked through these accusations. Thank you for being strong when my mind was under attack."

She stood up and put her arms around my chest. A hug never felt so good. At that moment, I knew what kind of person Debbie was. We had been through battle together, and we would emerge stronger than before.

*

Having Debbie back was the greatest joy of my life. Once again we could hardly stand to be apart. Even having coffee in the morning or saying good night on the phone with my head on the pillow felt more special than ever.

On the downside, we didn't see Rachel for about a month because she chose to stay with her mother. Maybe she was embarrassed by what had happened, or was sorting out what she might have heard. In the years ahead, Rachel and I would have misunderstandings leading to a long and painful estrangement that would only be healed when we both humbled ourselves and asked for forgiveness. But for now she did come back and join our household after that month away.

I could not wait any longer and had planned another surprise proposal, this time with no banners or big celebrations, nothing out of the ordinary. Just simple—Debbie, me, and the kids in our normal environment.

The kitchen was always the heart of our home. We played music there and danced with the kids and with each other. I often cooked two or three meals a day on weekends for the whole family so Debbie was used to seeing me busy with pans and skillets. On a Saturday in December, right under her nose, I cooked something special. Debbie had no idea what was coming. While she was out of the room for a moment, I lit candles and assembled the kids, forming them into a semicircle. Debbie walked back in and saw us smiling and waiting for her. I held up a ring box. The moment had arrived.

"Before we sit down and eat, I have something to say," I said. The kids beamed and giggled. Debbie stood apart, emotion rising in her face.

"Debbie, I love you with all my heart. I want you to be my wife. If and when we get married, I want us all to be one big family. Not your kid and my kids, but our kids."

I had gotten the kids together in the preceding days to talk to them about what our family would look like if Debbie and I married. I wanted to answer all their questions and deal with their concerns right up front. I had told Eryn, "You'll always have your dad. I would be your stepdad." I had told Rachel, Blake, and Heather that they didn't need to call Debbie mom if they didn't want to. After our conversations each of the kids had been enthusiastic about combining our families into one.

I got down on my knee and handed the ring to Rachel, who was right next to me.

"Debbie, I'm handing this ring to each of the children because I want you to be my wife and their mother," I said. "We will make this commitment as a family."

Rachel looked at the ring and started crying. She nodded happily and passed it to Eryn. Eryn took the ring in her fingers, her face breaking into a smile, and said, "Yes!" Heather couldn't be with us that weekend so it went next to Blake who gave his wholehearted affirmation. With a sense of honor, he handed it to Debbie.

Debbie received it like something rare and precious, which our love was. She held the beautiful ring in her hands, tears rolling down her cheeks. It was perfectly silent; a sort of divine calm had descended over all of us.

"Debbie," I asked, "will you be my wife and these kids' mother?"

She looked at each of the kids for a long moment, and if eyes could convey complete love, hers did. Then she looked at me and cut my suspense short.

"Yes! Of course I will!" she said.

With that it was like someone popped the cork out of a champagne bottle. We all erupted and started jumping around the kitchen. Something big had happened, and we all knew it. Each of us had survived our past to come to this moment. A larger purpose was unfolding right before our eyes.

It was obvious that my first plans—an airplane banner, a big public scene—would not have suited Debbie's personality well. She doesn't like over-the-top events, especially when they focus on her. I couldn't even picture what she would have done watching a plane fly by with a big "Will you marry me, Debbie?" banner flailing out behind it. She probably would have been horrified.

None of us will ever forget passing the engagement ring around and becoming a family. Life would still throw challenges at us—but we were ready to face them together.

NINE

A NEW DIRECTION

We planned a simple wedding. Blakc and I bought suits. Debbie took Eryn, Rachel, and Heather to a specialty dress shop in the country and got them all dolled up in the prettiest dresses you've ever seen, Heather in pink, Rachel in mint green, and Eryn in periwinkle blue with sparkles on them. (At the time, Heather had decided to stay plugged-in with us as her family; her biological dad was nowhere to be found.) On the big day we had a bunch of photos taken at a professional studio and then headed to a one-stop wedding shop in Kingsland.

There was just one problem: when we got there, the woman responsible for doing the blood work was gone. She just plain forgot about our appointment to get married. Not only that, but she wasn't answering her phone. "She just went over to Walmart. I'm calling her," the lady who worked there kept saying, but she had no success reaching her. We couldn't get legally married without blood work, so we stood around waiting for hours for this woman to return. After a while Debbie was almost in tears and I was thinking, *My wedding night hinges on some delinquent county employee who flaked off work to go shopping at Walmart? How uncool is this?*

Finally I had to take action or the whole night was going to go down the tubes. I turned to Pastor Ron, who had counseled us and was marrying us, and said, "Brother Ron, do you think it would be a sin to have the ceremony and get the blood work done later? They say we can get blood drawn elsewhere. Do you think God would still recognize this marriage even if the county doesn't?"

Ron scarcely missed a beat: "You know, Howard, God's law has been around a lot longer than the state of Georgia. I think it'll be fine."

So we went into the chapel and Ron performed the ceremony. Ron had been a friend throughout our engagement. At one point a few weeks before, I had panicked and told him, "I'm scared to death. I've already proven I'm the worst husband ever. How can I be sure I will make things work with Debbie? I failed so badly in the past. What do I do?"

Ron replied, "You'll do fine," and then gave me great words of wisdom on how to be a good husband. The one that stuck with me most: "You don't have to win all the time. It's not like combat. It's okay to compromise and give in when that seems the right thing to do. She can be right too."

So I calmed down and Debbie and I said our *I do*s, kissed the kids good-bye, and drove straight to a nearby hospital to get our blood drawn. We waltzed in wearing our wedding clothes and left with our sleeves pulled up and little bandages on the insides of our elbows. We must have looked a sight strutting into the Ritz-Carlton on Amelia Island. We certainly felt like royalty, and everyone there seemed to know our names. All the way to the restaurant we heard, "Congratulations, Mr. and Mrs. Wasdin. Have a good evening." In our room, chilled champagne and strawberries dipped in white and dark chocolate were arrayed on the table. From that day on we have celebrated every special moment with champagne, strawberries, and chocolate.

Ron told us that day, "When I marry people, I use good glue." I believed him. I never felt so sure that I'd made the right choice in my life.

DEBBIE

We came home from our honeymoon and lived on the other side of town in a little house I had bought four months earlier. It was a cute three-bedroom place. We converted the garage into Blake's room. Eryn's bedroom was next to mine and Howard's. We were a happy little family. Then one day Eryn, who was eleven, came to me and said, "Momma, you know I can hear everything from your room through those walls—everything." I blushed but only half believed her.

Then one day I lay down on her bed with a headache. Howard and Blake were in our bedroom watching a boxing match and wouldn't you know it, I heard every noise, every word, every creak of the bed frame coming through that wall. Eryn was right! The wall even seemed to amplify the sound like a giant speaker. The poor girl went from having parents who didn't sleep in the same bed to having parents sleeping right next door—and often not sleeping at all. We started looking for another house right away.

To me, one of the ironies of my life remained that less than twenty-four hours after signing my divorce papers, I found the man of my dreams. Not just my regular, practical dreams, but my wildest dreams. I went from "I don't think I'll ever get married again" at the beginning of our first date to "I think I would marry him right now" at the end of the night. It felt like God was blessing me for sticking it out in my first marriage and trying to do the right thing. To find love so fast seemed like God's way of saying, "I'm going to bless you immediately. You don't have to wait this time."

Friends used to tell me when I invited them out, "No, I want to spend the day with my husband." I used to think, *Really? You were with him all night. Don't you ever want to get away?* Now I say the same thing: "No thanks. I'd rather stay home with Howard and the kids."

I loved Howard not because he was some "tactical god." That kind of thing didn't go very far with me. It was because the man underneath all the pride and bluster was a terrific guy, a survivor, someone who had endured a rough childhood and a demanding career and unhealthy first and second marriages. He had come out the other side somehow, battle-scarred and rough, but with so much to give and so much love. I found him irresistible.

HOWARD

Marrying Debbie was the best decision I've ever made by a long shot. But I was still floundering professionally. The events of September 11 had left me high and dry, stuck in a used-car-salesman job that I didn't want and that demanded long hours. I worked Monday through Saturday from 8:00 a.m. to 6:00 p.m. and ate lunch at the dealership so I wouldn't miss a sale. I worked strictly on commission, so the pay was up and down. Still, God helped me sell twenty to thirty cars a month. I think it's because I put customers' pocketbooks first. I wasn't a smooth-talking salesman. I was just real. I'd tell prospective buyers, "I'm a single dad too. I know where you're coming from."

Saturdays and Mondays were our big days. We'd air up the

balloons, put them on the windshield wipers, and stand around waiting for people to come on the lot. On Saturday I often had customers
from that week coming to pick up their cars. We had a detail shop out
back where two guys worked. One was so injured in his knees that he
could barely walk. Though they were paid by the dealership—probably
not more than minimum wage—I slid them ten bucks whenever I
picked up a car to deliver to a customer. I know what it's like not to
have enough.

There was one aspect to selling cars that I didn't like at all. In
the industry they talked about "taking the customer's head off." That
meant making a lot of money on somebody. Some people were easier
to negotiate with than others. Interestingly, the people with the most
money knew how to negotiate the best, and they would nickel-and-
dime you down to the last penny. The ones who didn't negotiate well,
and who got taken advantage of more often, were the poor single
mothers who got stuck with a larger payment than they should have,
or who got a lot less for their trade-in than it deserved.

It affected me if I took unfair advantage of someone in a deal. I
couldn't sleep well knowing that someone was struggling until payday
like I did because of something I did to them. The right thing for me
was to give them a fair deal and offer what their vehicle was worth for
trade-in. I would tell my customers directly, "This is how much you're
giving me for this vehicle. This is what your vehicle is worth. This is
the price I can give you."

I butted heads frequently with my sales manager before I became
the sales manager myself. When I brought him an offer, he would say,
"No. That's a really nice piece. I want to keep it on the lot. Someone
else will come buy that for more."

I'd try to persuade him, "We're not going to make a lot on this deal, but the trade-in is real nice." He might say no on Wednesday and yes on Friday because not enough vehicles had sold. I had the pleasure of calling people back and saying, "Come on in. We're accepting your offer." At that point they knew they had a good deal. We were taught never to let someone walk off the lot. If you let them off the lot and called them later, that person got a deal.

My day was over when the last customers were gone from my desk. I was there often until 8:00 p.m., and back in the next morning at 7:30 in a shirt and tie.

Though I didn't drive hard bargains, I did well enough to get my own office, and then they made me a sales manager at a dealership in another town. That made it harder because it meant leaving at daybreak and coming home at dark, a routine that was quickly wearing me out. I knew it couldn't last.

As happy as I was to have any kind of job, selling cars did nothing for my pride. It was just a way of paying the bills, and it barely did that. All my training and expertise were being wasted day after day. Though my body was hobbled, my ambitions were not. The desire to do more burned within me.

It also weighed on me that I was a drain on Debbie's finances. She was now clearly the primary breadwinner in our marriage, and as a man, that didn't sit well with me. I didn't begrudge the money she made; I just thought that as a man, the load should fall mainly on me. My own finances were not in the best shape when we met. I was generous perhaps to a fault with people around me. I would pay for dinner or golf or movies when I went out with people and would buy my kids nice things even if it meant I starved for a week until my next paycheck. I liked to make everyone as comfortable as I could and didn't much care what that meant for me.

That shocked Debbie. She grew up with good parents who taught her how to handle money, to protect it and set it aside—even to create this mysterious thing called a "budget." Not me. When I had money, I gave it away or bought stuff. When I didn't have it, I waited for it to come in. On the positive side, I showed a lot of love to people with my money. On the negative, it meant I had virtually nothing left. I was always waiting for car sales to close so I could gather my commission. One week I might get a twenty-five dollar paycheck, the next week two thousand dollars. But I didn't have a long-term vision.

That's why the temptation to return to tactical paramilitary work was strong. Before meeting Debbie, I had gotten a call from Mike, the CIA guy who ran my Pasha safe house in Somalia.

"I've got a job for you in Brazil—Rio de Janeiro," he had said. "Diplomatic security detail. Pays really well."

The Brazil job offered two tantalizing solutions in one: First, it would solve my money problems, paying a couple hundred thousand dollars for a year of work. That would make me feel like a successful father and husband. It would also help me stay in the tactical world, which I desperately wanted to do. The choice seemed obvious: I could go to Brazil, do what I did best, and get paid well for it, or I could stay in Georgia, do something I wasn't as good at, and get paid a lot less while hating my job.

"Mike, that sounds great," I said. "Let me wind things down here and we'll start talking details."

"Is that a yes?" he said.

"It's a don't-offer-it-to-anyone-else-yet," I said. He laughed.

"All right," he said. "I've got a little time. Just don't think about it too long."

At that point other motivations were mixed in as well. As happy as I was, I probably still had a mild death wish. I loved Debbie from the start but deep inside there was a part of me that would have been happy to go to the frontlines, make a lot of money, get killed in the process, and have the people I cared about taken care of. That's how little I thought of myself and what I had to offer the world. If I died, the big insurance would come through. I would go out in a blaze of glory, join my buddies on the other side, and leave my family a big inheritance. Where was the downside?

Still, something about going to Brazil made me uneasy. I don't like the word *mercenary*, but in my line of work, once you're not working for Uncle Sam, that's what you are. You can try to convince yourself it's honorable work, but the bottom line is, it's usually about the money. As much as I soothed my conscience by saying it was the only thing I was good at, I wrestled with the thought of doing harm or taking someone's life on this private mission. Would it really be for God and country? Lying in bed at night, I had a hard time answering that one.

Private security is also cold and lonely work. The military, for all its foibles, offers a team environment where everyone has your back. You fight for an ultimate purpose: the defense of your country and the protection of your families and homeland. There's a sense of commitment, camaraderie, and *esprit de corps*. There is none of that in contract situations. You aren't defending the United States, just the guy who hired you. You often have no idea who the other guys on the Team are until you start working together. There is no history, no loyalty, no group training, and sometimes you wonder about the other guys' qualifications. Uncertainty means greater risk and lower satisfaction. In Brazil there would be no feeling of ultimate purpose, just a hollow professional success and a paycheck.

Looking past all that, I was determined to prove I was still a breadwinner and a tactical expert who hadn't lost his magic touch. I told Debbie and Blake early on that Brazil was in my plans, and just six months after we met, I asked Debbie if Blake could live with her and finish high school while I did this op. For a guy like me, who trusted hardly anyone, that was remarkable and showed how much Debbie was part of my life already.

Debbie was more than willing to have Blake live with her, but in her gentle way she pushed back against the whole idea of taking the op. Blake would suffer with me running all over the world being the guy in black, she said. I would be missing his senior year and his graduation. In fact, I might never really come back. Not that I would die in Brazil, though that was always possible. Rather, she foresaw that after Brazil I would take the next contract and the next and spend my life on various details, separated from her and the kids.

How would our relationship grow when we were not together? E-mails and phone calls wouldn't cut it. Who knew if we would be the same people when I got back? And what if something happened to me out there? Blake wouldn't have a dad and would essentially have lost both parents.

Those arguments were like a dagger in my heart, and Debbie knew how to patiently and quietly twist that blade. I was torn between the financial and professional fulfillment I now lacked and the family life I'd finally found. Debbie was right in many ways. Blake needed me. He was finally experiencing a stable home life. Eryn and I had just bonded. She was learning to love me like a father. I, too, had more peace and stability than I had ever dreamed of having.

But . . . , I kept thinking. *But . . . I have to go! It's who I am. This is what Howard Wasdin does.*

As if she needed a stronger argument, Debbie then brought up the money. The two hundred fifty thousand dollars I stood to make in Brazil filled my eyes. I thought it would get me pretty close to retirement. As an accountant, Debbie knew better. "You can't retire on that," she said. "First of all, you won't get the entire amount. There are taxes and Medicare and Social Security. It's not tax-free like they imply. Second, with inflation, the value of that two hundred fifty thousand dollars is going down every day. Pretty soon it won't buy nearly as much as it does now."

I, of course, didn't have any good responses to these things except to keep venting my frustrations. I also saw that Debbie was a different kind of partner. She never fought me head-on. If she had put her foot down and tried to say no, I would have been much more likely to get stubborn and insist on taking the job. But when she made those arguments and then put it back in my hands, saying she would go along with whatever I chose, I felt the weight of that responsibility. My family and my future were in my hands. Everyone was watching to see if I would be a selfish dummy. What would I do?

God sent a client across Debbie's path at just the right time to give us both a vision of the future I was considering. A man came to her office needing CPA services.

"I just got back from Iraq," he said.

"Oh," said Debbie, "are you in the service?"

"No," he said. "I went with a private contractor."

Debbie's antennae went up.

"You did?" she said.

"Yes, and it ruined my life," he said. "That's why I'm here. I had seven kids and a wife. I heard about these jobs driving trucks in Iraq where they pay you tens of thousands of dollars a month, and I thought that would be a way to make money we needed for our family. For the first two months it was great. I was sending home twenty, thirty thousand dollars. Then my truck ran over an IED. The explosion broke a bunch of my ribs, and I came home on a stretcher only to find that my wife had run off with another man and spent all the money I had sent her."

Debbie's jaw was on the floor, thinking of me going overseas in the same way.

The guy continued, "I didn't realize it, but when a spouse leaves, sometimes the only way the human psyche can deal with the possibility of them dying is to put up a wall and kill your own love toward that person," he said. "My wife went into protection mode with herself and the kids. I ended up injured, broke, and alone. Taking that job destroyed everything."

Debbie came home ruffled, to say the least. She told me the story and concluded, "I'd rather live in a teeny tiny house called Wasdin Manor and have you safe than have ten million dollars and be without you."

After that real-life story, I would have looked like a complete fool going to Brazil or anywhere else, so I did something I don't remember doing before: I yielded to someone else's wisdom on a career decision. As Pastor Ron would tell me later, relationships weren't combat and I didn't always have to be right. On this one I took a deep breath and gave in. Debbie probably didn't realize it was a major milestone for me to defer to her opinion and trust that she had my best interests in mind. We weren't even married yet.

Saying no to Brazil didn't solve my frustration, though. I tried to make the best of life in rural Georgia. For a series of reasons that had nothing to do with my job performance or me, I left the car dealership. That was a big shock to our finances. We were married at this point, but it wasn't looking good for us financially until my cousins Greg and Sonny helped me get hired at a chemical plant where Sonny worked.

I started on April 1, but the hard work was no joke. This plant produced specialized chemicals for foods and perfumes. It took turpentine, a natural substance in pine trees, and processed it into flavoring for chewing gums, hard liquors, and things like that. As a result, the plant smelled good all the time, like spearmint.

The job was a full-day workout. As the low man on the totem pole, I had to do all the grunt work nobody else wanted to do. It felt like being the new guy on the SEAL Teams, fetching beer and coffee for the other guys until a newer guy arrived. Work was scarce in the Southeast, and the plant didn't hire a lot of people. It was pretty good money for that area, and I worked a lot fewer hours than at the car dealership—five days a week, nine to five, rather than six days a week and never at home.

My duties included unloading fifty-five-gallon drums of the acidic and caustic chemicals that were used to refine the flavoring. With brute strength and my newly acquired forklift driving skills, I brought those drums into the warehouse and put them in their proper places. But my most important job was loading our refined essences onto tanker trucks after they were processed. Those liquid essences were caustic, meaning they could eat the skin off your body, so I had to wear a hazmat suit even in sweltering 105-degree weather. I started bringing my old CamelBak to work just to stay hydrated.

One tanker truckload of these refined chemicals cost four hundred thousand dollars. It took a lot of man-hours and processing to produce this stuff, and the essences were held to very stringent standards because they were consumables. By the time it left our plant, often to ship overseas, it was a very precise mixture. My job was to hook up a huge hose from our plant's tank to an empty tanker truck and run the liquid in at high pressures. It was a critical job because if anything went wrong, or if it failed quality assurance on the other end, the first person they would look to blame was my position.

I did everything methodically: chocked the truck, looked inside the tank to make sure it was completely empty, tested the tank I was loading from, hooked up the hose, watched the metering gauge on the tank and took the pressure down to certain level, pumped the essence in without running it over, sealed up the truck just right, took a last sample, and then put unique, stamped-aluminum seals on the top of the tank and over the valve at the bottom. If anyone tampered with those seals, we didn't get paid and heads rolled.

The big benefit of the job was that I got in the best shape I'd been in since the Teams. I ate whatever I wanted and sweated it all off. My six-pack emerged again and my arms got ripped. I was once again a hunk of burning love, which wasn't a bad deal for Debbie either.

Then they promoted me to a desk job inside. I became an administrative assistant, which is a fancy title for secretary, to the woman who ran the company. Nobody said it to my face, but through the grapevine I heard that my coworkers got big laughs out of that: "The tough SEAL Teams guy is now a personal secretary!"

My job was to keep track of shipments coming in, and if I'd done that alone, maybe it would have been fine. But I learned then that some guys just don't like to work, and they stick other guys with all the extra tasks. The young guys at the plant had developed a reputation for being difficult, and instead of kicking them in the rear and telling them to shape up, people basically stopped going to them for help. Instead, they came to guys like me, family guys who needed the job, and more or less demanded that we help out with extra duties. We had the incentive of supporting our families and also had a much better work ethic.

When they loaded essences into a truck, they often called me and I had to go suit up. I didn't mind too much because I like to work and the main loader who had trained me was an old Vietnam vet with whom I got along famously. When I looked out and saw him busting his hump at his age, I voluntarily threw on the hazmat suit and went out to help him.

Still, after eighteen months I felt my soul shriveling up. I called Debbie one day at her office and said, "I just can't do this. I hate this job. I feel like the president of Underachievers Anonymous. I was made for more than this. I'm not doing anything I'm good at. I'm a secretary. By the time I drive home and back, I'm not bringing much in anyway. I've got to do something else, something that fits me better."

"Okay," she said. "I'm listening."

"I'm going to call and see if the position in Brazil is still open," I said.

Silence. Debbie knew I brought up Brazil whenever I got aggravated at work. I would get e-mails from former colleagues dangling these high-dollar jobs before me. Most of them were in unstable parts of the world, the kind of places most sane people avoided.

"Gosh, Howard," she said, "I just don't want you to do that. I don't think you'll be safe."

"We can talk about it later," I said, "but I can't keep doing this. It's killing me quicker than a bullet in a foreign country."

Sometimes old habits and thought patterns float to the surface, maybe so God can skim them off and purify you a little more. The

Bible does say, "Fire tests the purity of silver and gold, but the LORD tests the heart" (Prov. 17:3 NLT). One of my impurities was this idea that in some mysterious way I was better than anyone else in a certain area. Anyone who's been part of an elite group like the SEALs naturally develops an elitist mentality: "I'm special. I'm different. Other people don't get who I am and what I can do."

That pride makes you confident in battle, which is good, but can drive you to make bad decisions in civilian life, which is a whole separate arena. In this case, with the years ticking away, I was reaching for a lifestyle that had been slipping away from me for a long time. Residues of pride and elitism and selfishness clouded my thoughts, along with my dissatisfaction at work.

I called Mike. The Brazil gig wasn't available anymore, but Iraq was suddenly full of opportunities. In 2004, Iraq was like the Wild West. Private security companies were hiring anyone—mall cops, campus security, local sheriff deputies—with any security experience to help train Iraqi police as the US government tried to prop up Iraq's government and infrastructure. Uncle Sam's money was sloshing everywhere. The job they were offering me paid four hundred thousand dollars a year. For a highly qualified guy like me, it was like winning the lottery—if I made it back in one piece to spend it.

Debbie was frustrated that I saw only one path to the future.

"It seems like you're trying to climb back into that world where you have some stature and some history, but the odds are worse than they've ever been," she said. "This is wartime now, not peacetime."

"That's right," I said. "That's what I am—a warrior. That's my training, my line of work. It's what I'm good at."

"Really?" she said. "That's all you are, some gun-slinging tactical guy taking down the bad guys? Gee, I thought you were my husband too. Or does that just get thrown aside? How could we spend that much time apart? We haven't gone hardly a day without seeing each other since the day after we met. I couldn't take you being gone for a year on a different continent and not knowing if you were alive or dead."

"It would only be for a year, and the money is great," I said.

"A year!" she said. "And then what—you'd come home and retire peacefully? If you came home at all?"

The discussion was more heated and more serious than it had ever been because now we were married. It's one thing when it's your girlfriend. When it's your wife, and you're both deeply in love and have committed the rest of your lives to each other, there's more on the line.

Debbie's resistance was palpable, and our discussion seemed to go in circles until finally she threw up her hands and said, "Can't you get this 'Howard Wasdin, tactical genius' stuff out of your head? Are you that one-dimensional? Haven't you ever considered doing anything else? You don't have to be stuck in this ex-SEAL thing for the rest of your life. You can do whatever you want. Think about it, Howard— what do you really want to do? If you could go back to school and get an education, what would you be interested in?"

I didn't expect the words that came out of my mouth: "I always wanted to be a chiropractor."

Where did that come from? I thought.

It was true that going to a chiropractor had restored my quality of life starting when I had lived in Florida. Still, I couldn't believe what I'd just said to Debbie. I quickly added, "But I'm too old to go to school."

"No, you're not," she said.

"Yes, I am."

"You know, Howard, you can start now and in five years be finished, or you can not start now and in five years look back and say,
'If I'd started then, I'd be finished now.' Then you'd live with regret."

Something happened in that moment that had never really happened before: I saw another path for myself. I didn't have to be the
tactical guy until the day I died. I didn't have to go into the coffin as
Howard Wasdin, ex Navy SEAL. I could choose something else. I
had the freedom to redefine my career and get out of the straitjacket of
my reputation. All this blaze-of-glory stuff was my way of not wanting
to consider change. Debbie's way of saying it made it safe to consider:
What else did I want to do? What else could I do? Could I really switch
careers at this age? Was I ready to start over at forty-three years old?

When the right answer comes in the middle of an argument, it
can defuse the whole thing and lighten the atmosphere. My mind
began to go over the possibility of what I had blurted out: being a chiropractor. At the very least it was a real alternative to risking my life
in Iraq doing guts-for-dollars work. I had some college credits from
Cumberland College in Kentucky, where I attended right after high
school, and then more credits from navy college courses.

Why not? I thought. *It's at least worth looking into.*

Debbie helped me get my transcripts together, and I was pleas-
antly reminded that I had gotten straight As, even in difficult classes.
Given that many were taken in the navy, they weren't classes you
would normally see on a transcript. But they were accredited and a
normal part of my college history.

We looked at a place called Life University in Atlanta, where one
of Debbie's friends who was a chiropractor had graduated. I called
Life and talked to someone in records about transferring my credits.
She was upbeat.

"This won't be a problem," she said after I had faxed her my records. "All this should transfer."

I was excited, and Debbie and I planned a drive up to visit the campus in person. The first place we stopped was the registrar's office, and there at the front desk was a young girl who eyed my transcripts and me somewhat suspiciously. She wasn't the one I had talked with on the phone, and she didn't seem to like the fact that I was ex-military. I was surprised at the chilly reception she gave us. I admit, too, that I wasn't your average undergraduate. How often does a guy in his forties come in saying he's a former Navy SEAL with a bunch of credits from navy campus courses and wants to enroll to become a chiropractor?

Still, she could have had more grace or people skills. After looking at my records, she launched into a litany of rejection.

"This won't transfer, this won't transfer, this won't transfer," she said, pointing to courses on my transcripts. "That won't work because you don't have a lab. I'm sorry but we really can't use any of this."

From the moment she started saying no, I had been shrinking in my seat, and now I was just angry.

"Are you kidding me? None of this works?" I said. "These are legitimate navy campus classes."

"Yes, but they don't meet our requirements," she said.

Debbie watched as my temperature rose.

"That's not what the lady told me on the phone," I said.

"I'm sorry," she said. "I don't know what they told you. I'm just telling you what I see here."

I swelled with frustration and in typical fashion decided this girl wasn't worth talking to anymore. I got up to walk out the door, but before I could turn, I felt a touch on my hand. It was Debbie.

"Sweetie," she said quietly, "let's just take a minute and talk this through before we leave."

The touch was like a grounding wire that drained the negative energy out of me. Maybe I wasn't seeing the entire picture. Maybe there was a way forward that I was overlooking in my anger. I sat back down.

"Honey, tell us, what is your role here?" Debbie asked. She had realized this girl had no authority and was just there to help people pick the right classes based on what they had taken before. She was no more than twenty-two and probably was a work-study student with little training.

"I'm a student here at Life and an assistant in the registrar's office," the girl said.

"So do you make the final decisions on what classes qualify to be transferred?" Debbie said sweetly.

The girl blushed.

"No, the registrar does that," she said.

"Do you mind if we talk to the registrar before we go?" Debbie asked.

"One moment," the girl said and walked to an office in the back. Moments later the registrar walked out, a guy who seemed relaxed and more reasonable than his front-desk help. He smiled, shook our hands, and invited us to his office. I put the transcripts on his desk, but he barely looked at them. In a kind and straightforward way he explained the credentialing process and how records are reviewed by the state.

"I'll have to look into those classes to see if they can be used here," he said. "But for now, would you folks like to get a cup of coffee and see the campus?"

Debbie and I were surprised but said yes, and minutes later were in the cantina talking informally with him over coffee. He asked about my background and seemed to be assessing my intelligence and potential as a student. Then we walked around campus. He appeared to enjoy hearing about my experience, both in the military and in the workforce. When we returned to his office, he said, "Thanks for your service, Howard, and thanks for coming down. I don't think these transcripts will be a problem. We'll work with you to make it happen."

He later became one of my favorite instructors.

In the car heading back to Jesup, Debbie and I were overjoyed at the future that was unfolding before us. Deep inside I mulled over what had happened in the young girl's office: If I had gone there alone, I would have stormed out and not even given myself a chance. Nobody else would have known about me or stepped in to help, and I would have returned home and continued to bounce around meaningless jobs.

Debbie had a way of helping me see the better way in any given situation. She knew that my frustration would kick in suddenly and I wouldn't give things a chance to work themselves out. She taught me to quit fighting things so fast and instead to look for doors that might open unexpectedly, then trust God that they would lead somewhere good. She taught me the skill of saying, "Let's look at this from another angle." Some people bring out the best in you. Thank God I found one.

Money was now the issue. If I went back to school, how would we pay for it on one income? Blake was in college; I would be living in Atlanta and not working while I attended school. As the more money-minded person, this part scared Debbie more than it did me. We really didn't know how to make it work but I was always optimistic, even when I had no reason to be.

Debbie, for her part, was methodical and relentless in coming up with solutions. One night she turned to me and said, "You're a veteran of a foreign war. Don't they have scholarships for that? Surely someone out there would want to help you get started on a new career." Before I knew it, she had drafted a letter from me to every Veterans of Foreign Wars post in Georgia and northern Florida. It read, "Hello, my name is Howard Wasdin. I am a recipient of the Purple Heart and Silver Star and am starting on a new career in the medical field. Do you offer scholarships for college students who are not graduating seniors?"

One VFW sent us $250, but more importantly several of them called the Veterans Administration without our knowledge and said, "You ought to take care of this guy." Debbie was shocked later when she realized I had never been to the VA for any benefits. When they discharged me medically, they gave me a low rating with my leg, even though I was using canes at that point and was in pain every day. For my part, when I walked away from the military, I walked away for good. I didn't want anything more to do with them. I felt burned, as if they had given me a couple of medals and then kicked me to the curb: "Here you go. Thanks for playing." Once you're not an asset in the military, you're a liability. I didn't need any more reminders of that.

One day the VA called our house and asked to meet with me. Debbie was nervous.

"Are we in trouble?" she asked. "Maybe sending out all those letters looked fraudulent, like a money-raising scam."

But the VA wasn't angry. I took the day off from work at the chemical plant and met with a very friendly VA representative. He had me fill out paperwork about myself and my disability. Then he stunned me with his words. "The VA has a program called vocational rehabilitation, which will pay for forty-eight months of college if you meet the criteria," he said almost casually.

"Four years of college?" I said.

"Yes," he said. "If you meet the criteria."

"Well, do I?" I asked.

"It looks like you do, but you have to submit the paperwork within a certain number of years of leaving the military. You've been out for a while," he said. "That may be a problem."

We looked into it and realized that if I had waited six more months, I no longer would have qualified. I was making it in just under the wire. I moved ahead and enrolled at Life University while the disability assessment dragged out for ten months. Once the vocational rehabilitation kicked in, it started paying for my tuition, books, supplies, and housing. It made our life so much easier. Debbie became a walking advertisement for "voc rehab" to other people in the military. Many just don't know it's there for them, so Debbie played career counselor to anyone who left the military and was looking for their next step.

I rented a place in midtown Atlanta. The area had been rejuvenated and had sushi and coffee shops nearby. The bottom level of this building was like a basement with half windows and was available for four hundred dollars a month. We could just afford that. We called it the Dungeon. It smelled like mildew and wrecked Debbie's sinuses every time she visited. To make it worse, the previous tenant had smoked a lot, but it came totally furnished and was within our budget.

It was owned by a spry, eccentric eighty-four-year-old Greek man named Pete. Pete had never married and lived with his dog. His nieces and nephews came around now and then to check on him. Pete introduced us to Greek food and culture, which was wonderful. He was sharp as can be and a hoot to be around. I'm convinced his advice helped Debbie's and my relationship, which surprised me because it came from a guy who'd never been married.

Pete's toenails were overgrown, and he didn't take good care of himself, so I promised him I'd help him. When I make those promises, I often go overboard. I took him to get a pedicure and made him shower every day. Pete was in the habit of wearing the same shirt all the time, so I helped him do his laundry. We got along great, but after a time his nieces and nephews became suspicious of me and all the time I was investing in their uncle. As Pete told me, "Greek people love drama. To us, argument is entertainment." So I had to quietly bow out of Pete's life and give his family more ownership of his situation, which was fine, as long as someone was doing it.

On the first day of classes I got up really early, before the sun, and ran through Atlanta in the dark. The whole run I prayed to God, *Please let me be smart enough to pass the classes. Make me smart enough to make it through.* It was a sincere prayer. I always thought I was somewhat smart, but it had been two decades since I'd been in a classroom. I was more afraid of finding out I was dumb than I was of being in any gunfight. I knew my way around a gunfight. Clearing a room of bad guys was a lot less intimidating than going back to school with an unknown quantity of brains.

My schedule was suddenly full of mandatory seminars, gross anatomy weekend labs, and study groups. I had permission to take extra classes, so I took Organic Chemistry 1 and 2 in the same quarter, which was horribly hard. I spent interminable hours in the Dungeon memorizing things like how the proton pump works on the membrane of the mitochondria to make ATP and understanding the Krebs cycle.

A lot of students split time between studying and enjoying the Irish pub right across from campus. In my old days, that pub would have been my living room, but now I told myself it was off-limits. What if I went in there and liked it and wanted to go there every day after school? I was a middle-aged man getting a hard degree. I didn't have any brain cells to spare. In previous days I would have led the charge, but not now. It was like a stumbling block, a temptation placed right at the gateway to campus. I went there exactly zero times and haven't been inside to this day. I'm probably the only guy at Life U. who can say that I wasn't in Atlanta to party; I was there to redefine my life. I thought about Debbie back home making sacrifices financially and personally so I could pursue this future. There was no way I was screwing it up. I soon noticed that the students who went to that bar were the ones who didn't perform well. I would watch them go there and drink after school and hear their sob stories later about how they failed this or that assignment.

The drive from our house in Jesup to my apartment in Atlanta was four hours and thirteen minutes. I stayed in Atlanta all week, and if I didn't have study groups or labs I would come home or, more often, Debbie would drive up. She insisted that she had the easy job: get up, get dressed, go to work, come home. But I didn't buy it. She was running our life without me while I had my head in a textbook most of the time.

We talked about her moving to Atlanta but ended up concluding that I wouldn't have time for her anyway, she would be bored to death and probably get her feelings hurt because I was always studying. So we pressed on as best we could. Sunday nights were the worst because she had to go home. Sometimes she would stay until 3:00 or 4:00 a.m. and then drive back so we could at least share a bed for a few more hours.

We were also in financial distress until the vocational rehabilitation support began. Debbie maxed out her credit cards and worked extra hours so I could stay in school. For a while it felt like we were hanging on by our fingernails. Not only did we miss the daily contact and support we had grown accustomed to, but our bank accounts were always touching empty. We couldn't even afford to go to dinner unless Pete took us to some fabulous Greek place he knew about—and paid for it.

The summer after my first year, I moved back to Jesup to help Debbie move into a new office. The sense of dislocation and challenge almost overwhelmed us at that point, and though I was doing well in school, I wondered if it was worth it to keep going forward. Could we handle another three years of this? Our whole life was balanced precariously on Debbie's practice, and we hated being apart. It would have been the perfect time to step out and try something else instead. I certainly felt I didn't deserve to have someone support me like Debbie was doing.

When we surveyed the situation calmly, we came back to our original commitment: I would stay in school and we would do our best, always looking toward that day when I would graduate. Late that summer, amid many tears, I drove back to the Dungeon and found that everything I had left there was covered in mold. I had to throw it all away and move somewhere else. Welcome back to school, Howard.

We remained in financial hardship most of my years there. That also allowed us to experience the kindness of people like Pete, who would treat us to dinner, and my cousin Greg, who would invite us down to Orlando. The second time Greg brought us to Orange Lake, we left the kids eating burritos and pizza at his condo and went to a nice steakhouse. I remember opening the menu and saying, "Uh-oh. If Debbie and I pay for this, it'll break us." I'll never forget that Greg picked up the check without even a word. That was true love.

Debbie had a friend who took us on a cruise with his staff because Debbie was their accountant. I tried to enjoy that vacation, but I had taken a test the day before and was scared to death of what it had done to my grade in Organic Chemistry. I found a place on the boat that had Wi-Fi and found out that I had gotten a B. That felt like the happiest day of my life. I gave Debbie a high five when I saw her next and we celebrated.

Apart from the generosity of friends, we lived without extras. We bought family-sized pork chop packs and boiled the bones to make soup. I was an old guy trying to hard-shift to another career and still make it happen for my family. Without Debbie, it never would have happened.

Debbie noticed changes in me during those years. My ego went down and my satisfaction and contentment went up. My identity was changing from Howard Wasdin, Former Navy SEAL, to Howard Wasdin, Future Chiropractor. Even my wardrobe changed. When I met Debbie, I was still wearing tactical pants every day, carrying a knife everywhere, and dressing all in black. Now I dressed like other people. She was slowly changing my wardrobe as well, talking me into other colors. She would often laugh that on our blind date she thought I was so well put together when the truth was, black just matched black. That was a no-brainer. Besides, black was tactical and "tactical" still defined my self-image at the time.

When I was finishing up at Life University and working in the student clinic, I had to wear dress pants, a dress shirt, and a tie every day. Debbie would take time on her weekend visits to match a shirt with a pair of pants and wrap a tie around the two hangers. She did this with all my clothes, putting together a week's worth of outfits. She only missed a few weekends during tax season when she was unable to come up to Atlanta. I had gone through all my clothes, and when I picked them up from the dry cleaners, they were all unsorted.

I had no clue what went with what. Debbie had brightened my wardrobe with all sorts of colorful shirts, pants, and ties, which I found amazing, but I had no idea how to pair any of them.

I decided to start safe with a pair of my favorite pants. They were black with a small blue square design going through them. *I've got this,* I thought. *Where's that black tie with the blue diamond design? There it is. Now how about a white shirt with blue stripes? Black shoes, black socks, and a belt—I'm ready to go.*

When I got to the clinic door, I walked past a female student who looked at me and giggled.

"That's funny," she said. "Where's your real outfit?"

What is she talking about?

I walked to the patient sign-in front desk and was quickly approached by two female students from my study group.

"Debbie didn't come up this weekend, did she?" one of them asked.

"No, I went to Jesup," I said. "How did you know?"

They looked me up and down and pointed at my ensemble.

"Because she never would have put all those things together," they said, then patted me on the back and walked off giggling.

From that point on I would call Debbie on my way to school and describe my clothes.

"I'm wearing those black pants with that solid blue shirt and such-and-such tie."

"Sounds good. What about your shoes, socks, and belt?"

"Beige socks, brown shoes, and a brown belt."

"What? You don't wear beige socks, brown shoes, and a brown belt with black and blue! Go back and put on black shoes, black socks, and a black belt."

"Okay."

I would turn the car around, go back up the hill, and correct my wardrobe blunders. To this day I don't have the hang of it. Debbie organizes my clothes for me. If you ever see me out in public looking like a clown, it's because Debbie was not around to dress me.

More important than my looks were my grades. My teachers had always told me I was smart when I was a kid, and I was relieved to find out they weren't entirely wrong. I was on the dean's list every quarter but one at Life University. They hired me as an assistant instructor for physiology and paid me to teach students things like kidney nephrons and electron transfer on a mitochondrial level. That class was taught by the toughest professor at Life U., which made my job harder. I was often called upon to get up in front of a dry-erase board and bring these complex concepts down to earth so everyone could understand them.

In SEAL parlance, that course had the most confirmed kills. But my cerebral side started coming out and I liked it. I would find myself teaching a classroom full of young people and thinking, *I can do more than pull a trigger and stay steady while getting a shot off. This is pretty cool.* A new guy was emerging, and he surprised even me.

Finally, after four years and nine months, I graduated cum laude with a doctor of chiropractic degree and a biology degree. I won the clinical excellence award for the student who interacts best with patients. That was a big deal to me. On graduation day Debbie was surprised almost to tears as so many people came up and told her, "If it wasn't for your husband, I wouldn't have made it through that class. He has the ability to take something complicated and break it down."

A transformation had taken place. I was no longer just the tactical expert. I was a doctor. It wouldn't have happened without a lot of praying and a lot of studying—and a lot of sacrifice.

That transformation opened my heart for another kind of healing I'd needed for a long time. And that led to a breakout success I never saw coming.

TEN

RUNNING FROM GHOSTS

We said it all the time in the Teams: "You win the op before you get there."

SEAL Teams briefings are all-consuming planning experiences. You actually walk through every step of the op together, brainstorming possibilities from every angle, considering everything that might happen and then coming up with contingencies beforehand. By the time you are in the op, it almost feels familiar, like you've been there before. You know what will happen at each step no matter what turn it takes. It's a comforting and empowering feeling and one of the big reasons SEAL Teams have earned the reputation they have today.

In the same way, I spent the fall of 2009 preparing to open my clinic. I thought through every single thing I needed to do, from securing my licensing to establishing relationships and procedures with insurance companies, buying equipment, choosing furniture and paint colors to how I would greet patients and what an appointment would look like. I often woke up at 2:00 a.m. to write down ideas, big or small. I knew the day the first brick would be laid, the day my first X-ray would be taken, how everything would run that first week, how I would advertise my services, and how many patients I should expect.

By the time I opened the practice in April 2010, I felt like I'd already won the op. People came in by the dozens per day. For the grand opening I offered free spinal screenings. I also had something unusual: digital X-rays. By the time patients had dressed and walked back into the exam room, I had the X-rays on-screen so we could look at them together.

I soon discovered that chiropractic is like SEAL Teams work in another way: it's about using multiple techniques, not just one silver bullet. The more tactics I had up my sleeve when we went into combat, the better off I was. The same tactic does not work in every situation. That also is true of people's bodies. Everyone's precise physical situation is different, and different solutions work for each person. In my new work I learned to adapt, improvise, and expect the unexpected as people came through the door with pains and problems they needed me to help heal.

On an even deeper level I saw that in both the Teams and my new practice, I had always worked for love. People don't usually understand that, so I have to explain that as much as my ego was wrapped up in the Teams, the thing that satisfied me was offering my life for the safety of others. As Jesus said, "Greater love has no one than this: to lay down one's life for one's friends" (John 15:13). Every time I went on an op, I was volunteering to give my life for strangers and for every guy on the Teams, even the ones I didn't like. In a gunfight I would prioritize everyone's life above my own. That's not about personal glory or being a hero. It's love of God and people and country.

As a chiropractor, my mission hadn't changed, just the venue. I still took the greatest satisfaction from laying down my life for everyone who walked through my office door. People's biggest complaint with medical doctors is the feeling of being rubber-stamped. "Hello. You've got X, Y, and Z. Here's a drug. Good-bye." So many doctors rely on prescriptions that they overlook people's very real need to be listened to, which produces a psychosomatic response in their physical bodies.

Listening became one of my greatest tools. I decided that no one would feel rushed out of my office. I spent extra knee-to-knee time with my patients and am convinced it did them as much good as adjusting them physically. I even offered to pray with some patients when I had done all else I could. Soon I was seeing a hundred people a week, not counting the people I prescribed manual therapy or massage.

It felt wonderful to change people's lives for the better. Unlike a medical doctor or surgeon, I didn't have to go through the difficult experience of seeing people die on the table. I had decided early on that I simply would not go into another profession that dealt in matters of life and death. If I performed an operation or prescribed a medication that had a harmful effect on someone, I couldn't have handled the pain it would cause them and cause me. I had spent the first half of my life in risky endeavors. Now I wanted to be the one bringing joy and relief, not pain.

Debbie helped immensely on this journey of discovering new levels of love. She's as loyal as I am, which is a pretty high standard. Aside from the guys on the Teams, I never had someone so loyal to me. I missed that kind of reciprocal loyalty in my life and had concluded that most women were incapable of it—hypocritical, I know, given the way I treated many of the women in my life. Still, I wanted to know that someone had my back and wouldn't just walk out when it got bad.

Debbie surprised me in that regard. She didn't believe in playing "leaving" games; for example, walking out the door during an argument or pretending to pack up her stuff. She told me one time, "If I ever leave, it's serious, because if I leave, it's for good." Her loyalty toward me gave me the stability I had craved for years. When we argued I still sometimes feared she would walk out. She finally reassured me, "I'm not going anywhere. If we have a fight we're still sleeping in the same bed. Nobody's going on the couch. We can disagree and life doesn't have to end." What a powerful statement of love and commitment.

When God grants stability in one area of life, it's often because he wants to operate on more delicate places that still need healing. That's what he did with me that fall. The last time I had confronted memories of what happened in Somalia was eight years earlier, in 2001, when the movie version of *Black Hawk Down* came out. I had sucked up my courage and gone to see it in a drive-in theater. A third of the way through, I had to leave. It was just too real. I ended up getting through the whole thing years later when my daughter Eryn was curious if the movie presented reality.

My conclusion was that the basic storyline was good, though some things were changed to make it more Hollywood. For example, the bad guy, Osman Atto, the man running the regime's finances, was depicted as a tea-drinking, cigar-smoking tough guy. In reality, he came up to my chin, was skinny as a rail, and couldn't drink tea without burning himself. We'd watched him for a long time through long-distance scopes as we kept track of his whereabouts. Yes, he was a sharp cookie, but not suave in any way. He certainly didn't lecture our general (as depicted in the movie) about how we would never win. He was scared to death of our forces, and I'm convinced a fifteen-year-old girl could have taken him down in a one-on-one face-off.

As for how the battle that day went down, the movie was fairly accurate. The biggest disappointment most of us felt, having talked to a lot of guys since then, is that the movie didn't show how America had tucked tail and run, giving up everything we had gained. Before that battle we were feeding people and keeping down Al Qaeda. When we left Somalia, it became an incubator for Al Qaeda and piracy. People began starving again. I also wished they had ended the movie by showing pictures of guys who died, like Dan Busch. The filmmakers would have gotten class points with all of us for that. Then the American people could say, "This wasn't just World of Warcraft or a Hollywood movie written by some pencil-neck writer at a keyboard in Burbank. People actually died that day."

Aside from the difficult experience of failing to sit through *Black Hawk Down* at the drive-in theater, actual memories of Mogadishu didn't haunt me much. I never had recurring dreams or nightmares, never slipped into another reality during the day and thought I was back on the battlefield. Sometimes as I was drifting off to sleep I would get a snippet of a memory—a quick image of something that had happened or a strong feeling from that day or the certain acrid smell as tires burned in the streets. But then I would sleep peacefully. I never woke up in a cold sweat. Indeed, Debbie was always amazed at how I could basically sleep on cue, a skill learned in the Teams as we put our downtime to best use.

Somehow, in spite of my violent childhood and violent career, I had developed a talent every warrior needs: the ability to go from high gear to low gear, from war footing to civilian life. I was never jumpy at loud noises or sudden movements the way some veterans understandably are. I knew how to go from aiming and firing at enemies to standing around the kitchen asking how things were going with the kids. It was a hard downshift for some guys, and yes, there were times I missed upshifting to war footing, but somehow, probably due to the way my childhood beatings shaped me, I knew how to travel between crises and normal life.

The one exception was early October and especially October 3, the anniversary of the Battle of Mogadishu. I would fall down a dark well that week, feeling mentally wrecked. When I was younger and that date rolled around, I would go on three- or four-day drinking binges, sometimes disappearing for days. Later, when I stopped drinking, a depression would set in around late September, and I would be overwhelmed with grief and beat myself up with questions: *Why me? Why did I survive? What is my life worth now?*

I had coped with this annual walk through hell as best I could, but while studying at Life University, it occurred to me that it wouldn't hurt to hear a different perspective on my state of mind and perhaps shine light into places that I had kept in the dark for too long. The Bible says that "God is light, and there is no darkness in him at all" (1 John 1:5 NLT); and "if we are living in the light, as God is in the light, then we have fellowship with each other, and the blood of Jesus, his Son, cleanses us from all sin" (1 John 1:7 NLT). I wanted to grab on to that promise, to walk in the light more than I had up to then. I felt I was missing a certain freedom and confidence by holding those dark things inside.

An opportunity came when I was serving as a supplemental instructor for a physiology class. I learned that right after my class met, a pre-counseling class met that also needed a supplemental instructor. I thought I might do that, and in preparation I filled out a personality questionnaire. I found, as I had when filling out Veterans Administration personality tests, that I had some weak areas. I was also taking psychology and sociology classes, which seemed to offer hope that my experiences with beatings and war, and the way they had shaped me, were not unique. A friend encouraged me: "There's a counselor at Life and she's easy to talk to. Just go see her. It'll help."

For the first time in my life, I was ready to talk to someone about my most horrible experiences. I had been ignoring those memories for decades and that hadn't done me much good. Outwardly I seemed normal, but I kept my guard up and didn't let people know I felt damaged. I stayed busy to avoid the pain, and if it hurt really bad, I worked harder. Now I told myself that asking for help was a strength, not a weakness. Jesus said his power is made perfect in weakness (2 Cor. 12:9). I was going to test that proposition.

Plus, the counselor at Life was free, a benefit I wouldn't have forever.

I went to her office one day, a nondescript little room on campus. Our first meeting was thirty minutes long and sort of uneventful. For me, thirty minutes talking to anyone is an eternity because in that amount of time you start to open up about yourself, something I always avoided. But I was surprised that the counselor wasn't some antimilitary, tree-hugging, overly emoting, overeducated weirdo. She didn't lay me down on a couch, didn't ask me about my mother, and didn't make sympathetic cooing noises as I spoke. She was like a little iron rod, all of four feet nine and 120 pounds and completely dispassionate as she sat behind her desk. I never saw her smile or frown, never heard her condemn or condone anything. The most sympathy she gave me was to slide a Kleenex box across the desk when I needed it, still offering no expression.

Within two sessions I was spilling my guts and crying my eyeballs out. Her quiet, professional manner disarmed me and made it safe to talk somehow. I actually started to feel better, putting this stuff into words. Her occasional responses made sense and her questions were thought provoking. I was learning a lot about myself just by conversing with another human who had no vested interest in me.

During the second and third sessions I really opened up and let the emotions flow. I told her I thought I was screwed up beyond repair, that something was really wrong with me. I cried so hard that I felt like a kid coming clean with his parents. My chest heaved uncontrollably, and I could only get out one word at a time. It was embarrassing, but I thought, *If I'm here, I might as well get it on the table and get it over with.* She handled it almost without response. She somehow knew I didn't want to be comforted. The best thing was to pass the snot rags and let me keep talking. Which I did.

The emotional release was physically exhausting, and I walked out of there wishing someone would prop me up and drive me home. But it felt so good, like an anvil had been removed from my chest. She told me during one of the sessions, "Howard, with what you've been through and what you've seen, you are very high functioning. It would be hard to blame you if you had turned into a serial killer, but you didn't. You simply have an inferiority complex because you feel you're living on borrowed time. You think you were supposed to have died a long time ago, but you're still here. You have survivor's guilt, meaning you feel guilty for being alive while others around you died. But in the big picture, you're doing pretty well."

It was the first time I had ever heard the term "survivor's guilt." I can't overstate what a relief it was to know that my feelings had a label and had been studied. People think of survivor's guilt as one-dimensional: "Other people died, so I shouldn't have lived either." But it involves a lot more than that, questions you entertain a thousand times while staring at the ceiling at night: *Did I do everything I could in that situation? What if I had taken a little extra time and shot the bad guy first? Would I have been able to save the other guys' lives if I hadn't been injured? Why didn't I do a better job as an elite warrior? Was I really good enough to be out there? Should I have taken a shot when I didn't? Did I take a shot when I wasn't supposed to? Did I shoot someone who wasn't in it by mistake?* It's amazing how a few hours of time, like that battle in Mogadishu, can define the rest of your life and shape your mind forever.

Her diagnosis was that I had a double scoop of posttraumatic stress disorder (PTSD) from my childhood abuse and the war, plus a side order of survivor's guilt. It was a huge victory for me to get those horrible memories out in the open, to know that these were actual disorders, and especially to know that I was high functioning, a comment I clung to like a kid to a lollipop. She even explained to me why I used to date a woman for a while and then get rid of her. She said it was because in my mind my mom had abandoned me when she should have protected me from my stepfather's violent punishments. As a result I wouldn't let women too far into Blake's life. It made total sense to me.

I saw the counselor for twenty weeks, twice a week at first, then once a week, then once a month. Sometimes she gave me "homework" to do between our meetings. The most impacting one was, "This week I want you to do something just for you and don't feel guilty about it." That was tough. I had so many things to do: study, get ready for Debbie coming to visit, be a dad—and now I was supposed to do something just for me? But the counselor wanted me to see that I didn't need to keep trying to save the world. All I could do was make the world around me better. I wasn't responsible for everything. So that day I went out and got myself something to eat and just enjoyed it. As simple as it sounds, that changed the way I saw the world and took a big weight off these narrow shoulders.

Debbie didn't know the specifics of what had happened in those counseling sessions until much later, though I wish I had told her earlier because my healing would soon go sideways. It would have helped Debbie to know that I had made some strides in processing all the stuff I hadn't even told her about. In the meantime, Debbie encouraged me to seek a relationship with God more than I ever had. She got me going to church more regularly and moving back toward the light.

But for all that movement in the right direction, God was preparing me for an even bigger step toward wholeness. It started when Debbie signed me up for Facebook and an old friend from my past changed both of our lives.

DEBBIE

"Mom, you should get on Facebook," Eryn told me for the umpteenth time.

She and I were spending a lot more time together while Howard was away at school, and some of her habits were rubbing off on me.

"I don't know what Facebook is," I said dismissively, wondering if it was just the latest fad for adolescent girls.

She explained what it was and said, "Here, I'll sign you up," in spite of my skepticism. Within days I was hearing from friends from college and high school who I hadn't seen in twenty years. I enjoyed reconnecting, sharing fond memories, and renewing friendships.

When I visited Howard in Atlanta, he was curious about my new obsession and started cruising my Facebook account when I wasn't looking. He would put comments on my friends' statuses, and I'd have to go back and say, "That was Howard, not me! Please disregard that." He teased me about being on Facebook all the time, but the truth was that he was on Facebook whenever he could be, using my account. I couldn't get him to leave it alone.

When he graduated and came back home, we were monumentally busy. He was trying to get medical approval from Medicare, construct a building, and get all his ducks in a row to open his practice, so at night we were both looking to check out our brains for a while. One night we were sitting in the den watching a Western I was not into, so I started checking Facebook. I noticed yet another comment Howard had left using my name.

"Howard," I said from my perch on the couch, "I'm going to create an account for you because I'm tired of you playing on mine."

"What? No, don't do that," he said. "I don't want my own account. It'll just waste time I don't have."

"But you're on mine all the time anyway," I said as I signed him up. It was quick and easy.

"There!" I said. "Now you are on Facebook."

Howard acted grumpy about it, but when I offered to delete the newly created account, he said, "No, no, don't worry about it." Soon he was reconnecting with people just as I had—classmates from school, people from the police force in Florida, friends from his hometown. One guy who "friended" him was Stephen Templin, who had been in the same BUD/S class as Howard in San Diego. Stephen had suffered a foot injury and moved to the BUD/S class behind Howard, but for a while they had roomed in the same bunkhouse.

Stephen was now living in Japan, working as an associate professor of literature and writing a blog. Some of his blog entries included stories about Howard in BUD/S. One told how they had been busting their butts all day long when at the end of the day Howard came into the room and said, "Who wants to go for a run with me?" Everyone looked at him like, "Are you nuts?" but then a couple of people joined him. Even then, Howard had a reputation for going not the extra mile but the extra ten miles.

By e-mail, Stephen asked Howard if he'd ever thought about writing an autobiography. It was a sore point with Howard because Howard had started writing such a book sixteen years earlier, right after Mogadishu, but never got past a couple of chapters. The hurt was still too fresh. Then, when *Black Hawk Down* came out, Howard felt like he'd missed his opportunity. Now Stephen reawakened that dream and offered to help write it. He had written e-books before and seemed to know how to pull it off, so Howard began Skyping with him every Sunday. During the week Stephen would write new chapters based on those interviews. It opened up a whole new era of our lives—with consequences we couldn't imagine.

Interestingly, a few weeks after I signed Howard up for Facebook, he deleted his account and hasn't been on since. It was as if God had used Facebook in those few weeks to put him in contact with the guy who would help to guide him in the next direction for his life.

We were cautiously excited about the possibility of having a book done, but it was also a busy time. Our life was a whirlwind. Howard was overseeing every detail of opening his practice—his own licensing and insurance relationships, light fixtures and carpeting, hiring, equipment, and so much more. We were building a new office that would house both his chiropractic practice and my CPA practice, so both of us were working with architects, bank people, and the Small Business Administration, not to mention hundreds of other details.

As cement was poured and framing went up, it also felt like we were laying a new foundation for our marriage. We had not lived together for nearly five years and now we were together daily in the same house. A friend of mine who has a counseling degree warned me, "I know you feel like you've got a good relationship, but you'll go through a honeymoon period at first and then living together full-time again might be harder than you imagine."

I laughed and said, "No, you just don't know us."

She was right. Howard and I had developed different habits and had to get to know each other again. At night he would come home and want to watch serious shows—"Weapons of Mass Destruction" documentaries; shoot-'em-up war movies; big, serious Westerns with horses running wild and guns firing. That stuff stresses me out. At night I don't want to watch people shoot each other. If I had the remote I'd set it on reruns of *Reba*, a show so silly that it drained the stress right out of my day. I'd stand there and cook and half watch. When Howard complained, I said, "My job is so stressful. If I watch something serious I can't unwind. Silly shows help me settle down."

Little differences like that weren't too difficult to iron out, but I soon noticed that Howard was more on edge than I remembered. One time we had friends over, and Howard was telling them he was writing a book. I added lightheartedly, "It's going to be great therapy for him." He jumped all over my comment: "Don't ever say that! I do not need therapy. I don't want to hear that again." Anytime I mentioned that the book might help him clarify what had happened in his life, he reacted strongly. I chalked it up to us being busy and the book being about sensitive topics, never dreaming what was hiding behind that response.

Then, a few weeks after starting the book, Howard started to disappear for days on end. As calm and steady as I am, I just about freaked out.

He had joined a group called Combat Veterans Motorcycle Association (CVMA), which is a good bunch of guys and their wives who understand the psychological effects of being in a war better than I did at the time. They draw comfort and strength from hanging around together. Howard liked going on their planned rides around Georgia and sitting around the campfire talking about their experiences. He told me later that he never went from laughing to crying to laughing again so quickly as with the CVMA guys. It was a nice break for him from our hectic lives.

But one weekend Howard went to Atlanta, to visit a friend and didn't come back that night like he said he was going to. Twelve hours went by—no Howard. A day went by. No Howard. Two days. No Howard. He wasn't even answering his phone. I was beside myself with worry so I called Tom McMillan in Atlanta and we started calling hospitals from Macon to Atlanta. We pulled up Howard's cell phone records and called people he had recently called to see if they had seen him. No success. The trail was cold, and my husband was nowhere to be found. Finally Tom and I decided I would drive to Atlanta and we would go on a mad search for Howard, scouring the area, looking in ditches and hunting down the back roads. It was futile, but we felt we had to do something.

Then Howard called.

"Hey, Debbie," he said somewhat remorsefully. "My phone died. Sorry about that. I'll be home soon."

My heart about stopped from relief and anger. When he got home I broke down in his arms, and he apologized for putting me in a panic. But within a couple of weeks it happened again. He left on a Friday, saying he'd be back that night. He came back on a Monday morning in time to get dressed and go to work. Not only that, but he hadn't called me once. Normally he was calling me twenty times a day to see what I was eating and where I was. Now he had shut me out and stopped communicating. Sometimes he would ride with no destination, no plan. More than once, after he was AWOL for two days, I would find myself looking at cell-phone records to see where he might be. Several times I was almost convinced he was dead in a ditch, the victim of some late-night accident on a farm road.

I had never questioned his fidelity or the stability of our marriage, but this sudden abandonment put doubts in my mind: *Was it me? Why was he wanting to leave every weekend? Was I doing something wrong? What was going on in his life that I didn't see? Was there someone else? Was I being blind?*

One weekend he told me he was riding to north Georgia, but somehow ended up in Florida with a guy he ran into who had served in the Teams. After he came back from Florida, I confronted him.

"It's bad enough you tear out of here leaving me to wonder where you are or what you're doing, but now I don't even know what state you're in?" I said, incredulous and angry.

"I was just on the A1A," he said. That was the highway in Florida that paralleled the Atlantic Ocean. Howard liked it because the ocean made him feel at home. Bikers go there a lot because there is no helmet law in Florida.

"I met a guy who was in the Teams," he continued, expecting me to be sympathetic. "We rode all weekend. The guy was in tears and having such a hard time. I never knew there were other guys like that out there."

"I get that," I said. "But it doesn't mean you don't tell your wife where you are. While you're out having guy time, I'm back here alone, freaking out."

He grimaced and shook his head.

"It's not like I'm losing track of time or that I don't want to be with you, Debbie," he said. "I've just got a lot going through my mind right now. I don't want to burden the family with it. It feels better just to get away."

I felt it was time to lay down the law.

"I get that you need to get away sometimes," I said. "We all do. But I am not going to be that wife married to that guy who just disappears whenever he wants to. This is a deal breaker for me."

His eyes steeled up, and he gave me the answer he had started giving lately: "You just don't understand."

And it was true. I had little idea what was going through his head. He wouldn't explain himself, wouldn't reveal what was troubling him. He would just say, "I've got to get away." And I wouldn't see him for three days.

As close as we were, I knew very little about Howard's past life with the SEALs. He wouldn't talk about Somalia or his childhood. To this day it's hard for me to envision him as a sniper. I didn't see him shoot a gun until ten years after we were married. It just wasn't part of his life anymore.

People naturally got excited when they found out he was a SEAL, but he would never talk about Somalia. He was happy to talk about BUD/S training and how difficult it was, but never combat. He also wasn't in contact with many Teams guys, which I didn't quite understand. He spoke so fondly of his time in the Teams that it didn't make sense why he had cut away from that community so completely. I figured it was difficult to lose something he enjoyed and he was trying to shove it into the past.

Unlike other veterans, Howard never had flashbacks, as best I could

tell. One CVMA wife told me her husband would wake up scream-
ing and that she would take the gun and hide it. She had learned not
to get close to him when these episodes came so that he couldn't grab
her. She stood across the room and called his name softly. Compared
to that, I hadn't really gone through anything with Howard, and I felt
for the women and their husbands who walked that road.

But for months, Howard shut me out of his private life. I learned
to pray in a different way—ceaselessly, turning to God whenever I felt
doubts creep in, offering prayers throughout the day. "This, too, shall
pass," I told myself, praying that it would really be true.

I drew strength from another place too. Early in our marriage I
had gone through a tubal pregnancy and emergency surgery. I lost
so much blood that I nearly died. Doctors said if I had gone to sleep
that night instead of into the emergency room, I wouldn't have made
it to morning. That had been a wake-up call for me: I was human. I
could die.

It had been hard for me to confront my mortality. I had always
lived by the rules and thought that exempted me from danger. But I
believe that brush with death happened for a reason. God puts you in
situations to build strength for what's ahead. Surviving that medical
scare gave me confidence that it wasn't my time to go, and it helped
me relate to Howard in a way I never had before: as a survivor.

Finally, when I could stand the doubts no longer and my trust
was fraying to the breaking point, I sat Howard down.

"You have got to tell me what's going on," I said, looking him in
the eye.

He shifted a little and did his typical gestures that were his way of
avoiding a subject. I didn't back down but stared right at him, waiting
for him to put the truth on the table.

"This cannot go on," I said. "This running away, this hiding from something, this shutting me out. It's hurting us. It's hurting me."

He waited a moment to speak. What he said surprised me.

"It's not easy, writing this book," he said. "Maybe you think it's a walk in the park going back and remembering this stuff, but it's not. I haven't thought deeply about it forever. A lot of times it's like reliving it all over again. I can hardly take it."

"That's what this is about?" I said. "Not about us, not about the business?"

"No, it has nothing to do with that," he said. "If anything, you and my work give me the stability I need to fight my way through these things. Debbie, when these emotions rise up from the past, I'm not sure what to do with them. I go into self-preservation mode. It's selfish, but at those times I don't even consider that someone is worried about me back home or that I should check in. I just ride and try to forget.

"These CVMA guys, they get that side of me. They let me know I'm not weird or weak because of what I've gone through after combat. They had family problems, too, and trouble fitting in with 'normal' people. They know how all this stuff goes. If I didn't have them, I don't think I could keep writing this book. I'm certain of it, because it's the most painful thing I've done in a long time."

When I saw the hurt and vulnerability in his eyes, I felt almost guilty for not sympathizing a lot more than I had. I didn't come from a military family, so I had no background with that kind of trauma, and he had hidden these emotions so well for so long that I didn't know they were there. Writing the book was churning up every emotional struggle, every loss, every awful memory he had kept at bay for years. Stephen, like any writer, pressed him for details: "Tell me more about this. Clarify this. Dig deeper here." By facing his past, Howard couldn't hide anymore. Strong emotions came with each of those memories and now they were bursting forth, seemingly out of control in his own mind. He didn't know how to deal with them except to get on his bike and ride.

Howard Wasdin is running from ghosts, I realized.

I put my hand on his, and for a moment I thought he was going to cry. Then we embraced. That was the last time he left without notice or a plan. My concern seemed to tether him to a stable place. Trust slowly returned to our marriage. He didn't spill his guts and tell me everything, but now I knew how he was struggling when he walked out of a Skype call with Stephen. I knew when to leave him alone and when to offer a gentle word or touch of support.

Over time he shared with me the questions that had dogged him for so long: Why had he suffered at the hands of his stepfather? Why didn't his mother intervene to spare him the beatings? Why did other men die in Mogadishu while Howard survived? Why had that op gone so terribly wrong? In my own weak way, and with little knowledge of how best to care for him, I showed the love I felt for him and listened when he decided to share what was going on in his mind.

But it wasn't until I read the first draft of the book that I got the full story. I cried so hard on so many occasions that I had to compose myself before continuing.

This makes sense of everything, I thought. *This explains who Howard is and why he feels the way he does. Why didn't I see it before?*

For most of our marriage, I had wondered why Howard argued so viciously whenever we had a disagreement, and why he wanted me to fight that way too. I told a friend once, "When we argue, even if it isn't anything big, it's almost like he gets to the point where he wants someone to cut him down to size. He's begging me to abuse him verbally. I just don't want to." On those occasions, when in exasperation I would burst out in anger, it seemed to give Howard a strange peace. He'd quiet down and say, "Okay," and we would soon resolve whatever it was. In some twisted way he wanted someone to push him down to where he thought he deserved to be.

Now it made sense: that was the way he'd been taught to fight, with overwhelming force one way or the other. Either you totally win or you totally lose. When he'd been beaten, he was the recipient of that force. When he was on the offensive, he was determined to win and no rules of combat would stop him. Howard is a sweet person, but when we argued, he would say harsh things I didn't expect. He didn't know how to fight fair. When we fought, he went on the attack and said anything he had to say to win.

Every page of that first manuscript told me why. I didn't realize how much anger remained in him about his childhood. When I finished my first read-through, Howard was in the bathroom shaving.

"What do you think?" he asked, turning off his razor.

"If people only knew you from this book, they would think you were the angriest person on the planet," I said. "But you're not. I think you need to tone some of this down."

So began the editing process for *SEAL Team Six*. Normally a proposal includes a chapter outline and a few sample chapters, but Howard and Stephen had written the whole thing. Maybe Howard needed to, for his own sake. Now we went through it time and again, balancing things out and adding clarity or grace wherever we could.

Once the writing was finished, Howard became a different person—rather, he became the Howard I knew and loved. He quit riding on weekends so much, and his sweet, sunshiny demeanor returned to brighten our home. His practice was in full swing, and he had a new direction and identity he could be proud of. Life was settling down, and we were starting to enjoy the benefits of the normal life we had tried to build. We had no idea if anyone would even want his book, now that Mogadishu was so far in the past, but Stephen sent the manuscript off to several agencies to see if any agent expressed interest.

The first response was not promising. An agent wrote and said, "There may be something to work with here, but you have to be willing to scrap the whole book. Blow it up and start from scratch." That insulted Howard and Stephen after spending so much time editing it.

Thank God for the second agent who called.

"Scrap it? Are you nuts?" he said. "This manuscript is fantastic."

Within days major publishers were in a bidding war for the book, and it finally came down to two. The bidding war ended with a sale on April 15, 2010—always a significant day for me as a CPA. There were other eerie parallels: the literary agent was from Trident Media Group, whose logo is a three-pronged trident very similar to the SEAL insignia. Plus, Stephen had graduated from Trident University International. Three tridents had converged. Go figure.

It felt like God was directing our lives very purposefully again. We didn't know the half of it.

ELEVEN

BIN LADEN AND THE BOOK

Having sold the book, we splurged and spent Christmas 2010 in St. Lucia with Eryn and a friend. We weren't making a lot of money but decided to do something special anyway. Debbie and I spent much of our time on that beautiful island with our noses in manuscript pages. We all came back with Christmas tans.

We were surprised to learn from our editor that there was no other book named *SEAL Team Six*. We settled on that title, though at the time SEAL Team Six as a unit was generally unknown. It turned out to be yet another providential choice whose outcome we couldn't even begin to see. Our main concern at the time was how the book would stand out from the dozens of other books by snipers and special forces members, which were now saturating the market. To break out from the pack was going to take a small miracle.

We got one.

On May 1, 2010, two weeks before our publication date, I took Eryn with me on a flight up to Vidalia. I had started taking flying lessons and was recertified as a private pilot. Vidalia had a fly-in air show and heading up there sounded like a fun way to spend a Sunday. On the way, once we were airborne, I gave Eryn the yoke and let her fly the plane for a while. Then we landed and watched the air show before flying back home. The book wasn't much on my mind that day. We didn't know what kind of reviews or attention it would get. Most books don't sell well, and the odds were not any better for ours. Like any first-time author, I was hoping it would just make its advance money back.

We lived in a house right across the street from the pastor of our church. Dr. Mike Von Moss, pastor of First Baptist Church in Jesup, is a laid-back guy with a great sense of humor. The morning after the air show, I was taking it easy, getting ready to see patients later that day. I was sitting around in my pajama pants. I had just fed the cat and was getting ready to take the dogs for a walk when Mike came to the door walking his Schnauzer named Max. He spoke to me through the doorway.

"Hey, neighbor," he said casually. "Just wanted to tell you 'Happy bin Laden's Dead Day.'"

My skin bristled.

"What did you say?"

"Oh, you didn't hear? SEAL Team Six stormed his compound and shot him dead. See you later."

He turned around and walked off.

When I heard him say that SEAL Team Six was involved, I just about jumped out of my drawers. I ran out after him, bursting through the door.

"What?" I said. "SEAL Team Six killed bin Laden?"

Mike turned with a grin. He was playing it low-key just to have fun with me. But he wouldn't lie about something like this.

"Yeah, a SEAL Team Six member shot him in the head. Have a great day."

I ran back in the house and turned on the TV to see that it was true. On May 2, 2011, in Pakistan, Osama bin Laden was killed by SEAL Team Six in an early-morning raid. My old unit. A sniper. A guy a lot like Howard Wasdin. Twenty years earlier and it might have been me.

I was so excited I didn't know what to do with myself. I started pacing the house, calling whomever I could who was still in the game and asking what had happened on that raid. I admit, I wished I could have been there with them. If for some cosmically unlikely reason they had asked me to suit up and go on the raid, wild horses and chains couldn't have kept me home. As it was, having SEAL Team Six do the honors was the next best thing. It felt like vindication for me, since the three bullets I'd taken in Somalia were from fighters supported by bin Laden. It was also the perfect op to counterbalance what had happened in Mogadishu, where two helicopters had gone down and we didn't get our man. With the bin Laden raid, one helicopter went down but no Americans lost their lives. It felt to me in some way like we had finished the job.

I carefully watched the news that day, and when I saw diagrams of the compound that had been raided, I started thinking like a SEAL. *That's where I would have put my sniper station. That would be my infil place. That would be my exfil place. That's where I would put the blocking force. If I were planning the op, I'd have my assault team in the compound and a containment team on the outside. I would be worried about reinforcements coming in to rescue bin Laden. I'd put snipers there and there to give us the power to reach out and touch someone approaching from a distance.*

The raid took a full forty minutes, which is a long time when you're engaging an enemy and worried about someone shooting at you. I marveled at everything I was hearing about this well-executed hit on the world's most wanted man.

After watching the news for a while, it dawned on me and Debbie that the biggest headline of our times was going to impact us in a very personal way. For the first time in history, SEAL Team Six was being thrust into the global spotlight—and my book of the same name was scheduled to hit stores two weeks later. Not only was America's foremost enemy dead, but now "SEAL Team Six" was going to replace "sex" as the top search engine term, at least for a couple of days. My book was going to show up on millions of computer screens across the world. Everyone, it seemed, was asking, "Who is SEAL Team Six and how did they just find and kill the world's most notorious terrorist?"

Talk about timing. You can't convince me there's no such thing as divine intervention. I've never had a better manager than God. It helps when someone on your team knows the future.

Life accelerated much faster than I expected and became a mad rush of publicity. My publisher called within hours and said they were pushing the book's publication date up to May 8, six days after bin Laden was killed. And now a little-known chiropractor from south Georgia was in demand by major TV networks.

"*Good Morning America* and Fox News want you on," said the publisher's publicist by phone. "We need you to get to New York right away."

"Sure. Can I bring Debbie?" I asked.

"Absolutely," he said.

Overnight I was about to become the face of SEAL Team Six to a lot of people. That meant Debbie and I had to consider that our lives were going to be scrutinized—and possibly endangered. Who knew if terrorists would respond to the death of bin Laden with crazy assassination missions? Our home address was listed publicly, and it was just possible that some anti-American nut would see me on TV, think I was in on the raid, and retaliate against our family. For that reason we took Eryn with us to New York, locked the doors of the house, and prayed no harm would come while we were away.

In the meantime, small-town gossip had started to spread that I was in Pakistan and had helped take bin Laden down. People around Jesup were saying, "I haven't seen Howard Wasdin for a couple of days. Do you think—?" If they had just poked their heads in my office they would have seen me adjusting, X-raying, and consulting with people the week before. Now, of course, I was heading to New York and would be away. People seemed to like it when they thought I was living a secret life. I only wish it had been true.

It was my first time in an upscale hotel in New York City, and it felt surreal to pull back the curtains and see Central Park. A private car drove us to ABC News for my first big interview, *Good Morning America*. As I was sitting in what they called the green room, a woman came in and said, "We're going to bring you back to makeup now."

I looked at her like, "I'm the SEAL Team Six guy. Maybe you didn't get the memo, but I don't do makeup." I made some comment about not really wanting to have makeup put on me. She sweetly said, "Okay," and rolled a monitor in front of me. "This is what you'll look like on camera," she said. It was me on the screen but I looked shiny, white, and pasty, like some sort of zombie.

I said, "Where's that makeup place again?"

Soon I was caked up, powdered up, and talking to Robin Givens in front of millions of people. Actress Betty White was on right before me, which added to the fun but strange feeling, going from a beloved actress to a sniper in the space of a commercial break. For reasons I still don't understand, the whole experience felt natural to me. I enjoyed hanging out with the hosts and crew. I had no stage fright and Debbie told me my personality came across well on camera, which was a relief. You always wonder what you'll look like under those bright lights. I guess being a straight shooter was finally going to serve me well.

After the show my phone buzzed with a text from a SEAL buddy in Tennessee: "Hey, sissy, we could tell you were wearing makeup." I laughed and thought, *Thanks for the congratulations.* Then a text popped up from a buddy from the SWAT team in Florida. "I know what you were doing with Betty White before you went on," he wrote. I just rolled my eyes. I could tell who watched what show by who shot me texts over the next few days.

After *GMA*, the car sped us off somewhere else and the day turned into a blur of radio interviews, TV interviews, interviews in the car, interviews at the hotel. The publicist kept shoving journalists in front of me—the *New York Times*, the *New York Post*, and many others. In a moment of national celebration, I somehow became one of the spokesmen for the winning team, though I had nothing to do with killing bin Laden. It all went back to the title and the timing of the book, and of course to my background on the Teams.

I had the advantage of being able to speak more freely than guys who were still active, though I kept my comments limited to protect them and their work. The journalists asked the same questions over and over: "How come we've never heard about SEAL Team Six? Do these ops go on all the time? What have you done that you can't tell us about?"

I tried to keep it humble: "Guys in SEAL Team Six are normal people who love our country and try to do an extraordinary job for our fellow citizens." I started practicing how to answer the questions I wanted to answer instead of just reacting to what the interviewer put on the table. Every interviewer knows what he or she wants you to say and tries to phrase questions to get the answer they want. I was learning the art of the interview.

After day one, Debbie and Eryn called it quits. "We can't keep up," Debbie said. "We're going to stay in the hotel tomorrow." That night after I came back, we lay in bed flipping channels and Debbie said, "Oh my gosh, there you are!" We watched me talk on some network for a while, then flipped the channel and there I was on a different show. It's funny to me now how we sat up and listened to what I said so intently, as if we'd never heard it before.

My impromptu media tour was supposed to last three days, but the requests kept coming in, so I decided to stay in New York while Debbie and Eryn went home. On Debbie and Eryn's last night in the city, I went on Sean Hannity's TV show for the first time and had a blast. I've been on three times now, and Hannity is a classy, fun guy. He signed one of the footballs he throws after a segment and gave it to Debbie and Eryn. I also had the privilege of being on his Great American panel and opining about a particular presidential wartime decision I disagreed with. I was having the time of my life.

Between interviews I had to do some quick shopping for more clothes. I'd only brought enough for the shows I thought we were doing. I couldn't wear the same thing everywhere, so we bought some more twenty-dollar shirts like the ones that already filled my closet. The book was preselling but we weren't exactly rolling in cash.

The night after Debbie and Eryn left, I dined alone in the nice hotel the publisher had put us up in. To my surprise, I saw Jon Bon Jovi sitting a few tables over. Debbie is an absolute Bon Jovi freak. If at this moment he knocked on our door and asked for her hand, I have to wonder what she would say. I like the band, too, and "Living on a Prayer" was my Hell Week song.

So I got up, went over, and said, "Mr. Bon Jovi, I want to let you know that I really like your music. When I went through BUD/S, your song was our official Hell Week song, 'cause we were going through hell and we needed prayer." I would like to say that his face brightened and he smiled and said he appreciated my little story, but he must have been tired of having people come up to him. He shook my hand half-heartedly and didn't make any eye contact. I thanked him and drifted back to my table, a little abashed at what I had done.

Just as I was texting Debbie that I had met and been mostly ignored by her teenage heartthrob, a gentleman came over who had been staring at me from across the restaurant for a few minutes.

"My wife told me you're that SEAL Team Six guy we saw on Hannity last night," he said. "Is that you?"

"Yes, sir, I'm Howard Wasdin," I said, standing up to shake his hand. "Glad to meet you."

He turned around.

"Honey, it's him," he said to his wife so loudly that every other patron could hear. "It's the SEAL Team Six guy we saw on TV."

Within moments half the restaurant was lined up to shake my hand, pat my shoulder, and give me napkins and other things to sign. In the midst of it I looked over at Jon Bon Jovi, who was looking at me like, "Who is that? Wasn't that guy just over here? Did I blow off somebody famous?" For fifteen minutes I was more popular than the rock star.

Debbie was upset to miss her rock-and-roll idol. She has said a hundred times since, "If only I'd stayed one more night . . ."

My favorite TV appearance was the *Daily Show with Jon Stewart*. Jon was not how I expected him to be. He was not cynical and sneeringly liberal, but openly patriotic and thankful for my service. The biggest surprise that night was when I walked out before my first live audience. The place went crazy. I couldn't believe how much love they showed me. In reality they were cheering for America and I just happened to be the guy in the spotlight, but it felt so good. During the interview Jon and I had a particular exchange that literally left him speechless. His producer told me later that it was the first time he had seen Jon without a comeback. I was proud of that and had a great time on his show.

My second favorite experience was on the *Imus in the Morning* TV show, another surprise. I had heard that Don Imus was cranky, said controversial things, and baited his guests, so I told my literary agent and my publicist, "I'll do the show, but if he says something insulting to me like he has done to others, I might snatch his butt from across the table." They said to go on and not worry about it. They were probably thinking it would make good television.

Imus was a card. He'd been a US Marine but not a warrior; he played in the Marine Band. "I've never understood you SEAL guys," he said. "I spent my career trying to get out of stuff, and you guys spend your lives getting into stuff."

Then he asked me, "Dr. Wasdin, do you think it's a good idea to have more than one wife?" He was referring to Osama bin Laden, who apparently had had several wives living in his compound with him. I started to explain that with Muslims it's as many wives as you can afford, but Imus interrupted and said, "The reason they want more wives is so they have more people to throw in front of them when SEAL Team Six comes knocking."

I liked the guy.

Not only that but his show incorporates guests' favorite songs for its bumper music. Audiences got to hear my top four: "Hunk of Burning Love" by Elvis, "Living on a Prayer" by some guy I saw at a restaurant one time, "Pour Some Sugar on Me" by Def Leppard . . . and "Drowning" by the Backstreet Boys. It was a little embarrassing to be on national television and have "Drowning" come on as one of my life songs but hey, it was true. I wasn't going to lie and get uppity about it.

A week later, spent and all talked out, I returned home. I had hired another chiropractor to run my practice for me while I was away, but when I came back I learned that some of my patients would drive by looking for my car in its normal spot and would drive away if I wasn't there. That made me feel good and bad. It's nice to be loved, but I wanted them to get the care they needed.

SEAL Team Six sold by the truckload. Barnes & Noble bookstores ran a big promotion for Memorial Day. For months I was doing interviews from home. As just one example of how different our life had become, one night friends asked us to dinner so they could catch up on all our excitement. I heard Debbie say on the telephone, "Oh, we'd love to but CNN's going to be at the house, and then the Discovery Channel is coming by. How about tomorrow night?" We looked at each other and started laughing with our friends about how ridiculous it was to hear those words coming out of our mouths.

Life never went back to normal. Suddenly we weren't just living on a prayer, we were living our dreams.

While I think *SEAL Team Six* is well written and deserves its popularity, it's clear that divine intervention made it a best seller.

Nobody could have timed it to come out within a week of bin Laden's assassination. Nobody could have known that the actual military unit SEAL Team Six would carry out the op that took bin Laden out. I was gratified with the book sales and the victory our country had scored, but it also had a deeply personal effect on me. The timing and success of the book made me even more confident that God had kept me alive for a reason.

I did have a message to share, something to impart to people. The Bible says we comfort others with the comfort we have received. I felt that was true. After all, the book was just as much about my life and painful childhood as about the flashy ops. God had used his perfect timing to get that message of hope to people who were desperate to hear it.

I began to receive letters and e-mails from all over the world from people who had experienced similar things—violent childhoods, various forms of abuse, PTSD. Many said the book was helping them heal from their past hurts. Some wrote simply, "Thank you for your service." The most amazing responses, like the one I received from a young man in Poland, said, "I didn't know God until I read your book. After reading it, I gave my life to Jesus."

I was amazed by that. I had always wondered how a guy like me from a rural town in Georgia, especially as a Christian, could impact people. Now I saw that God would do exactly what he wanted with my book. The many letters and e-mails frequently brought tears to our eyes.

I toured Europe to promote the book. One woman even had me sign her Kindle device with a permanent marker. I was treated so well in countries like Germany, Poland, France, and Holland. They recognized that I hadn't written a chest-thumping tale of war but a simple story of a young boy who, through great pain, had taken an extraordinary journey. The publisher also produced a youth-adapted version of the book called *I'm a SEAL Team Six Warrior*, which was chosen as a "Quick Pick for Reluctant Young Readers" from the American Library Association. Many teachers sent us messages saying, "Kids who never read before are devouring your book."

Most important to me, the publicity led to opportunities to do good. The Boys and Girls Clubs of America have always been dear to my heart because they give kids role models and a positive place to be—things I wish I had more of when I was growing up. I love how the clubs encourage kids, help them with their homework, and organize fun activities and field trips for them. I was invited to be on the board of the local Boys and Girls Club, and we held fund-raisers for them.

One was a book signing and another was the "SEAL for a Day" day camp where we set up fun games and tests of skill for the kids, simulating a scaled-down version of my own BUD/S training. At a BB gun shooting range, they shot at targets from standing, kneeling, and prone positions. They did "KIM" games, which stands for "keep in memory." They were shown ten objects and had to describe or draw them. There were stations for sit-ups and push-ups and other things. The kids who won were remarkable. Some of them had perfect scores in shooting. It was so successful that we immediately began talking about making it an annual event.

One of the more exciting connections for me took place in Texas. A book that deeply impressed me when I was young was *The Cross and the Switchblade* by David Wilkerson. I was a preteen when my grandmother, who was also my Sunday school teacher, gave me the book. I read about this man in New York City who slept in his car and woke up to find it on blocks—vandalized overnight. I read about him going to gangs and trying to pull kids out of bad lifestyles and heroin use. It made a lasting mark on me.

I was profoundly moved that the very first speaking presentation I did was at the ministry property owned by David Wilkerson in Texas, a place known as Little Jerusalem. I spoke to a group called Teen Mania, six hundred high school students getting ready to go out on missions all over the world. My hosts were A. C. Musgrave and Ron Luce.

A. C. is the biggest Christian philanthropist I know. He told me he can't give money away fast enough because it comes back. He drove me around that big ranch, showed me where David Wilkerson bought his first piece of land, and told me how God had told him to give his possessions away—when Wilkerson died in a car wreck in 2011, the only thing he owned was the car he was driving. Listening to A. C. recount God's work there was like sitting at a grandfather's knee.

Luce was a real inspiration. I have great respect for the guy. He founded Teen Mania, which motivates kids to live their faith out in real, tangible ways. Also headquartered there is the ministry of Mercy Ships, which sends relief all over the world via large ships.

Later I flew a guy down there whose name is familiar to a lot of people: country singer Travis Tritt. Travis had read *SEAL Team Six* and sent me an autographed picture of himself with a nice note saying, "I feel ya, Howard. Thank you. You're a real American hero." He invited my family and me to come to a show in Columbus, Georgia, and when we got there, he brought us backstage and then onto his bus. I learned that Travis grew up poorer than I had and learned to sing by going to a black church. We discovered we had a lot in common.

Travis's friend Steve Johnson had bid on and won the shooting lesson offered as a fund-raiser by the Boys and Girls Club. As a result of that connection, I ended up traveling with Travis and Steve out to Texas for the visit to A. C.'s ranch. After the ministry and the tour were done, A. C., Travis, Steve, and I were hanging out at a lake house cooking steaks. Travis found a guitar and began giving us a free concert.

I thought to myself, *I can't believe this is happening. I'm grilling steaks with these great guys, and Travis Tritt is giving us a private show at this beautiful lake house. There are people with all sorts of money and privilege who don't have something this special.* I couldn't believe a poor kid from Screven who used to mow grass barefoot for three dollars a lawn was having such a cool experience.

While in Texas I also taught Travis to shoot long distances, and as a result he made his first long shot, a one-thousand-yard shot with a .338 Lapua gun. I flew us back home and was seeing patients again the next day. It felt surreal but awesome. At some point I expected someone to pinch me and wake me from this beautiful dream.

My speaking schedule filled up fast—perhaps too fast. Suddenly I was being invited to speak to corporations, churches, and colleges around the country. They often wanted to hear about team building. A major automobile manufacturer flew me to Las Vegas where they were having a seminar on the top floor of Mandalay Bay. They told me that in their company they had a couple of people "on their own agenda," and they wanted me to talk some sense into them about working as a team. Again I was amazed that a redneck, premature little boy from Screven was telling these corporate leaders how to improve their company.

The events I really enjoyed were in churches. I spoke at a "Breakfast Bowl" event for men the day before the Super Bowl at a church in

Philadelphia. Three thousand people showed up to hear me talk about my journey from darkness to light. I told them what Tom had told me, that if you ever find yourself in a dark space, it's not the light that moved. I told them that our generation feels entitled to things we don't deserve. I showed photos of little boys and girls in Somalia and reminded the group, "Nobody in this room did a thing to deserve to be an American. By the grace of God you wake up in the morning and turn on the hot water. Nobody's entitled to anything."

Then I encouraged them to get help if they needed help, the way I had done with the counselor at Life University. I told them not to be ashamed to ask, because we all need a hand at some point. After the event the pastor told me, "I've never had this happen, but eight men told me they're having problems at home and need help."

Sudden "fame" led to wonderful new opportunities. But there was still reconciliation to take place with people I loved.

TWELVE

LAST BATTLES

It would be nice to reach a place in life where all the battles went away and you made perfect decisions every time, but I've discovered that life is more often about struggle, learning, and growth. As the publicity ramped up and stayed up, my old familiar response was to say yes to every speaking engagement and interview while adding patients at the clinic and trying to be a good father and husband. I loaded my schedule, then loaded it even more, like an overstuffed box bursting at the seams. I still wanted the approval of those around me, and by working hard I felt I could prove myself and my worth. When you've lived like that for decades, it becomes automatic.

The wear and tear started to show. A good friend spent the weekend with us, and while we were heading back home he told me, "I've watched you lately, Howard. I know you can handle a lot of stuff, but I'll be honest: I'm worried about you. You're tired and worn out and stressed."

It was true. I would get done with one interview and get ready to travel to a speaking engagement. Then I would come home and without a day off start seeing patients again. I was running myself ragged. Debbie sat me down one day and told me all these speaking engagements were starting to have an impact on our relationship—and I knew right away that she was right. It was the Brazil conversation all over again: I could try to save the world, but what good would it be if I lost my family and my happiness?

"We do better when we're together than when we're apart," she told me. "I'd rather have my husband than all the money you could make running around the country."

Success offers more opportunities to get off course than normal because you're trying to accomplish so much. You think, *Now's the time. I'm a national figure for the moment, but it may not last very long. I should accept every engagement and every interview to keep this going.* It's not bad to do the most with the doors God opens for you, but as with piloting an airplane, you always have to check your heading.

Debbie and I had gotten out of balance and were starting to snap at each other more often. The ease of our relationship wasn't there. Instead, we were both rushing around, increasingly consumed by our own lives and careers. When Debbie said she thought we were suffering because of my schedule, it rang true. I had to be more selective. I didn't have to say yes to everything. I could shape and fashion my own life and not be ruled by whatever invitations came in. The top priority was to care for my home and family first. I realized that even if I had never written a book, I still had a really good life. It was worth protecting.

As part of slowing down and getting back to our first love, we found a condo in Florida that we could afford and made it our weekend retreat. After just one weekend there, I saw how wound up I was.

I hadn't truly relaxed in a long time. Now we had a place we could slow down, take naps, laugh, cook, or do whatever we wanted. Fun returned to our relationship. The condo was close enough that we went down every Friday after work and stayed until Monday morning. What a difference! It was like being reborn every weekend.

I stopped doing interviews by phone and stopped accepting non-paying speaking engagements except for the Boys and Girls Club and some ministries. To reduce the number of inquiries, I raised the price I asked to come and speak. I started doing fewer events with greater impact and it felt great.

The other incentive to slow down was a baby girl named Emma, Eryn's daughter and our first grandbaby. Nothing brought me such joy as holding that baby girl. She was a living, breathing manifestation of God's love and goodness to us. I had been so absent during my own children's upbringing that it was like God gave me a do-over. I got to see and experience things I had missed the first time around, simple things like helping her up a ladder so she could go down a slide. I even cut down trees and resodded my backyard so she would have grass to run on. Anyone who's ever had a grandchild knows of what I speak. Patients, friends, and relatives tried to tell me what it was like but now I know. I'm putty in her hands.

After the book came out, I also came into contact with Dan Busch's son, Paul, who was in college and was a baseball player. He thanked me for the way I portrayed his dad in the book. I wrote back to tell him how proud I was of what he was doing with his life. I sent him photos of his dad. When Paul e-mailed pictures of himself, I was amazed how much he resembled Dan. It brought tears to my eyes— tears of remembrance and tears of joy. I told him that to this day I try to emulate Dan and his easy-going, upbeat manner.

Dan lived half the number of years I have lived and had more impact on people than I probably ever will. Just the other day I was upset with someone for parking their car behind mine in our driveway and I barked at the person about it. On the way to work I considered my words and realized I'd done wrong. I knew that Dan Busch would not have said the words I did and that if he were in my position he would apologize when he came home, which is exactly what I did. It was so good to share those things with Dan's son.

Maybe this is another reason God had me stick around, I thought. *To tell this young man what a wonderful father he had.*

Dan's wife, who had remarried, told me later, "Paul looks like his dad, sounds like him, acts like him, and has the same weird sense of humor. It's eerie." I fully expect that Paul will carry on his dad's great legacy of friendship and service to those around him, whatever path he chooses to take.

God also brought me into a season of reconciliation with those closest to me. I had always wanted to know who my biological father was but also dreaded learning the truth about him. Was he a bad seed who ended up in prison as my mom's family said? I was curious to find out, but for years I had left it alone out of respect for Leon. As much as I had suffered at Leon's hands, I also recognized that he had fed me, given me a home, and treated me as his own son. Yes, the beatings wounded me inside and out, but I'm convinced he didn't know any better and that he was doing the best he knew how. Out of respect for Leon I had never sought to meet my real dad. I felt it was better to leave it alone for the time being.

Leon had mellowed in his later years, and we reconciled as much as two men can who never talked about feelings. He even told me, "I want to be your first patient when you become a chiropractor." But he never got to keep that promise. Leon died shortly before I graduated. I remember sitting on the back porch with Debbie soon after his funeral and saying, "I think I'd like to meet my biological father now."

She was encouraging.

"He is probably the same age as Leon. If you don't do it soon, you may never get to," she advised.

I knew my dad's name was Ben Wilbanks, but I had no idea where to find him, and I didn't move too quickly on it. I was still hesitant about what I might discover. Then one night Blake and I were sitting around and he asked, "Don't you ever wonder what your biological dad looks like? You've told me a hundred times that if you passed him in Walmart, you wouldn't know who he was."

I said, "Yeah, I've thought about it for years."

Blake hopped on the computer and within minutes had tracked down my father. Ben Wilbanks lived in the same state we did, near Athens. Before I could think about it, I picked up the phone, called him, and got his answering machine.

"Hello. I don't know how to say this, but this is your son, Howard," I said. "I'd like to meet you and talk to you. Here's my number."

The next day I was on pins and needles until the phone rang. When it did, I heard a man in tears.

"I can't believe you contacted me," Ben said. "I'm so glad to hear from you."

Blake and I drove up to Athens to see him. I didn't take anyone else because part of me was suspicious, given all that I'd heard about this man over the years. I didn't want our first meeting to be in front of family because if everything I'd heard was true, I might punch his lights out in front of everyone. The only sympathetic view of Ben I had heard while growing up was in a single conversation with a drunk uncle when I was fourteen or fifteen. When no one else was nearby, this uncle asked me, "If you saw your dad, what would you do?"

I thought he was talking about Leon, so I said, "Dad's back at the house."

He said, "I mean your real dad."

I thought a moment and said, "I would walk up and punch him out, given what I've been told." This uncle, who had worked with my dad at the same dairy for a while, said, "I wouldn't do that. I would have a conversation first and hear him out." Those were the only positive words I had heard as a boy about Ben Wilbanks, and now I clung to them on the hope that they were true.

We met at a gas station. I saw an older man standing under the eaves as Blake and I pulled up. When he saw me, he walked right up to us and without a word hugged me and Blake. I was taken aback. Hugging other men was definitely not the Wasdin way. I could feel him shaking with emotion and saw tears in his eyes. In that moment I knew where I had gotten my affectionate personality.

"I'm so glad to see you," he said. "I'm so glad you called."

We went to his house, met his wife, Linda, and talked for a few hours. This man who had been the object of such scorn from my mom refused to say a single bad thing about her or her relatives. "She was young," was all he would concede. His conversation was so gracious. The only time I saw him get firm and deliberate was when he rebutted the idea that he had abandoned our family.

"I didn't know where your mother had gone with you," he said. "The last I knew you were living over at the dairy camp and the next thing you all were gone. I had no idea where to find you."

I realized then that my mother had basically abducted me. Nowadays when people separate, there is a custody agreement, child support, and so on. Back then there was none of that. Ben was just cut out of our lives. My mom married Leon, who adopted me, and we moved to Screven.

When I told Ben I had grown up in Screven, he was visibly upset— he had lived in Baxley, half an hour away, and never seen me for all those years. The stories about him being a terrible father and husband did not seem credible. The man before me was affectionate and kind. I saw my own mannerisms in him. He told me he had been so grieved by the divorce that he refused to marry again right away and never had more children of his own. Instead, he became an active and supportive uncle to his nephews and nieces and a father to his stepchildren.

"You don't know how difficult it was to never be part of your life," he told me. "I prayed for you all through the years."

It occurred to me that we might have lain in our beds on the same nights miles apart, crying for the relationship we never got to have. I had to wonder if his prayers had kept me alive, kept me safe, kept me somehow moving in the right direction even when I seemed determined to go the wrong way.

What surprised me even more was how Ben and Linda began reaching out to our family regularly. They didn't miss sending cards on every holiday and birthday. They called on special occasions, and Dad still sends me texts every week saying, "I love you and God loves you. Have a good morning." He sings in a gospel group, plays guitar, and has a CD out. My own personality made a lot more sense having met him.

I could not help but ask God why I had not been raised by this tender, affectionate man. Life would have been so different. I mourned for the childhood that could have been, but I also recognized that if I had been raised by Ben, I probably would not have had the career I did, either as a SEAL or a chiropractor. For all its pain,

Leon's influence had given me the tools and habits I needed to succeed in extremely demanding situations. Though questions about my real father had haunted me for years, my mourning was relatively brief once I had met him.

You can't regain lost years or take the road not traveled. You have to simply be thankful for the path God gave you and walk it the best you can. I do believe it is a wonderful thing to know the man who had such a profound influence on me simply by passing on his genes. He influences me even now. But I have thrown my regrets into the sea of forgetfulness. I am free.

Let me pause to say to fathers like Leon who have made mistakes or treated your kids more harshly than you should have: there is always room for a second chance. I have forgiven Leon for the way he treated me. I have accepted that it built qualities into my character that God used for good. If my experience is any indicator, your child probably has a greater capacity to forgive you than you think. I encourage you children who have suffered abuse to forgive easily and build on the positive qualities you received. No human is totally evil. Let God heal your relationship with your parents and restore your hearts.

On the same subject of reconciliation, my daughter Rachel had been missing from my life for eight years. Gone were the days we would vacation together and I would cook for her when she came over. Gone were the days of working out together on the Bowflex machine and running before work and before bed. When Rachel hit adolescence, we started stumbling into more hurtful arguments. She told me later that she blew them out of proportion, and of course I was still learning to be a dad. Her main complaint was that I was too strict. At age sixteen or so she just decided to stop coming around. For the next eight years, there was no meaningful contact between us.

Rachel's stepdad stepped up wonderfully for her. Rachel did nothing but praise him, and I was grateful for the home and good upbringing he and Katherine provided her. Still, every little girl eventually misses her dad.

One day when Rachel was in her early twenties, she went shopping for Father's Day cards at Walgreens. I had sent her a birthday greeting in a roundabout way through her grandmother a couple of months earlier, and so she stood there looking at the cards and pondering the future. Before leaving she grabbed an extra one, just in case she built up the courage to send it to me. The next day she wrote, "Love and miss you" and sent the card to me.

I was so overjoyed to get the card that I sent a response in that day's mail saying how happy I was she had reached out and that I would love to see her. My response convinced her it was time to straighten out our relationship, and so she accepted my invitation to fly down to Jacksonville together. We spent the weekend getting to know each other again without the distraction of other family members around. The more you talk, the more stuff comes out and the more tears flow. That evening bonded us together again.

Our relationship was reborn, and it has been wonderful. Whenever you don't have a family member in your life, it feels like you're missing something. Now we don't feel that void anymore. Rachel told me later that she never thought she needed her dad, but that time had showed her differently. It's important to have both parents, even if you do have wonderful stepparents.

For one thing, you see the inherited similarities. It blew her mind to see her own mannerisms in someone else's body, from the way we play games to the way we do last touch-ups before walking out the door. We also saw the same personality characteristics in each other:

a hard work ethic, a desire to do things perfectly and efficiently, a stubbornness that needs to be tempered. Like she said, it's almost a relief to see someone going through life with the same strengths and weaknesses.

I'm a lot different now than I was when our estrangement began, and so is Rachel. I cry more easily whenever we talk about soft subjects, especially my children and grandchild. I'm better at handling people's emotional sides, and I constantly remind the people around me that I love them.

Rachel not only got her dad back, she got her brother. When she was estranged from me, she essentially lost Blake too. They picked up right where they left off, competing with each other over everything. We started a new tradition. Every Wednesday Rachel drives down from Statesboro for family night. She usually comes by the clinic where Blake, Eryn, and I work, and then we go eat somewhere or I cook. We sit around the table and cut up and have a good time. Blake brings his girlfriend and Rachel brings her boyfriend. It's like making up for lost time, and it's a lot of fun. Sometimes we go with Debbie, Eryn, and Emma to the condo, or I take her to a presentation I'm giving and we have daddy-daughter time.

Reconnecting with Rachel even helped change her career path. I encouraged her to follow my example and go back to school. I also offered to help pay for it. So she reenrolled at the university to study psychology. Her goal now is to get her doctorate in psychology and work with PTSD patients and their families. She wants to join the army, live on a base, and be part of the soldiers' lives.

She obviously saw what a big impact PTSD had on our family and what I went through just to fit back into "normal" society. She also has friends in the military who come home and wake up every night with nightmares. They don't connect with their children and wives because they are going through such hardship. Rachel has a soft heart and wants to help the soldiers and their families, because when a parent suffers from PTSD, the family suffers as well.

One of the high points of my life was reconnecting with Rachel and discovering that we could pick up where we left off. That was demonstrated the moment we went onto the dance floor on a trip we made to Florida. I had always done special dance moves with each child. With Blake it was the monkey flip. With Rachel it was a swing and dip on the right side, a swing and dip on the left side, and then stand her up and spin her into me. We hadn't done that move for years, but the moment we got onto the dance floor, we fell into it naturally—swing and dip, swing and dip, spin and hold. We hadn't even planned it. We looked at each other and started laughing.

Just as reconciling with Rachel was so important, the relationships I have with my other children are also important. Blake works with me at the clinic as my X-ray technician and chiropractic assistant. Eryn works with me as well as a chiropractic assistant. She writes me such moving Father's Day cards that I can't read them without tearing up. The great thing is that I know I'm not smart enough to make things work out as well as they have. When I humbled myself and showed the love I felt, relationships around me started healing. That's worth a lot more to me than being right.

The Bible says that "love covers a multitude of sins" (1 Peter 4:8 NLT). I have seen that in action. For a guy who wielded some of the most powerful weapons of warfare on earthly battlefields, I can tell you that none are as powerful as love. I even believe that many of the problems I used to think were best solved with a bullet could ideally be solved with some counseling, patience, and love. Of course that's no way to defend a country, but it sure does work on the civilian side.

When I speak to people in corporations or churches, my message is the same: you've got to love and forgive. As long as I wanted to point the finger, I was trapped. The minute I decided that Howard Wasdin was going to take responsibility and not blame others for his life, I became a better man. I'm not bitter at anyone anymore. I let myself out of that prison. My ex-mother-in-law is even a patient of mine; I just helped her after a knee replacement surgery.

For a guy who never expected to make it to forty, I am blown away by all the blessings God has given me. Even being shot in Mogadishu has made me a better doctor today. When people come in, I don't discount their pain. I'm sympathetic in a way that only happens when your own journey has been hard.

I leave every audience with a message of love. I finish every presentation by saying that what we're missing as a country is love. Nobody expects a guy with my background to say that. Ask anyone in my neighborhood who the biggest sucker is and they'll tell you, "Howard Wasdin." They expect a hard-hearted, steely-eyed guy, but instead I'm the guy who feeds stray cats that other people chase out of their yards. I don't know if it's a gift or a sickness, but it feels a lot more life-giving to share the love.

Even on Hannity's show I disagreed with him when he was arguing for the release of the photographs of bin Laden's corpse. I said no, that's not the right mentality. You don't treat your enemy that way. My colleague Eric Greitens—former SEAL and author of the great book *The Heart and the Fist*—agreed with me, but we couldn't persuade Sean. Maybe it's because of what we've been through. God gave us new eyes.

C-SPAN carried one of my presentations in which a World War

II veteran stood and burst into tears because of what I had said. I couldn't help crying, too, moved as I was that someone in the audience had needed that message. Those kinds of things happen more frequently and help me see why God kept me alive that day in a ditch with the enemy just a stone's throw away.

My day-to-day life now is less about being on TV and more about adjusting people's bodies in Jesup so they live more happily and productively. I can't believe I get to be the guy giving such relief. Not only that, but recently the American College of Chiropractic picked my migraine research paper for presentation in Washington, DC, which was a huge honor.

My thesis was that we can resolve migraine headaches without narcotics. Billions of dollars are spent on chronic pain. To me, using drugs is like making a thousand-yard shot—it might help, but it's not really the best way to go about solving the problem. Instead, I have more than a hundred patients who have resolved migraine pain because I did certain things. I never get tired of people telling me, "I feel so much better. I'm sleeping better; I concentrate better." Sometimes I feel guilty getting paid.

Debbie and I are careful to thank God for what we have and everything he's done. I'm especially thankful that he brought me a spunky redhead to help put me on the right track. When I met Debbie, I was a pompous used-car salesman with no future and an ego the size of a hot air balloon. She saw good in me when I didn't believe it was there. She helped me get out of debt and supported us while I went to school. She had nothing to look forward to with me unless I sold my car quota to pay the bills. And she took on my personal baggage. Even now my patients and friends joke that the only reason Debbie married me is because I can cook.

Without Debbie I would not be a doctor, would not have written a best-selling book, would not be talking to Fortune 500 companies, and wouldn't have such a great family around me. I don't think finding Debbie was an accident. I think it was all in God's plan. God sometimes shoves you on the path you're supposed to be on. I think of the night we first went out. I had never had dinner with Philip and Connie before and we never did again after that night. But for some reason, that day they thought it was important we meet. That was a lot more than chance.

Meeting Stephen Templin on my brief time on Facebook was another divine appointment, along with getting the attention of Trident Media Group, and of course the miraculous timing of the book's release. Debbie's and my paths may not have always taken us where we wanted to go, but in the end it's been much better than what we would have done otherwise. My advice is to have faith, be patient, and if it doesn't work out, don't sweat it. God has something much better in store. Now when we're going through a hard time, we say, "Lord, we know you're teaching us something. Help us get through this time."

Debbie was the best gift God ever sent me. Every man wants a wife like her. I wake up sometimes, roll over, and think, *Why on earth is she with me? She could have had anyone in the world and chose me. Thanks, God.* It's still humbling. She saw something in me that I couldn't see in myself.

The lingering difficulty for me was always October 3. Even in the context of my stable life, the memories would bombard me and I would slip into mourning and regret. I would be on edge that week and break down crying for no apparent reason. Recently I was invited by the Boys and Girls Club to give a presentation on October 3 for a community fund-raiser. I was nervous about accepting the invitation because I know my own state of mind, but this time the sorrow was outweighed by something else: hope. The scales had tipped and for the first time I believed that God had kept me alive not randomly but for a purpose. Helping the Boys and Girls Club was part of that purpose, so speaking that day would help close the circle on why I was still alive.

I couldn't predict how I would do at that podium. I thought there was a real chance I would break into tears in front of everybody and have to walk off. I stayed in a back room until it was time. Then, nervously, I stepped up to say what was in my heart.

"We have it so good as Americans that we've forgotten what it's like to have it bad," I said. "What America is missing today is love. We have forgotten what it is to love each other. We have been desensitized by video games, texting people without seeing their faces. We have forgotten how to love each other as Christians, neighbors, and friends. That's why our country is in a tailspin now."

For the first time I spoke publicly in my hometown about what I had gone through after Mogadishu. I talked about Dan Busch, and how I had wondered for years why he was killed and I was spared. I talked about Cliff Wolcott, one of helicopter pilots who went down in Mogadishu. He had on the side of his bird the words "Velvet Elvis" because he was an Elvis impersonator. Whenever you flew with him he sang all the Elvis songs. One thing he liked to do was sing "hunka hunka burning love" while bouncing all the SEALs and Delta guys in the back up and down. Eventually it wasn't hunks but chunks back there if you weren't careful.

"Cliff Wolcott and Dan Busch are just names to some people, or guys from a movie," I said. "But these were more than movie characters. They were heroes. Let me tell you some things about those guys that Hollywood never will."

Then I talked about the Boys and Girls Club and how I was that kid desperately looking for someone to give me encouragement. At that point I choked up and had to stop for a moment. Emotion tugged at my throat and I didn't know if I could continue. Then I took a deep breath and finished what I had to say. As they applauded and I stepped down, I knew it was a huge personal victory to publicly talk about those events.

As Debbie and I walked out, I whispered, "How was that?" Just then a young lady came running out to catch us before we left. She had tears in her eyes and she thanked me for my service and my heart for children in need. Then she went back into the luncheon.

"I guess I said the right thing," I told Debbie.

There are always battles left to fight and will be until we all go home, because that's what life is about: surrendering to God and letting him bring us through places of great pain to places of even greater victory. I still believe that as long as there is life, there is hope.

In the end it's all about love and forgiveness.

ACKNOWLEDGMENTS

I thank God for all the blessings and life I have enjoyed, the greatest of which is being born an American. I ask him to continue to watch over our military members as they defend America's precious way of life. I would personally like to thank everyone who is serving or who has ever served our country. These people, not the politicians, are the reason we enjoy our freedom.

Special thanks to Dr. Ron Wilcox for his counsel and Dr. Mike Von Moss for his mentoring. Thanks to the late Colonel John F. Parker, who taught me that respect and leadership do not have to be beaten into children.

To the people of Wayne County, Georgia, and my patients: thanks for your support of me as a military man and your continued support of me as a local doctor.

All families go through trying times and ours is no exception. I want Blake, Rachel, and Eryn to know I am proud of them and how they have overcome adversity and have made and are making a bright future for themselves.

Finally, thanks to my wife, Debbie, who against the odds and with God's help showed me that I deserved to survive and encouraged me to start life anew.

Howard Wasdin

In all things I am thankful. I thank my heavenly Father for loving me, forgiving me, and giving me the gift of salvation. I would also like to thank him for blessing me with a set of loving parents, a wonderful husband, great kids who are healthy and happy, and our beautiful grandchildren.

I would like to thank my parents for teaching me, guiding me, supporting me and encouraging me in childhood, and even today. I would especially like to thank my mother and stepfather for being loving parents to my husband and for providing him the nurturing from parents that he has always longed for.

To my sweet children, Eryn and Blake, thank you for coming together from the beginning and helping Howard and me form a loving family. You have both endured right beside us, even through the darkest of times, and your love and loyalty are priceless. You, also, made this story have a happy ending.

A special thank you to my sweet friend and mentor, Antonia Harris, who will never realize the impact her words have had on my life and on my marriage. Thank you for helping me understand so much that I never would have been able to understand or relate to.

And a huge thank-you to my husband, Howard, who took a woman who had given up on ever finding true love and gave her a life filled with love, affection, challenges, and adventure. I may have taught you how to love, but you taught me how to live. I praise God for bringing us together and placing us on his path. I thank him for sparing your life so you could save mine. I love you more than human words could ever express.

Finally, a huge shout-out to my granddaughter Emma, and my grandson Tripp. I'm so happy God blessed me with such wonderful grand-blessings!

Debbie Wasdin

ABOUT THE AUTHORS

Deborah S. Wasdin, CPA, has been a practicing Certified Public Accountant since 1991. In 2008, she joined the board of directors of Wayne County Protective Agency, Inc., a shelter providing services to victims of abuse and their children. Deborah has worked with her husband, Howard, on various fund-raising events for the Boys and Girls Clubs of the Altamaha Area, Inc., as well as previously serving on the board. Having witnessed the difficulties of soldiers transitioning from the military into the civilian workforce, she has become an advocate of vocational rehabilitation programs offered by the VA and educates all retiring or discharging eligible veterans she comes in contact with on the importance of participating in vocational rehab, education, career choice, and the impact education can have on their future, not only from a career fulfillment standpoint, but a financial standpoint as well.

Howard E. Wasdin, D.C., was a top sniper with SEAL Team Six. Howard served in the US Navy for twelve years, nine as part of the SEAL Teams. Howard was awarded the Silver Star for gallantry in action against an enemy of the United States and the Purple Heart for injuries sustained in Operation Gothic Serpent in Mogadishu, Somalia. Howard now lives in Jesup, Georgia, where he is a practicing chiropractor. In 2012, he was inducted into the Jeremiah Milbanks Society of the Boys and Girls Clubs of America. Howard is the author of *SEAL Team Six: Memoirs of an Elite Navy Seal Sniper*, a *New York Times* best seller for twenty-two weeks. He coauthored a fictional series, SEAL Team Six Outcasts. Howard also travels the country as a motivational speaker.

Joel Kilpatrick is an author, journalist, and humorist whose work has been featured in *Time* magazine, the *Washington Post*, and CBS Radio. He lives in Los Angeles.